Contents

Body Image

Body Image reviews current research on body image in men, women
and children and presents fresh data from Britain and the United
States. Sarah Grogan brings together perspectives from psychology,
sociology, women's studies and media studies to assess what we know
about the social construction of body image at the end of the twentieth century.

Most previous work on body image concentrates on women. With
the male body becoming more 'visible' in popular culture, researchers
in psychology and sociology have recently become more interested in
men's body image. Sarah Grogan presents original data from interviews with men, women and children to complement existing research,
and provides a comprehensive investigation of cultural influences on
body image.

Body Image will be of interest to students of psychology, sociology,
women's studies, men's studies, media studies, and anyone with an
interest in body image.

Sarah Grogan is Senior Lecturer in Psychology at Manchester
Metropolitan University.

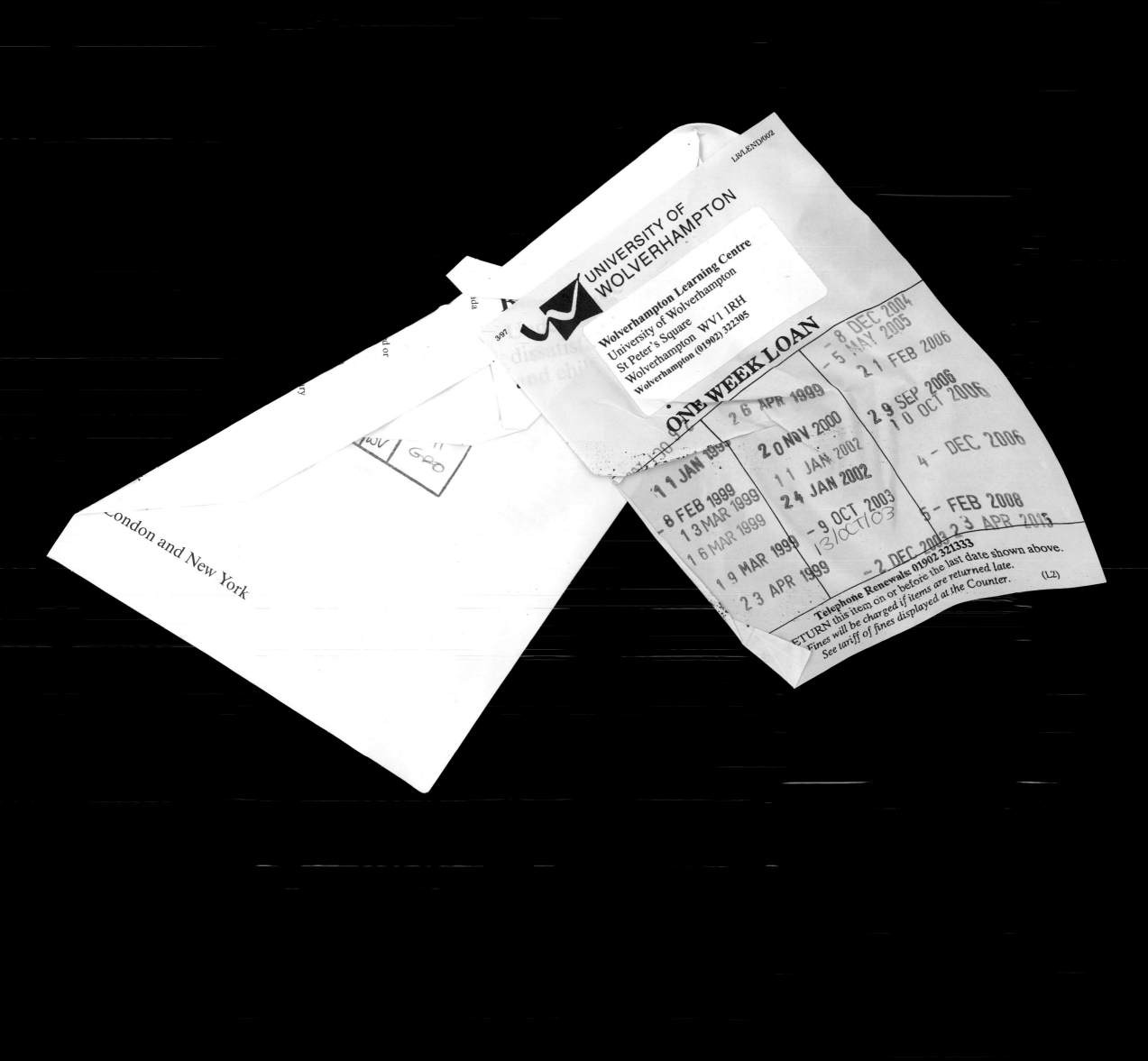

First published 1999
by Routledge
11 New Fetter Lane, London EC4P 4EE

Simultaneously published in the USA and Canada
by Routledge
29 West 35th Street, New York, NY 10001

Typeset in Times by Routledge
Printed and bound in Great Britain by
Biddles Ltd, Guildford and King's Lynn

British Library Cataloguing in Publication Data
A catalogue record for this book is available from the British Library

Library of Congress Cataloging-in-Publication Data
Grogan, Sarah, 1959–
Body image : understanding body dissatisfaction in men, women and
children / Sarah Grogan.
Includes bibliographical references and index.
1. Body image. 2. Body image—Social aspects. 3. Body image—Social
aspects—Great Britain. 4. Body image—Social aspects—United States. I. Title.
BF697.5. B63G76   1998
155. 9'1–dc21
98–4036

ISBN 0-415-14784-0 (hbk)
ISBN 0-415-14785-9 (pbk)

Illustrations

Plates

Figures

Table

Preface

This book reviews current research on body image in men and women, and presents some fresh data from interviews, questionnaires and experimental studies carried out recently in Britain and the United States.

It is intended for students studying psychology, sociology, women's studies, men's studies and media studies. It will also be useful to anyone with an interest in body satisfaction and the factors that contribute to it. It is not a text on anorexia or bulimia, although these are discussed in Chapter 7. It is primarily designed to bring together work from disparate disciplines, along with some fresh research mate-rial, to assess what we know about men and women's body image at the end of the twentieth century.

Most previous work on body image concentrates on women. This text summarises what we know so far about body image in men as well as in women. The study of male body image is a fairly recent phenomenon. Researchers in the 1980s and 1990s have started to be interested in men's body image largely due to the fact that the male body is becoming more 'visible' in popular culture, leading to interest in the psychological and sociological effects of this increased exposure. This book aims to produce a fresh summary of research on body image that addresses disparate perspectives within body image research, and that looks at body satisfaction and body size estimation. In particular, it presents data from qualitative and quantitative studies within psychology, sociology, cultural studies, women's studies and media studies, to demonstrate how they can complement each other, and how they can lead to a better understanding of body image in men and women.

Most of the data presented here come from previously published research from Britain, the United States and Australia. Where there are gaps in the existing literature, fresh data have been collected specifically for this book. Some of these new data have been collected by research students in Britain (Manchester Metropolitan University) and the United States (Santa Fe Community College) who have run interviews or administered questionnaires. It is intended that these fresh data will complement existing research to provide a comprehensive investigation of cultural influences on body image.

Acknowledgements

I would like to thank all the people who have given their expertise and their time to make this book possible. Thanks to all those who agreed to be interviewed or to complete questionnaires and who shared their experiences of body dissatisfaction. Thanks to students at Manchester Metropolitan University, Manchester, England (Penny Cortvriend, Lisa Bradley, Helen Richards, Debbie Mee-Perone, Clare Donaldson, Wendy Hodkinson and Nicola Wainwright), and at Santa Fe Community College, Florida, USA (Jacqueline Gardner, Renee Schert, Melissa Warren, Harry Hatcher, Damien Lavalee, Timothy Ford and Rhonda Blackwell), who agreed to run interviews and administer questionnaires to their peers. I am also indebted to Paul Husband for running interviews with steroid users, and to Geoff Hunter for advice on anabolic steroids.

Thanks to colleagues, friends and family who have read various drafts and provided invaluable suggestions and support. In particular, thanks to Alan Blair, Jane Tobbell, Carol Tindall, Emma Creighton, Edward Grogan and Joanne Wren for their feedback on full and partial drafts. Thanks to Marilyn Barnett for typing the body-builders' transcripts. Thanks to Viv Ward and Jon Reed for their advice during the preparation of the manuscript, and to Nicholas Mirzoeff and Michael Forester for their helpful reviews.

Thanks to the following for permission to include plates, figures and tables: Musée du Louvre for Plates 1 (*Bathsheba*), 10 (*Study of two nude figures*) and 12 (*The Turkish bath*); Musée d'Orsay for Plate 2 (*The artist's studio*); Sterling and Francine Clark Art Institute for Plate 3 (*Blonde bather*); Mary Evans Picture Library for Plate 4 (Flapper fashion); Staatliche Museen zu Berlin for Plate 8 (*St Sebastian*); the British Museum for Plate 9 (*The Battle of Cascina*); Kobal for Plates 5 (Marilyn Monroe), 11 (Dolph Lundgren) and 14 (Arnold Schwarzenegger); Retna Pictures Ltd for Plates 6 (Twiggy), 7 (Kate

Moss) and 13 (Claudia Schiffer); Select Press for Figures 3.2 (Female body shapes), 6.2 (Female stimulus figures varying in breast size) and 6.4 (Male stimulus figures varying in chest size); Lippincott-Raven Publishers for Figures 3.1 (Female silhouette figure rating scale) and 4.1 (Male silhouette figure rating scale); the American Psychological Association for Figure 6.1 (Female stimulus figures varying in WHR) and Figure 6.3 (Male stimulus figures varying in WHR); Ashgate Publishers for Figure 7.1 (Percentage of men/women taking part in activities involving physical effort); the Health Education Authority for Figure 7.2 (Frequency of children getting out of breath and sweaty playing games or sports in free time); and to McGraw-Hill for Table 2.1 (Height–weight tables for adults).

Most of all, thanks to Mark Conner for reading several drafts without complaint and for consistent encouragement and support whilst I was writing and researching this book.

1 Introduction

Interest in the psychology and sociology of body image originated in the work of Paul Schilder in the 1920s. He was the first researcher to look at body experience within a psychological and sociological framework. Prior to Schilder's work, body image research was limited to the study of distorted body perceptions caused by brain damage. Schilder developed this work to consider the wider psychological and sociological frameworks within which perceptions and experiences of body image took place. In *The Image and Appearance of the Human Body* (1950) he argues that body image is not just a cognitive construct, but also a reflection of attitudes and interactions with others. He was interested in the 'elasticity' of body image, the reasons for fluctuations in perceived body size, feelings of lightness and heaviness, and the effects of body image on interactions with others. He defined body image as:

> The picture of our own body which we form in our mind, that is to say, the way in which the body appears to ourselves.
>
> (Schilder, 1950: 11)

Since 1950, researchers have taken 'body image' to mean many different things, including perception of one's own body attractiveness, body size distortion, perception of body boundaries, and accuracy of perception of bodily sensations (Fisher, 1990). The definition of body image that will be taken for this book is:

> *A person's perceptions, thoughts and feelings about his or her body.*

This definition incorporates all the elements of body image originally identified by Schilder: body size estimation (perceptions), evaluation of body attractiveness (thoughts), and emotions associated with body shape and size (feelings); and is adapted from a definition produced by Thomas Pruzinsky and Thomas Cash (1990). Body dissatisfaction is defined here as:

A person's negative thoughts and feelings about his or her body.

In recent years, there has been a noticeable increase in academic and popular interest in body image. The sociology of the body has become an established discipline in the 1990s, with Bryan Turner (1992) coining the term 'somatic society' to describe the new-found importance of the body in contemporary sociology. The popularity of Mike Featherstone and Bryan Turner's journal *Body and Society*, set up in Britain in the mid-1990s, demonstrates the high level of interest in the role of the body in social theory. Psychologists have also become more interested in the psychology of body image, with an increase in research into psychological factors predicting body satisfaction. Newspapers and magazines in Britain and the United States are replete with stories about plastic surgery, 'eating disorders', reducing diets (and the dangers of dieting), and critiques of the use of skinny models to advertise products (often placed adjacent to pictures of skinny models in advertisements!). The end of the twentieth century is clearly a time of enhanced concern with body image.

In this book, body image will be investigated from psychological and sociological viewpoints. This is because body image is a psychological phenomenon which is significantly affected by social factors. To understand it fully, we need to look not only at the experiences of individuals in relation to their bodies, but also at the cultural milieu in which the individual operates. Only by investigating the psychology and sociology of the body will it be possible to produce an explanation of body image that recognises the interaction between individual and societal factors.

Body image is conceptualised here as subjective, and open to change through social influence. There is no necessary link between a person's subjective experience of their body and what is perceived by the outside observer. This is obvious in distortion of body size (e.g. many young women who experience *anorexia nervosa* believe they are much heavier than they really are), and in cases of 'phantom limb' phenomena (in which people who have had limbs amputated report still 'feeling' the missing limb). It is also relevant (though less obvious) in the large number of women and girls who 'feel fat', although they are objectively of average (or below average) weight for their height; and in men who feel too thin or too fat although they are objectively of average size.

The image that an individual has of his or her body is also largely determined by social experience. Body image is elastic and open to change through new information. Media imagery may be particularly important in producing changes in the ways that the body is perceived and evaluated, depending on the viewer's perception of the importance of those cues. It is likely that some viewers are more sensitive to such cues than others. For instance, it has been suggested that adolescents are especially vulnerable because their body image is particularly 'elastic' while they undergo the significant physical and psychological changes of puberty. Other groups who attach particular importance to body-related imagery (e.g. people with eating disorders, body-builders) may also be sensitised to media cues. Research has suggested that most people have some reference group that furnishes social information relevant to body image (which may be friends, family or the media). Body image is socially constructed, so it must be investigated and analysed within its cultural context.

This book investigates men's and women's body image, focusing in particular on cultural influences on body image, and on degree of body satisfaction and dissatisfaction in men and women of different ages. Theory and data from psychology, sociology, women's studies and media studies are integrated to address the question of how men and women experience body shape and weight. It will be argued that body dissatisfaction is normative in women in the Western world from eight years of age upwards, and that this has a significant impact on behaviour such that most women try to change their shape and weight, and many women avoid activities that would involve exposing their bodies. Body image in men will also be investigated. Data show that boys from as young as eight years old also show concern over being the 'right' shape, and many adult men's self-esteem is related to how good they feel about their body shape.

Chapter 2 reviews current research on culture and body image. It is argued that Western culture prescribes a narrow range of body shapes as acceptable for men and women, and that those whose body shape and size falls outside this range may encounter prejudice, especially if they are heavier than is culturally acceptable. The debate as to the basis for current Western cultural ideals is reviewed. Arguments from the biological determinist perspective (suggesting a biological basis for body shape preferences), and from social psychology and sociology (stressing cultural relativity), are evaluated. An historical review of trends during this century shows how cultural ideas of acceptable body shape have changed radically over the years, particularly for women. Myths about weight and health are questioned, and the impact of the dieting industry on the lives of men and women is examined. Chapter 2 provides a backdrop for the data on body dissatisfaction presented in Chapters 3, 4, 5 and 6, demonstrating the extent of socio-cultural pressures in Western society.

Chapter 3 looks specifically at body dissatisfaction in women. Different techniques that have been used to assess satisfaction are evaluated, along with findings based on each technique, to determine the extent of body dissatisfaction and the reasons why women are dissatisfied. Women's attempts to modify their bodies through plastic surgery, dieting, exercise and body-building are investigated, reflecting on data from psychology, sociology and women's studies. The chapter ends with a review of cultural pressures on women to conform to the socially acceptable 'slim but shapely' body shape, drawing mostly on work from contemporary feminist writers on the social construction of femininity.

Chapter 4 focuses on body satisfaction in men. Most previous work on body satisfaction has focused on women. A review of men's body satisfaction is timely in the light of recent arguments that there has been a cultural shift in the 1980s and 1990s such that men are under increased social pressure to be slender and muscular. Men's satisfaction is evaluated, using work from sociology and psychology and introducing fresh data from interviews with young men, to determine whether men seem to be aware of societal pressures, and whether these pressures impact on their body satisfaction. Current work on body-building and anabolic steroid use is reviewed, to understand the psychological and social effects of becoming more muscular, and the motivations behind taking anabolic steroids in spite of negative side effects. Work on the social construction of masculinity is reviewed, to produce a picture of social pressures on men, and to evaluate the extent of recent cultural changes on men's acceptance of their body shape and size.

Chapter 5 looks directly at studies of the effects of media pressure. Theory and data from psychology, sociology and media studies are discussed in relation to effects of exposure to idealised media images of attractive photographic models. Content analyses of media portrayal of the male and female body are reviewed. Mass Communication Models are then evaluated, with reference to 'Effects' and 'Uses and Gratifications' models. Empirical evidence of the direct effects of observing media imagery is reviewed and evaluated, with special reference to two of the most influential psychological theories in this area: Social Comparison Theory and Self Schema Theory. Data from laboratory experiments are complemented by data from interviews to evaluate the mechanisms through which media role models may affect body satisfaction in men and women. Recent developments are discussed, in which representatives of various media have reflected on the use of slender models, along with ideas for reducing the effects of media imagery based on current psychological and sociological theories.

Chapter 6 investigates the effects of age, ethnicity, social class and sexuality on body satisfaction. Questionnaire studies which have charted changes in satisfaction throughout the lifespan are discussed, along with relevant data from interviews carried out with children and adolescents specifically for this book. Dissatisfaction is identified in the accounts provided by children as young as eight years old, and reasons for this dissatisfaction are discussed. There is discussion of ethnicity and body dissatisfaction, evaluating claims that black women are more satisfied with their body shape and size in the context of a sub-culture where plumpness may be perceived as attractive and erotic. Social class differences in body satisfaction are discussed within a social context that associates slenderness with the middle and upper classes, especially for women. The historical link between slenderness and social class is explored. Finally, differences in body satisfaction in heterosexual men and women, gay men and lesbians will be investigated. Research from sociology and psychology, looking at different sub-cultural pressures, will be investigated, and this section will include an evaluation of evidence suggesting that the lesbian sub-culture protects against body dissatisfaction.

In the concluding chapter, arguments presented in the earlier chapters will be summarised, with an exploration of their implications. This chapter aims to summarise factors that seem to predict either dissatisfaction or satisfaction with the body, to try to identify ways to counter social pressures and develop positive body images through raising self-esteem and perceptions of control over the body, and by developing images of the body based on function rather than on aesthetics.

2 Culture and body image

This chapter explores the effects of cultural influences on body image. Cultural prejudice in favour of slenderness and against overweight is placed in a psychological and sociological context, with a critical evaluation of the roles of biology and culture in promoting the slim ideal.

The idealisation of slenderness

In affluent Western societies, slenderness is generally associated with happiness, success, youthfulness and social acceptability. Being overweight is linked to laziness, lack of will power and being out of control. For women, the ideal body is slim. For men, the ideal is slender and moderately muscular. Non-conformity to the slender ideal has a variety of negative social consequences. Overweight (for both men and women) is seen as physically unattractive and is also associated with other negative characteristics.

Tracing the social meanings attached to slimness over the years, Susan Bordo (1993) shows how, starting at the end of the last century, excess flesh (for men and women) came to be linked with low morality, reflecting personal inadequacy or lack of will. This has continued into the 1990s, where the outward appearance of the body is seen as a symbol of personal order or disorder. Slenderness symbolises being in control. The muscled body has recently lost its associations with manual labour and has become another symbol of will power, energy and control. The firm, toned body is seen as representing success. Most people do not have slim, toned bodies naturally, so they have to be constantly vigilant (through exercise and diet) so as to conform to current ideals. Bordo argues that the key issue in the current idealisation of slenderness is that the body is kept under control:

The ideal here is of a body that is absolutely tight, contained, bolted down, firm.

(Bordo, 1993: 190)

This links the spare, thin, feminine ideal with the solid, muscular, masculine ideal, since both require the eradication of loose flesh and both emphasise firmness.

People who do not conform to the slender ideal face prejudice throughout their lifespan. Thomas Cash (1990) argues that overweight people are treated differently from childhood. Children prefer not to play with their overweight peers, and assign negative adjectives to drawings of overweight people. This prejudice continues into adulthood, when overweight people tend to be rated as less active, intelligent, hardworking, successful, athletic and popular than slim people. People who are overweight are likely to find more difficulty renting property, being accepted in 'good' United States colleges and getting jobs, than are their slimmer peers.

In an interesting psychology study by Marika Tiggemann and Esther Rothblum (1988), large groups of American and Australian college students were asked about their stereotypes of fat and thin men and women. They were asked to rate the extent to which eight qualities were typical of thin men and women and fat men and women. Men and women in both cultures reported negative stereotypes of fat people. Although fat people were seen as warmer and friendlier, confirming the traditional stereotype of the fat and jolly person, they were also viewed as less happy, more self-indulgent, less self-confident, less self-disciplined, lazier and less attractive than thin people. These differences were more marked for judgements of fat women than fat men. The results indicate negative stereotyping of fat people, especially fat women, in these college students (Tiggemann and Rothblum, 1988). What was particularly interesting was that there were no differences in stereotyping between students who were fat and those who were thin. Even those who were overweight had negative stereotypes of fat people.

The tendency to link physical attractiveness with positive personal qualities has been documented since the 1970s, when Dion and colleagues coined the phrase 'What is beautiful is good' (Dion *et al.*, 1972: 285). They suggested that people tend to assign more favourable personality traits and life outcomes to those that they perceive as attractive. In an updated review of evidence in this area, Alice Eagley and colleagues (1991) suggest that the effects of the physical attractiveness stereotype are strongest for perceptions of social competence (sociability and popularity). Negative stereotyping of overweight people may be a specific aspect of the physical attractiveness stereotype that refers specifically to assignment of negative traits to those who have a body size and shape that is not considered attractive by dominant groups in Western culture.

It is likely that causal attributions affect responses to overweight people. If overweight is seen as being caused by factors within the individual's control (through overeating, lack of exercise) then overweight people are more likely to be stigmatised. Christian Crandall and Rebecca Martinez (1996) compared attitudes to being overweight among students from the United States and Mexico. The United States was chosen because it has been considered to be the most individualistic culture in the world (Hofstede, 1980). That is, US culture (in general) values independence, and tends to perceive individuals as responsible for their own fates. Mexico, on the other hand, was rated thirty-second out of the fifty-three countries rated for individualism by Hofstede, and is generally perceived to be a culture that emphasises interdependence and connection, with more focus on external, cultural influences on behaviour. Crandall and Martinez predicted that Mexican students would be less likely to see being overweight as within an individual's control, and less likely to stigmatise someone for being overweight. They supported both these hypotheses, finding that anti-fat attitudes were less prevalent amongst Mexican students and that Mexican students were less likely to believe that weight gain is under personal control. US participants were more likely to agree that fat people have little will power and that being fat is their own fault. Crandall and Martinez argue that anti-fat attitudes are part of an individualistic Western ideology that holds individuals responsible for their life outcomes.

The Crandall and Martinez study is typical of others in the literature, since it stresses that prejudice against overweight is culturally bound and depends on attribution of blame. Within Western ideology, being overweight is perceived to violate the cultural ideal of self-denial and self-control. In fact, there is a growing body of evidence suggesting that overweight results, at least in part, from genetic factors (Stunkard *et al.*, 1990; see Appendix). However, people still tend to hold on to the erroneous belief that the individual is 'to blame' for increased body weight because it fits ideological beliefs of personal responsibility. This results in prejudice against people who do not conform to the slender cultural ideal.

The basis of body shape ideals

There is an ongoing debate about the reasons why Western culture shows a preference for slenderness. On the one hand, biologists and some psychologists have suggested that these body shape preferences derive from biology. They argue that these ideals are based on the fact that slenderness is more healthy than overweight. On the other hand, theorists who have looked at cultural differences in body shape preferences at different times and in different cultures have tended to suggest that biology plays a minor role in the idealisation of slenderness, and that it is largely learned. These two views will be evaluated here.

Body weight and health

Biological arguments stress the importance of slenderness for health (and the unhealthiness of overweight). Slenderness has not always been linked with health. At the start of the twentieth century, thinness was associated with illness in the United States and in Britain, because of its link with tuberculosis (Bennett and Gurin, 1982). More recently, extreme thinness is coming to be associated with AIDS. Indeed, AIDS is known as 'slim' in some African countries. The cultural effects of this association between thinness and illness in Western industrialised countries may become apparent over the next decade, but at present thinness does not produce the generally negative stereotypes that are found in poorer nations. Instead, there is a general belief that to be plump is unhealthy, and that thinness is an indicator of good health.

In order to determine the health risks of overweight, it is important to draw a distinction between mild to moderate overweight and obesity. Obesity is almost certainly harmful, and is associated with heart disease, hypertension and diabetes (Brownell and Rodin, 1994; Taylor, 1995). According to Kelly Brownell and Judith Rodin (1994):

> Obesity is a major cause of morbidity and mortality. To argue that greater levels of excess weight are not associated with increased risk is to dismiss an abundant and consistent literature.
>
> (Brownell and Rodin, 1994: 783)

However, there is considerable controversy as to the precise degree of overweight at which risk begins to increase. Estimates range from 5 per cent overweight to 20–30 per cent overweight (in Brownell and Rodin, 1994).

Many authors have argued that 'overweight' represents no significant risk, whereas 'obesity' presents significant health risks, but there is very little agreement as to the cut-off point between these two categories. Although it is generally believed that 'obesity' is an objectively defined medical condition, definitions vary so that the same person may be considered overweight, obese or within the normal range, depending upon which measure is used, and when the measure is taken. For instance, a person who was considered 'obese' in relation to norms for 1960 may not be considered 'obese' by current norms, since average weight has increased over the last thirty years (Brownell and Wadden, 1992).

In the United Kingdom the most widely used measure is the Body Mass Index (BMI; also known as Quetelet's Index). BMI is obtained by dividing weight in kilograms by squared height in metres. The normal range of BMI is between 20 and 25. Those with BMI between 25 and 30 may be classified as 'overweight', and those over 30 as 'obese' (British Heart Foundation, 1994). The advantage of BMI is that it controls for a person's height. However, the scale is only valid if it is assumed that adults should not gain weight during adulthood. Moderate weight gain with increasing age is healthy (Andres *et al.*, 1993). This means that classifications of older people as 'obese' need to be interpreted with caution.

A measure of body weight that is still widely used in the United States is based on the person's weight relative to their 'frame' size (small, medium or large). Weight is compared with a standard weight table, and obesity is commonly defined as weight that is at least 20 per cent above the 'ideal' weight for a person's frame size. Different levels of obesity are sometimes defined: 21–30 per cent above ideal weight – mild; 31–50 per cent – moderate; 51–75 per cent – severe; 76–100 per cent – massive; and 101 per cent or more – morbid (see Hanna *et al.*, 1981). The standard table, shown here as Table 2.1, originated in *Desirable Weights for Men and Women*, published in the United States by the Metropolitan Life Insurance Company.

As a standard, this has been extensively criticised. Norms are based on life insurance applicants in 1959 who were white, male, middle-class, and of Northern European descent (Bennett and Gurin, 1982), and are not necessarily applicable to other groups. The norms assume no change in weight after age 25, and that people can be categorised by 'frame' size, with little guidance as to how to do this. The norms were revised in 1979, and results indicated that the 'ideal' weights were now at least 10 lb heavier than they had been in 1959. This change meant that some people who had previously been labelled 'obese' no longer fell into this category, emphasising the cultural specificity of the classification scheme.

Table 2.1 Height–weight tables for adults

Men			Women		
Height (ft)	Ideal weight (lb)	Overweight (lb)*	Height (ft)	Ideal weight (lb)	Overweight (lb)*
5'1"	131	157	4'9"	112	134
5'2"	133	160	4'10"	114	137
5'3"	135	162	4'11"	117	140
5'4"	138	165	5'0"	119	143
5'5"	140	168	5'1"	122	146
5'6"	143	172	5'2"	125	150
5'7"	146	175	5'3"	128	154
5'8"	149	179	5'4"	131	157
5'9"	152	182	5'5"	134	161
5'10"	155	186	5'6"	137	164
5'11"	159	190	5'7"	140	168
6'0"	162	194	5'8"	143	172
6'1"	166	199	5'9"	146	175
6'2"	170	203	5'10"	149	179
6'3"	174	209	5'11"	152	182

Source: Adapted from Taylor (1995), with permission.

Note: * denotes 20% above ideal weight.

Yet another way of defining obesity is in terms of the extent of subcutaneous body fat rather than general body weight. Skinfold thickness measures involve applying callipers to various target areas of the body to measure the thickness of the fold. This gives a direct measure of body fat, but assumes that people do not gain fat with age. This means that the norms (derived from young adults) are not valid for older adults. This may be a particular problem when assessing women, who carry more subcutaneous fat than men. From birth, the thickness of subcutaneous fat is greater in females, and this increases through the lifespan. By age 55–9, women (on average) have skinfold thickness between 42 per cent (triceps) and 79 per cent (subscapular) thicker than men (Greil, 1990). Estimates of obesity in older women may be inflated if norms based on younger women are used, because of the significant progressive increase in fat distribution in women that is normal through the lifespan. Also, the measure has low inter-rater reliability (i.e. different raters produce varying estimates), is uncomfortable for the person being assessed, and is time-consuming (Rothblum, 1990). Largely because of these problems, most researchers use either the BMI or the Metropolitan Life Insurance Company Tables to decide whether a person should be categorised as 'obese'.

In addition to problems over definitions of obesity (and, by inference, the level at which overweight represents a health risk), there are
also important shortcomings in research design in this area.
Evaluation of research is difficult because of reliance on correlational
data. Most studies have looked at mortality and target health factors
in a sample of people (usually men) of different weights. It is obvious
that extraneous variables may operate to confound the relationship
between weight and health, such as frequency of stringent dieting in
the obese which may itself be deleterious to health (Rothblum, 1990).
Also, it has been suggested that body fat distribution may be as important as degree of overweight in predicting health risks (Taylor, 1995).

Although definitions vary, and methodological restrictions do not
allow definitive estimates of the exact extent of overweight that presents
a significant health risk, most researchers in this area would agree that
people with a BMI of greater than 30 (and/or body weight 20 per cent
above ideal weight on the Metropolitan Life Insurance Company Tables)
have increased mortality and morbidity associated with heart disease,
hypertension and diabetes (Brownell and Rodin, 1994). Statistics on the
prevalence of this degree of overweight suggest that about 13 per cent of
men and 15 per cent of women in England meet this criterion
(Department of Health, 1993). This is a significant increase from the 6
per cent of men and 8 per cent of women recorded in 1980. Prevalence
estimates in the United States are higher, particularly in women. Recent
data suggest that at least 14 per cent of men and 24 per cent of women in
the United States are in the obese range (Taylor, 1995).

The health risks to those who are overweight, but who have BMI of
between 25 and 30, is still a matter for debate. Some authors have
suggested that moderate overweight carries no significant health risks,
and may even be advantageous to health. Tom Sanders, a British nutri-
tionist, argues that being slightly overweight can have positive effects
on health, particularly for women. He argues that being plump means
that the heart has to work harder during exercise, which might explain
why more overweight people than thin people survive heart attacks.
Plumper women are less likely to experience early menopause, heart
disease and osteoporosis than thin women. He argues that the health
advantages of being slightly overweight have been largely ignored
because of cultural prejudice against overweight (in Sanders and
Bazelgette, 1994). Esther Rothblum (1990) also argues that there is no
conclusive evidence that being moderately overweight is bad for health.
She suggests that medical concern with overweight is grounded on
cultural prejudice against people who are overweight, rather than on
realistic health risks.

Clearly, this issue has generated controversy. The most parsimonious explanation of the data as they stand at present is that severe overweight represents a health risk, but moderate overweight (BMI 25–30) probably represents a minimal health risk, or may even be advantageous, particularly to women. Relatively few people are overweight to an extent that would be expected to impact on their health. The belief that slenderness is more healthy than moderate overweight is not borne out by medical research. This suggests that social pressures to be slender are based on culturally based aesthetic preferences as well as health concerns.

Culture and body shape preferences

Many authors have argued that cultural differences are primarily responsible for body shape ideals. Data mostly derive from studies of historical differences in body shape preferences, and from studies of differences between different cultural groups. Here we will review evidence for historical changes in body shape 'fashions' in the Western world, followed by some evidence of cultural variation in body shape preferences.

Historical trends: portrayal of the female body

There is general agreement that the social pressure to conform to the slender ideal is greater in the West on women than on men. The idealisation of slenderness in women is often viewed as the product of an historical evolution that has occurred over the past century. Within Western industrialised cultures, there have been many changes over the years in the body shape and size that is considered attractive and healthy, especially for women. It is possible to trace a cultural change in the 'ideal body' from the voluptuous figures favoured from the Middle Ages to the turn of this century, to the thin body types favoured by the fashion magazines of today.

Plumpness was considered fashionable and erotic until relatively recently. From the Middle Ages the 'reproductive figure' was idealised by artists. The fullness of the stomach was emphasised as a symbol of fertility (Fallon, 1990). The female body was frequently represented with full, rounded hips and breasts. This trend is represented in the fleshy bodies painted by Rubens in the 1600s, and in Rembrandt van Rijn's *Bathsheba* (1654) which portrays a woman with a plump body and represented the aesthetic ideal of its time (Plate 1, p. 80).

In the 1800s the idealised form was still voluptuous and plump, as, for example, in Courbet's *The artist's studio* of 1855 (Plate 2, p. 81).

Manet's (1863) *Olympia* (which he considered his masterpiece) was denounced when it was shown in the Paris Salon in 1865. The picture represents a reclining nude woman of average size. The picture was said to be 'obscene' because (amongst other reasons) the subject was not considered sufficiently plump to be erotic (Myers and Copplestone, 1985). *Olympia* contrasts with the fleshy nudes painted by Renoir around the same time. Renoir's (1881) *Blonde bather* (Plate 3, p. 82) portrays a healthy looking, plump figure. The ample and curvaceous woman's body was idealised as the antithesis to the taut male body portrayed by neo-classicists such as Jacques-Louis David.

The idealisation of slimness in women is a very recent phenomenon, dating from the 1920s. It is often argued that the thin ideal is the outcome of successful marketing by the fashion industry, which has become the standard of cultural beauty in the industrialised affluent societies of the twentieth century (Gordon, 1990). Clothes fashions were represented by hand-drawn illustrations until the 1920s, when they started to be photographed and widely distributed in mass-market fashion magazines. These magazines presented a fantasy image of how women should look. The fashions themselves demanded a moulding of the female body, because each 'look' suited a particular body shape (Orbach, 1993). The 'Flapper' fashion which originated after the First World War demanded a boy-like, flat-chested figure to show off the straight, low-waisted dresses to advantage (Plate 4, p. 83).

At this stage middle- and upper-class women began binding their breasts with foundation garments to flatten their silhouettes (Caldwell, 1981). They used starvation diets and vigorous exercise to try to get their bodies to the pre-adolescent, breastless, hipless ideal (Silverstein *et al.*, 1986). Winners of the 'Miss America' beauty contest at this time had average bust–waist–hip measurements of 32–25–35.

In the 1930s and 1940s ideals moved towards a more shapely figure, epitomised by Jean Harlow and Mae West in the 1930s and Jane Russell in the 1940s. The mean measurements of 'Miss America' winners changed to 34–25–35 (an increase of two inches in bust size from the previous decade) in the 1930s, and to 35–25–35 in the 1940s. Breasts became fashionable, along with the clothes that emphasised them. Lana Turner and Jane Russell became famous as 'sweater girls'.

In the 1950s this trend continued, when the Hollywood film industry and the fashion industries promoted large breasts (along with tiny waists and slim legs). Marilyn Monroe personified this trend (Plate 5, p. 84), and was the first *Playboy* centrefold. 'Miss America' winners increased in bust and hip measurements in the 1950s, and reduced in waist measurement, so that the body was (on average) an exaggerated hour-glass shape of 36–23–36. In the 1950s there was also a significant move towards slimness. Grace Kelly and Audrey Hepburn were slim (rather than buxom) and were portrayed to cinema-goers as symbolising sophistication (rather than sensuality). They became role models for some young women, and slimness became associated with the upper classes (Mazur, 1986). The trend for slimness became particularly acute in the 1960s, when the fashion model Twiggy became the role model for a generation of young women (Plate 6, p. 85). She had a flat-chested, boyish figure, and weighed 96 lb (Freedman, 1986).

Slimness came to exemplify unconventionality, freedom, youthfulness and a ticket to the 'Jet Set' life in 1960s Britain, and was adopted as the ideal by women of all social classes (Orbach, 1993). 'Miss America' winners also became slimmer and taller in the 1960s than in the previous decade, with an increase of about an inch in height and a weight loss of about 5 lb by 1969 (Mazur, 1986). This trend occurred across Europe and the United States. Studies of the portrayal of the female body in the media have reliably found that models became thinner and thinner between the 1960s and 1980s. For example, models in *Vogue* magazine became gradually thinner, and even *Playboy* centre-folds become taller and leaner so that, although their breasts remained large, 'Playmates' became slim and nearly hipless in the 1980s (Fallon, 1990). This trend for thinness as a standard of beauty has become even more marked in the 1990s than it was in the 1980s. In the 1980s, models were slim and looked physically fit, with lithe, toned bodies. *Time* magazine, in August 1982, argued that the new ideal of beauty was slim and strong, citing Jane Fonda and Victoria Principal as examples of the 'New Ideal' of beauty. In Britain and the USA, the slim, toned figure of Jerry Hall epitomised the ideal. The 1990s have seen a departure from this trend with the emergence of 'waif' models who have very thin body types, perhaps the most famous of these being Kate Moss (Plate 7, p. 86), who has a similar body shape and weight to Twiggy from the 1960s. Although the three most highly paid super-models of the mid-1990s were not 'waifs' (Cindy Crawford, Claudia Schiffer and Christy Turlington), designers and magazine editors often choose to use extremely thin models such as Kate Moss to advertise their clothes and beauty products.

The late 1990s have seen the rise of 'heroin chic', where fashion houses have taken very thin models and made them up to look like stereotypical heroin users, with black eye make-up, blue lips and matted hair. In a *Newsweek* article of August 1996, Zoe Fleischauer, a model who is recovering from heroin addiction, tells the interviewer that models are encouraged to look thin and exhausted:

> They [the fashion industry] wanted models that looked like junkies. The more skinny and f—ed up you look, the more everyone thinks you're fabulous.

(Schoemer, 1996: 51)

More recently, model Emma Balfour has publicly condemned the fashion industry for encouraging young models to take stimulants to stay thin, and for ignoring signs of heroin addiction (Frankel, 1998), and US President Clinton has denounced 'heroin chic' in the wake of fashion photographer Davide Sorrenti's death from a heroin overdose. This is yet another fashion trend that glamorises extreme thinness, and may give cause for concern because of the potential negative effects on young women's body image.

Historical trends: portrayal of the male body

Representation of the male body also has an interesting history. Myers and Copplestone (1985) note that sculptors in ancient Greece were keenly interested in the problems of representing the anatomy of the human figure in a realistic form, and that it was at this stage that life-like male nudes started to appear. Men were often presented nude, whereas women were represented clothed in cloaks (*himation*) and undergarments (*chiton*). The male body was revered and considered more attractive than the female body. In the seventh century BC there developed a trend for a broad-shouldered, narrow-hipped ideal that has become known as the 'Daedalic' style, after the mythical Daedalus of Crete who was according to legend the first Greek sculptor. At this stage the male body was idealised and presented in a strictly stylised way, with emphasis on clearly defined muscles which were carved into a surface pattern on the marble.

Idealisation of the male body can also be found in the art of the Roman Empire, where the epitome of physical beauty for the Romans, who hated obesity and idealised slenderness in their paintings and sculpture, was the slim, muscular male warrior. In Renaissance art, too, the male body was traditionally presented nude, emulating the physique represented in classical Greek sculpture. A good example is Sandro Botticelli's (1474) *St Sebastian* (Plate 8, p. 87). The naked, muscular male body which represented this aesthetic ideal can also be seen in the work of High Renaissance painters, such as Michelangelo's *The Battle of Cascina*, painted in 1504 (Plate 9, p. 88), and Signorelli's (1503) *Study of two nude figures* (Plate 10, p. 89).

The male body continued to dominate art until the mid-1800s, when artists such as Courbet shifted the erotic focus from the male body to the female body. From then until the 1980s, the male body was rarely idealised in art, except in paintings and photography aimed at a gay male audience. However, there were exceptions. Thomas Eakins in the late 1800s (in the series *Thomas Eakins at 45 to 50*) photographed his own body nude, in defiance of the convention that male bodies should not be shown to a heterosexual audience. However, his body is not presented in an idealised form. On the contrary, it is seen as mature and fleshy, without the firm muscles usually portrayed in pictures of the male body.

Another notable exception to this general trend is the idealisation of the male body in Nazi propaganda of the Second World War. Leni Riefenstahl's photographs of the 1936 Olympic Games (*Schönheit im Olympischen Kampf*) were modelled on classical Greek poses, and were idealised by the Nazi propaganda machine as representing the Teutonic ideal. This ideal (highly muscled, engaged in athletic pursuits) is echoed in images in the specialist body-building magazines that emerged in Europe in the 1940s (Ewing, 1995).

Yet a further exception to the trend was the portrayal of male Hollywood idols in the 1950s. In publicity photographs explicitly aimed at a female audience, Rock Hudson, Kirk Douglas and James Dean were portrayed semi-clothed, in poses designed to flatter their muscularity (Meyer, 1991).

However, it was not until the 1980s that idealised images of the naked (or semi-naked) male body started to become common in mainstream Western media. The 1980s and 1990s have seen an increase in the objectification of the nude male body in photographs which follow the conventions of photographing the female nude (eyes or face averted or not visible). Some of these photographs have been specifically aimed at gay men, such as those by Robert Mapplethorpe, but many have been admired by a wider audience (Pultz, 1995).

The advent of such magazines as *For Women*, together with the appearance of male erotic dance troupes such as The Chippendales and The Dreamboys who play to all-women audiences, have blurred the traditional boundaries between men as viewers and women as the viewed. Muscular actors such as Arnold Schwarzenegger, Jean-Claude Van Damme and Dolph Lundgren exemplify the well-muscled male ideal as portrayed in the popular media (Plate 11, p. 90; Plate 14, p.93).

The male body as an object seems to be losing its originally homo-erotic connotations, so that advertisers now feel happy to use the naked male torso in mainstream advertising to sell everything from ice-cream to perfume and orange juice. Lisa O'Kelly (1994) discusses the influence of gay culture in making men's bodies more visible, showing that the iconography of gay culture has moved into the mainstream, blurring the edges of men and women's sexual identities, and extending the range of images that are considered acceptable for men:

> Once advertisers would have been fearful of linking their products with images that might have been thought homoerotic. Now even Marks and Spencer advertises its socks with pictures of hunky men. . . . Mainstream women's publications such as *Marie Claire* regularly feature articles on men and their bodies and have no qualms about including revealing pictures.
>
> (O'Kelly, 1994: 32)

The muscular physique is still preferred by advertisers, although male 'waif' figures are also starting to make an appearance, including Kate Moss's younger brother Nick. Greg Buckle (head of the male division at Storm, the model agency which handles Kate Moss) confirms that the new look for men is:

> Slimmed down – the male waif is what everyone's after.
>
> (O'Kelly, 1994: 32)

Peter Baker (1994) argues that there are sound commercial reasons for this increase in the visual portrayal of the male body in the media. Cosmetics companies have recently come to realise that there is a gap in the market for male cosmetics, and that men need to be persuaded to buy them.

> They had to find a way of persuading men that it's actually macho to use a moisturiser and not fey to have a facial, hence the pictures of hunks splashing on the perfume.
>
> (Baker, 1994: 132)

Baker argues that the portrayal of idealised images of men's bodies in the media is likely to lead to increasing problems with self-image and body satisfaction in men.

There is a growing preoccupation with weight and body image in men, which parallels this increased 'visibility' of the male body

(Gordon, 1990). Clearly the social pressure on men is different and less extreme than that on women, since men still tend to be judged in terms of achievements rather than looks (Chapkis, 1986; Orbach, 1993). However, there is a growing interest in men's body shape and size. Men are under increased social pressure to conform to the muscular, well-toned, mesomorphic (medium-sized) shape, and Mishkind *et al.* (1986), amongst others, predicted a cultural shift in the 1990s towards increased body-shape concern amongst men.

Cultural variations in body shape preferences

Few researchers have considered body image in non-Western cultures. Work that has been reported indicates significant cultural differences in the meanings associated with thinness and plumpness. In poorer cultures, thinness is often seen as a sign of malnutrition, poverty and infectious disease, and increased weight may be viewed positively, as an indication of health, wealth and prosperity. Research in Latin America, Puerto Rico, India, China and the Philippines has shown that increased standard of living is reliably linked with increased body weight, and that in these cultures increased body weight is linked with wealth and health (Rothblum, 1990). Plumpness signals wealth, since the plump person has been able to eat to excess. In many countries, obesity is more prevalent in the higher social classes and is viewed as an indicator of high status (Sobal and Stunckard, 1989).

Some work has looked directly at what happens to body weight preferences when people move from one cultural context to another. There is some evidence that, when a person moves from a culture where plumpness is valued to one where slenderness is the cultural ideal, this may lead to a shift in body weight preference. In one cross-cultural study (Furnham and Alibhai, 1983), Asian women living in Kenya and Asian women who had emigrated from Kenya to Britain were asked to rate line drawings of women of different body weights. The Asian women who were living in Kenya gave more positive ratings to line drawings of heavy women than the women who had emigrated to Britain. Although not conclusive, these data are suggestive of a cultural shift in body weight preferences. Furnham and Alibhai suggest that the women who had emigrated had absorbed the British cultural prejudice against overweight.

April Fallon and her colleagues (in Fallon, 1990) asked American and Indian women to indicate their current and ideal body sizes. The American women reliably chose an ideal that was significantly thinner than their current size, whereas the Indian women reliably chose an ideal that approximated their current size. American and Indian men chose an ideal larger than their current size. Clearly the Indian women, living in a culture that does not generally idealise slenderness, were more satisfied with their current size than the American women living in a 'culture of slenderness'.

In a cross-cultural study in the 1970s, Iwawaki and Lerner (1974) looked at the characteristics assigned by college students to different body types. They found that Japanese college students tended to assign more negative stereotypes to thin bodies than to fatter body types, whereas American students showed exactly the opposite pattern of stereotyping. They concluded that the Japanese culture at that time did not idealise slenderness, whereas the American culture showed a preference for slenderness and a prejudice against overweight.

Even between Westernised cultures, some subtle differences are apparent. In the Tiggemann and Rothblum (1988) study, the authors compared Australian and American students on body consciousness. They found that the US students were more self-conscious about their bodies, showed a higher frequency of dieting, and were more concerned with weight than were a matched group of Australian students, suggesting that body consciousness was particularly extreme in US culture.

There can be no doubt that the idealisation of slenderness varies depending on cultural factors. Poorer cultures (where thinness may signify negative factors such as poverty and/or disease) are more likely to value plumpness; whereas affluent cultures (where thinness may be associated with self-control and self-denial in the face of plenty) are more likely to value slenderness.

The diet industry

One of the most powerful social forces in the promotion of thinness in Western society is the diet industry. Books, slimming plans and diet foods are all sold to a public which 'feels fat'. Of course, a proportion of that public *is* overweight, to a degree that will impact on their health. However, many more people diet than need to do so for health reasons, and most do so for aesthetic reasons. About 95 per cent of women diet at some time in their lives (Ogden, 1992), and recent surveys (e.g. Horm and Anderson, 1993) have shown that about 24 per cent of men and 40 per cent of women are dieting at any one time, and at least 37 per cent of men and 52 per cent of women feel they are overweight.

'Dieting' means different things to different people. It usually means a reduction in the intake of calories for the purpose of weight loss. However, approaches differ in numerous ways, from drastic weight-reduction programmes such as the 'Slim Fast' (low calorie meal-replacement drinks) and 'Beverly Hills' (fruit) diets to the relatively more gentle approaches such as the 'Hip and Thigh' (low fat diet with exercise) and F-Plan (high fibre, low fat) diets.

Jane Ogden (1992) argues that the dieting industry is the perfect industry, because it creates a problem (body dissatisfaction) and then offers to solve it:

> By creating a market for itself it ensures that women will continue to feel fat and will continue to support the dieting industry.
>
> (Ogden, 1992: 48)

She suggests that dieting is often a state of mind, where a person thinks about dieting and counts calories but does not eat significantly less than a non-dieter. However, some dieters use more extreme strategies for weight loss. These include smoking (which acts as an appetite suppressant), vomiting, laxative use, exclusive use of very low calorie drinks, diet pills, and fad diets such as all-fruit diets. All threaten health, and none work in the long term. She argues that all are particularly dangerous when used by normal-weight individuals who 'just feel fat'.

There has been a well-publicised debate about the long-term efficacy of dieting. Pro-dieting lobbyists argue that dieting leads to long-term weight loss, and generally that weight loss improves health. When assessing the effectiveness of diets, it is important to distinguish between dieting in normal-weight individuals in order to reach an aesthetic ideal, and dieting in those whose degree of overweight may be injurious to their health. The latter group is likely to be better motivated and better supported (clinically and socially) than the former, and diets that work with obese people will not necessarily be effective (or appropriate) for those who are not obese.

Even the most positive outcome data suggest that diets only lead to significant long-term weight loss in about 25 per cent of obese people (Brownell and Rodin, 1994). This has important implications for understanding the effects of diets on normal-weight people who are dieting to reach an aesthetic ideal. Researchers have generally found that dieting only works in the long term for around 5 per cent of non-obese dieters (Brownell and Rodin, 1994). This means that the other 95 per cent are likely to feel that they have failed. Nickie Charles and Marion Kerr (1986) interviewed over 200 women about their experiences of food and dieting, and found that most had tried and failed to keep to a diet, leaving them feeling guilty and dissatisfied with their will power, and with their body shape and size. It is not surprising that these women felt like this, given the marketing of diets which emphasises that will power is all you need to lose weight.

Anti-dieting lobbyists argue that dieting may actually lead to an increase in weight. The tendency to gain weight after successful dieting is well-established in the medical and psychological literature. It is suggested that when people diet the body interprets this as a period of starvation and slows down metabolic rate to make more efficient use of the calories that they do eat. When they come off the diet, the body sends out signals to store extra fat that can be used in the next famine. So they put on the weight that they lost and some extra, because the body is now more efficient at storing calories. They then go on another diet and lose the weight that they put on, and then the whole cycle starts again. Kelly Brownell and colleagues used the term 'weight cycling' to describe this phenomenon (Brownell *et al.*, 1986), and it has become known colloquially as 'yo-yo dieting'. Weight cycling can lead to chronic weight increase due to decreased metabolic rate and more efficient utilisation of calories.

Some anti-dieting lobbyists have argued that dieting presents more of a health risk than being overweight. Esther Rothblum (1990) presents evidence that it is weight-reducing diets, rather than being overweight, that result in health problems. She argues that weight-reducing diets lead to 'dieter's hypertension' when overeating, since the stress of deprivation can lead to raised blood pressure. This is supported by studies showing that weight-loss diets may lead to a variety of problems, including heart problems (Polivy and Herman, 1983). Also, epidemiological studies have shown increased mortality in obese individuals who lose weight (Wilcosky *et al.*, 1990). However, other authors have reported the opposite pattern of effects. For instance, Wannamethee and Shaper (1990) found that there was a 10 per cent reduction in mortality caused by heart disease in a group of over 7,000 British men who lost at least 10 per cent of their initial body weight. The reduction in mortality rose to 50 per cent for obese men.

Kelly Brownell and Judith Rodin (1994) provide a useful summary of the data relating to weight loss and health. They conclude that it is not possible to evaluate the effects of weight loss on health on the basis of existing data because of problems in the ways that studies have been designed. Most studies have taken self-selecting (obese) groups of people, and compared mortality in those who lose weight and those who do not. Factors such as body fat distribution, dieting history and disease-related factors may be confounded with weight loss. Only a study with random allocation of participants to weight-loss or non-weight-loss groups would enable a realistic evaluation. Brownell and Rodin also argue that the risk-to-benefit ratio must be assessed separately for individuals of different weights (and with different health risks), and that the decision to diet should be based on likely health outcomes (and not aesthetic ideals). Anti-dieting arguments are often based on the assumption that people are marginally overweight, or only overweight by some arbitrary aesthetic standard. Severe overweight may lead to more severe health problems than may dieting. However, for people who merely 'feel fat' and are not significantly overweight, dieting may represent a health risk.

Recent cultural trends

The anti-dieting movement is helping to make people aware of the potential dangers of dieting, and is starting to reduce the power of the dieting industry. Campaigns by groups such as Diet Breakers in the United Kingdom are helping to raise public consciousness in relation to the dangers of dieting and the importance of healthy eating; a holiday firm in Britain has recently produced a humorous advertisement that satirises those diet advertisements that promise 'A New You In Two Weeks'; and women's magazines and the popular press carry articles warning of the dangers of crash dieting ('Breaking the diet habit', *Daily Mail*, May 1992; 'Diet addiction: your ten point recovery plan', *Options*, January 1993).

In the late 1990s the pressure to be slim is still apparent. Models are as thin as they were in the 1980s. However, slimming articles are being replaced by articles on weight loss through exercise ('Four weeks to your best body ever', *New Woman*, July 1995). The cultural preoccupation with weight and body shape is as strong as ever, although the new cultural trend is to attain the perfect (slim) body through exercise rather than diet. Overweight is still linked to lack of will power and laziness, but in the 1990s this relates to lack of exercise rather than diet-breaking. This may be a generally positive move in terms of encouraging a healthy lifestyle for people who are within the normal range of weight, by encouraging them to exercise. Although exercise does not burn calories as efficiently as many people believe (Bray, 1986), it has other benefits including toning the body by strengthening muscle, and can lead to increased feelings of well-being and increased energy levels (Furnham *et al.*, 1994). It may also lead to benefits for cardiovascular health, although frequent, very intensive exercise is probably necessary to produce any tangible improvement (Cox *et al.*, 1993). However, for people who are overweight (and particularly those who are obese), exercise is made difficult because of the cultural prejudice against exercise in fat people (Bovey, 1989). So, although this trend may be generally positive for people who just 'feel fat', it is unlikely to benefit those who are overweight.

Summary

- Western society promotes slenderness for men and women. Women are expected to be slim and shapely; men to be slender and muscular.
- There is some disagreement amongst theorists as to the basis for these cultural ideals. Psychologists working within a biological framework have stressed the healthiness of the slender ideal. However, there is evidence that being slightly overweight may have health benefits for women, and that being very thin may impact negatively on health.
- Social psychologists have emphasised the importance of cultural factors in determining what is attractive, demonstrating that the slender ideal is relatively recent, and has become thinner over the last few years with the emergence of the (male and female) 'waif' model in the 1990s.
- The diet industry promotes a thin ideal, although dieting may lead to health problems and is unlikely to lead to long-term weight loss.
- The anti-dieting lobby is actively involved in promoting the dangers of dieting and is reducing the power of the diet industry.
- The Western ideal remains slender in the late 1990s, although exercise is replacing dieting as the socially acceptable means to the slender ideal.

3   Women and body satisfaction

Slimness is seen as a desirable attribute for women in prosperous Western cultures, and is associated with self-control, elegance, social attractiveness and youth (Orbach, 1993). The ideal female shape is epitomised in the slim but full-breasted figures of models Elle MacPherson, Helena Christensen and Claudia Schiffer. Chapter 2 showed how body shape ideals for women have changed this century. Despite changes in the feminine ideal, one thing remains constant through the decades. Women have always been encouraged to change their shape and weight to conform to current trends. Through the ages, women have undergone pain to attempt to conform to the current ideal. This is clearest in relation to procedures such as foot binding and the wearing of restrictive corsets, where women suffered discomfort and immobility in the name of particular fashions. In Western society in the 1990s we have replaced these practices with strict diets (which weaken and debilitate) and cosmetic plastic surgery (where women undergo painful procedures to try to attain culturally-defined attractive body shapes).

This chapter evaluates evidence from Britain, the United States and Australia to investigate the extent of body dissatisfaction in women in these cultures. Researchers have used a variety of different techniques to study body satisfaction and have concluded that most women in Western cultures are dissatisfied with their body weight and shape. These techniques will be discussed in turn to illustrate how body satisfaction has been investigated, and how such work helps us to understand women's experiences of body dissatisfaction. The second part of the chapter will look at ways in which psychologists and sociologists have tried to make sense of women's dissatisfaction with body shape and weight.

Assessment of body satisfaction

Psychologists and sociologists have used a variety of different measures to assess body satisfaction. Many of these techniques were originally produced to assess body dissatisfaction in women who have problematic relations with food. This text aims to look at body image in women who have 'normal' relations with food rather than those who have been classified as anorexic or bulimic. Readers with a special interest in anorexia or bulimia are referred to Chapter 7 in this volume, and to Susie Orbach's excellent review of body image and eating disorders (Orbach, 1993). The studies discussed here are ones that have looked at body image in women picked at random, or on an opportunity basis, rather than those referred to professionals as a result of problematic relations with food. As such, these women's experiences constitute majority views, rather than those of a more specific group. However, this does not imply that the women who are discussed in this chapter have unproblematic relationships with their bodies. As will be demonstrated here, evidence shows that most women experience levels of concern about weight and body shape suggesting a problematic relationship.

Silhouette studies

The silhouette technique is one of the most widely used quantitative measures of degree and direction of body dissatisfaction. Using this technique, silhouettes ranging from very thin to very fat are presented to the participant, who is usually asked to choose the silhouette closest to her own body size and that representing her ideal size. The discrepancy between the two figures is seen as an indication of (dis)satisfaction.

Studies using this technique have found that women show a reliable tendency to pick a thinner ideal than their current figure. This effect has been replicated in the United States, Australia and Britain. In the earliest published study using silhouettes, April Fallon and Paul Rozin (1985) asked 227 women studying psychology at the University of Pennsylvania to indicate their 'ideal figure', their 'current figure', and 'the figure that most men would find attractive' using Stunckard et al.'s (1983) scale. This scale is a set of nine figure drawings arranged from very thin to very heavy figures (Figure 3.1). In general, women picked a heavier figure for their 'current figure' than for 'the figure that most men would find attractive', and an even thinner figure for their 'ideal figure'. Fallon and Rozin conclude that women's perceptions put pressure on them to lose weight.

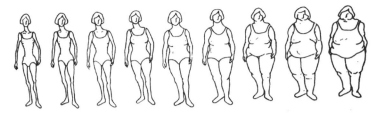

Figure 3.1 Female silhouette figure rating scale

Source: Adapted from Stunckard *et al.*, 1983, with permission.

Sue Lamb and her colleagues (1993) administered silhouette scales to thirty-four women enrolled on American degree courses who were studying psychology (average age 20), and to forty-two older women (average age 47) who were American public (i.e. state) school teachers, or who were chosen from a middle-class pre-retirement village. They were each given the scale used by Fallon and Rozin, and were asked a series of questions including their perception of their current and ideal body sizes, and the figure they expected men to find most attractive. Older women were objectively heavier, and perceived themselves to be heavier than the younger group. Both groups presented an ideal that was much thinner than their perceived size. The younger group had a significantly thinner ideal than the older group. Both groups believed that men favoured an extremely thin ideal body size for women. One of the interesting things about this finding is that body shape dissatisfaction is not confined to young women. Women in the older group were aged between 40 and 60, and none were obese. Yet they wished to be slimmer.

Perhaps this degree of dissatisfaction is limited to the body-conscious United States? Recent Australian studies have put this hypothesis to the test. Marika Tiggemann and Barbara Pennington (1990) gave questionnaires to fifty-two undergraduate women (average age 23) which contained the Stunckard *et al.* silhouette drawings. Participants were asked to indicate the figure that most closely approximated their current figure, the one they would like to look like, and the one that they thought would be most attractive to the opposite sex. Women rated their current figure as significantly larger than both their ideal figure and the figure that they thought would be most attractive to men. These data show that discrepancy in size between how women perceive themselves and how they would ideally like to look is not a specifically American phenomenon.

Gail Huon and colleagues (1990), in another Australian study, used photographs of women varying in size from very thin to very fat instead of the silhouette pictures, and found very similar results to the silhouette work. Forty young women were asked to pick one photograph that represented their own size, one to represent their ideal, one that they thought most men would prefer, and one that they thought most women would prefer. They were also asked to rate each photograph they had chosen along five 7-point scales (beautiful–ugly, liked–disliked, controlled–uncontrolled, energetic–lazy, and successful–unsuccessful). The 'ideal' photograph chosen was significantly thinner than the picture chosen as the 'actual size'. This discrepancy in size between 'actual' and 'ideal' bodies was mirrored in favourability ratings, which were higher for the ideal. It was interesting to note that women perceived 'most women's' ideal to be thinnest, followed by 'most men's', followed by their own 'ideal', followed by their 'actual size'. Huon suggests that this shows that women who wish to be thin are mostly influenced by what they think other women prefer, rather than by what they think that men prefer. However, the perceived men's preferred size was thinner than the 'ideal' reported by these women, suggesting that pressures are perceived from men as well as from women.

British work has also found that women want to be thinner than they actually are. Jane Wardle and her colleagues (1993) investigated body satisfaction in 274 white and Asian women using the Stunckard *et al.* drawings. Participants were asked to indicate the figure that looked most like themselves, the figure they thought men would find attractive, the figure they would most like to look like, and the figure that most women would find most attractive. There was a consistent tendency to chose a slimmer 'ideal' than 'current' shape, with 'shape that men like' coming somewhere in between, and 'shape that women like' being slimmest for both white and Asian groups. The investigation demonstrated that normal-weight young British women tended to feel fat and wanted to lose weight.

Studies where women have been asked to pick 'ideal' figures reliably demonstrate that most women would like to be slimmer than they perceive themselves to be at present. This suggests that most women perceive themselves as heavier than they would ideally like to be.

Questionnaire studies

Another way to assess body (dis)satisfaction is to ask women to complete self-report questionnaires. Body satisfaction questionnaires are designed to provide a quantitative measure of body satisfaction. Most ask respondents to indicate degree of agreement or disagreement with statements relating to satisfaction with particular body parts or with the body as a whole.

The Body Cathexis Scale was developed by Secord and Jourard in the 1950s (Secord and Jourard, 1953). It is one of the earliest measures for assessing the degree of satisfaction with the body and is still one of most widely used. Participants indicate satisfaction with a wide variety of body parts, and the scale is scored so that each person ends up with a score indicating body satisfaction. Secord and Jourard argued that body satisfaction was highly associated with general self-esteem, so that a person who scored highly on the body satisfaction scale would also be likely to score highly on self-esteem scales. This link has been confirmed in many studies in women, men and children (see Ben-Tovim and Walker, 1991, for a review). Recently, researchers have tended to modify the scale, losing the items that relate to height, ankles, calves and neck length which tend to produce unreliable results, and adding other body areas. For instance, Adrian Furnham and Nicola Greaves (1994) added lips, ears, biceps, chin, buttocks, arms, eyes, cheeks, legs, stomach, body hair and face. Fifty-five British women aged 18 to 35 were asked to rate, on a 10-point scale, how satisfied they felt with each body part (where 1 = complete dissatisfaction and 10 = complete satisfaction). Compared to a sample of forty-seven British men in the same age range, the women were significantly less satisfied with all body parts, and especially with thighs, buttocks and hips. Dissatisfaction with the lower part of the body, where flesh tends to accumulate in women, is widely documented in studies using a variety of different methods, as will be seen below.

The Body Areas Satisfaction Scale (Cash *et al.*, 1986) is part of the Body–Self Relations Questionnaire, and asks about dissatisfaction with a variety of parts of the body. In a survey of readers of *Psychology Today* magazine, 55 per cent of women were dissatisfied with their weight, 45 per cent with muscle tone, 32 per cent with upper torso, 57 per cent with mid-torso, 50 per cent with lower torso, and 38 per cent with overall appearance (Cash *et al.*, 1986). The areas of the body that presented most concern were mid-torso (stomach) and lower torso (hips and bottom). Again, the hips and bottom were identified as 'problem' areas. The 'stomach' also presented cause for concern in these women. This is another body area where women store fat once they have passed through puberty, and another part of the body widely documented to cause concern.

An awareness that women tend to be most unhappy about the lower parts of their bodies has led to the development of scales clearly derived from the Secord and Jourard scale, but with a narrower focus. David Garner and colleagues developed the Eating Disorders Inventory to assess eating and body image in people with problematic relations with food (Garner, Olmstead and Polivy, 1983). One of the sub-scales is the Body Dissatisfaction Scale. This scale consists of items asking whether the lower parts of the body are just right or too big, and one question that asks about overall satisfaction with the whole body. At least 50 per cent of women register a 'dissatisfied' response on this scale (Garner, Olmstead and Polivy, 1983).

The Body Shape Questionnaire (Cooper *et al.*, 1987) was specifi- cally designed to study body image in women with 'eating disorders'. It includes thirty-four questions relating to antecedents and conse- quences of body shape concern, and asks the respondent how she has felt over the last four weeks, to look at long-term dissatisfaction. Items include 'Have you felt ashamed of your body?' and 'Have you pinched areas of your body to see how much fat there is?' Evans and Dolan (1992) have produced shortened versions of the scale with sixteen and eight items, which retain the reliability and validity of the original version but have the advantages of greater ease of completion for participants. In a population of normal-weight women with no history of 'eating disorders', 17 per cent scored high levels of body shape concern on the original Cooper *et al.* (1987) questionnaire, showing – as might be expected – that body shape concern is not restricted to those women with 'eating disorders' but affects a significant propor- tion of women with no history of such problems.

The Body Attitudes Questionnaire (Ben-Tovim and Walker, 1991) covers six distinct aspects of body experience: feelings of fatness, self- disparagement, strength, salience of weight, feelings of attractiveness, and consciousness of lower-body fat. The scale is specifically designed for women, and produces separate scores on each of the sub-scales, and covers a wider range of body-related attitudes than alternatives such as the Cooper *et al.* (1987) scale. Example questions include 'I worry that my thighs and bottom look dimply' and 'I try to avoid clothes that make me especially aware of my shape'. They found that concern about being fat was central to women's attitudes about their bodies, and that this was particularly marked in relation to concern with the lower half of the body. They also found that 'body disparage- ment' (where the woman agrees to statements like 'My life is being ruined because of the way I look' and 'I prefer not to let other people see my body') was common in their sample of 504 Australian women respondents.

Questionnaire studies suggest that many women are dissatisfied with their bodies, particularly the lower half of the body (stomach, hips and thighs). These data support the results of silhouette studies, and also add detail on the specific body areas that present cause for concern. One of the problems with the silhouette work is that women are forced to make a choice of whole body silhouette, which obscures perception of individual body parts. Questionnaires that ask specifically about different body parts allow a more detailed assessment of satisfaction with different parts of the body, and reveal that most women participants in the studies may be quite satisfied with the top half of the body while being dissatisfied with the lower torso and thighs.

Interview studies

Another way to find out how women feel about their body shape and size is to ask them how they feel in a semi-structured or unstructured interview. Using these techniques, interviewers talk to women in an informal way about experiences of body (dis)satisfaction, usually guided by a list of topic areas that the interviewers want them to discuss. The advantage of doing this (rather than asking women to complete a questionnaire that asks specific questions) is that women are given the freedom to express how they feel, rather than just answering pre-planned questions. This allows them to set their own agenda and address issues that are important to them, giving this technique more flexibility than questionnaire work.

Nickie Charles and Marion Kerr (1986) carried out an interesting study using the semi-structured interview technique. As part of a study on eating in the family, they interviewed 200 British women about their attitudes and experiences of dieting, and their satisfaction with their current weight. Their results showed that most women were dissatisfied with their body image. Of the 200 women that they interviewed, only twenty-three had never dieted or worried about their weight. Of the 177 who had been concerned about their weight, 153 had been concerned enough to diet. When speaking about their ideal body image, most were dissatisfied with the way that they looked at the time of the interview. Charles and Kerr conclude:

> What emerges from these comments is a strong dissatisfaction with their body image, a dissatisfaction which was not confined to women who were dieting or trying to diet but was shared by almost all the women we spoke to.
>
> (Charles and Kerr, 1986: 541)

The women who were interviewed by Charles and Kerr seemed to have a mental yardstick for how they would like to look. For some of them this was how they had looked when they were younger. For many, losing a 'magic half-stone' was the goal. Most had not managed to accept their bodies as they were. The areas of the body that caused most dissatisfaction were breasts (too small or too large), legs (too fat or too thin), abdomens (not flat enough) and buttocks (too flabby or too skinny). Not all women felt too fat, but the majority did. Although being slimmer was linked with good health, women cited looks rather than health as the main reason for dieting. One woman needed to diet for medical reasons, but said that the main reason for losing weight was to look better.

The interview data in Charles and Kerr's study suggest that adult women tend to be dissatisfied with the way their body looks, and that they see the main way to change body shape to be dieting. Charles and Kerr link body dissatisfaction to women's inferior position in society, seeing control of the body as a realisable goal for women who may find it impossible to exert power externally:

> Women are constantly trying to reduce, or increase, their body size so that it will conform to the ideal, abnormally slim conception of female beauty which dominates our culture. At the same time their social position is often one of powerlessness and the body, something which can be brought under control and which power can be exerted over, bears the brunt of women's rage and feelings of impotence.
>
> (Charles and Kerr, 1986: 570–1)

In a series of interviews with women carried out at Manchester Metropolitan University, it has been found that women of a variety of ages report body dissatisfaction. Fifty women, ranging in age from 16 to 63, were interviewed in semi-structured interviews in which they were encouraged to talk about their experiences around body shape and weight, diet and exercise. Most of the quotes below come from interviews carried out by Penny Cortvriend, Lisa Bradley, Helen Richards and Debbie Mee-Perone between 1994 and 1996. Women reliably report dissatisfaction with stomach, bottom and thighs. For instance, here are some short, representative extracts from interviews. Since these women's ages span almost fifty years, and since these interviews will be discussed again in Chapter 6 in relation to age and body satisfaction, their ages (in years) are indicated after the quotes in parentheses.

All my bottom part. From my knees upwards and from my chest downwards. My um, my what's it called, trunk. The whole of my trunk I am dissatisfied with.

(35)

I'm getting better, but I don't like my legs and bottom.

(25)

Yes I would say from the waist downwards, I would like to be a lot less.

(43)

All the blub around my belly. I don't like that one bit.

(34)

I'd like my thighs to be smaller. And my bottom's too big.

(17)

These findings support those from the quantitative questionnaire work, suggesting that stomach, thighs, bottom and hips present most concern to women. Such comments were presented in almost all the interviews, irrespective of the objective size of the woman who was being interviewed. Both slim and heavier women of all ages reported concerns that their hips, bottom and thighs were too big. In fact, there is some evidence from work on body size estimation that women also tend to over-estimate the size of these body parts (see pp. 39–41). They are areas of the body where women store fat, and also areas which are often the focus of media attention in advertisements for slimming products (Bordo, 1993).

We have been interested in the discourses used by women when asked to talk about their bodies. Most women objectify their body. Most are able to describe what is 'wrong' with their body with no difficulty, but find it difficult to identify any part that is satisfactory. Most of the women we have interviewed, irrespective of their body size, report that they would be delighted to lose half a stone. For instance, one 26-year-old woman said 'I'd kiss you!'; another, aged 25, said 'I'd be so delighted'.

Most women believed that their life would change for the better in some way if they lost weight, usually identified as an increase in self-confidence. Many women reported that they would change the way that they dressed if they lost weight. For instance:

> Yes. I'd be confident as hell. Oh, I'd wear stuff that was shorter and tighter.
>
> (26)

> I'd completely change. My clothes, everything. I'd be a different person.
>
> (27)

Women who had experienced weight loss reliably reported increased confidence. For instance:

> I remember once I did a diet from a magazine going back, er, fourteen years now when I was so slim. I felt so good, I felt like a different person. I felt so confident.
>
> (43)

> I'm more confident when I'm slimmer.
>
> (30)

Feeling slender and feeling confident were intrinsically linked for most of the women we interviewed. This was the case for heavier and slimmer women.

When asked to imagine putting on half a stone (7 lb) in weight, many women said that this would make them feel like hiding away and not going out. This negative impact on sociability is expressed clearly by these women:

> Oh God, no, I'd be gutted [really upset]. I wouldn't go out.
>
> (26)

> I wouldn't go out. I'd stay in. I wouldn't want to go out if I weren't feeling right about myself.
>
> (27)

These feelings were expressed by women across the age range, who said that they would 'feel fat' and avoid social activities if they put on half a stone in weight. The significant social effect of this relatively small increase in weight shows the importance of not increasing weight to most of the women we interviewed. It is particularly interesting, since researchers have shown that judges do not rate women's attractiveness higher when they lose (compared to when they gain) between 0.5 and 18 lb (Alley and Scully, 1994).

Many women reported that they felt happiest about their body first thing in the morning (before they had eaten), when they felt lightest and slimmest. For instance:

> First thing in the morning when I am still lying on my back I can feel my bones.
>
> (34)

> When I first get up my tummy looks flatter but then as soon as I have had a drink or a slice of toast or something, there it goes, there it is [*laughs*].
>
> (32)

Most said that they are self-motivated to lose weight. For instance:

> I don't diet for anyone else. Just me.
>
> (63)

Some reported that their partners encourage them to lose weight. Many women reported experiencing anxiety and depression when their partners commented negatively on their weight or shape. For instance:

> He said 'God, you aren't half getting fat'. The cheeky pig. I cried and slept downstairs that night.
>
> (32)

> I cry. He says it a lot and it really upsets me.
>
> (25)

Women referred to media models as influences on body satisfaction. Many women said that models (in general) were too thin. For instance:

> I used to think, oh models, perfect figure. And now sometimes I look at them and I think no. Too skinny. Definitely too skinny.
>
> (17)

However, other women tended to be ambivalent about skinny models, saying that they were too thin, but also that they would like to look like them. For instance:

They make me sick. They are too thin. But I would kill for one of
their bodies.

(25)

Some [models] I think, no I wouldn't like to be like that. But I
suppose the Naomis and the Claudia Schiffers, and things like
that . . . that seems reachable. You know, I mean obviously you
couldn't get the youth and the flowing hair and that lot. But they
make you sick really don't they [*laughs*]? Why her not me?

(35)

The idea of 'skinny but shapely' being the most attractive body shape
was a recurring theme. For instance:

I like a balance. A bit of curves but skinny curves.

(17)

I don't like thin thin at all. I mean I would hate to be like that. But
the shapely slim models I might look at them and think it would
be nice to look like that.

(43)

Women of all ages cited models as influential in determining body
satisfaction. The ideal body for women from 16 to 60 was the tall, slim,
cultural ideal. For instance:

I'd like firm breasts, thin legs, little tiny hips.

(26)

Many women cite pressure from the fashion industry to be slim,
saying that fashionable clothes only come in small sizes (UK size 14
or below), so that to dress fashionably you have to be slim. For
instance:

Fashion dictates really what size you are, because none of them go
over a size 14 anyway, so you couldn't be fat and fashionable.

(26)

It is the way fashion is at the moment. You couldn't go out in
what's fashionable if you were fat.

(27)

Many women said that the fact that their clothes became uncomfortable if they put on weight acted as a motivator to lose weight again. This was seen by many women as more important than how much they actually weighed. For instance:

> The fact that clothes get uncomfortable really. That's basically what it is, cos I don't look in the mirror to see how fat I am. And when I put on clothes that are tight around the waist. And the clothes that I've got that are nice but that I can't get into. That's what motivates me to get my weight down. It's clothes.
>
> (63)

> I don't have an ideal weight. I just have to feel comfortable in my clothes.
>
> (35)

> I don't feel comfortable at the moment in my jeans. That three pounds [recent weight gain] has made a tremendous difference on a skirt or a pair of jeans. That's the only thing. If you've got a pair of jeans, three pounds makes a difference on the waist. That's the only thing that I would diet for if I went out of my clothes size. I would have to diet, because I could never afford to replace all my clothes. If I was growing out of my clothes I would definitely try and cut down.
>
> (46)

> I don't long to be under nine stone again, because I think that is an unrealistic weight for me, but I think just so that my clothes fit me nicely. Do you know what I mean? And I think that the emphasis has changed now in that I don't really weigh myself that often because it is not actually the weight that matters to me. It is how I feel myself and what I feel I look like.
>
> (27)

The physical changes associated with the after-effects of pregnancy presented particular concerns. Women felt that their bodies had become less aesthetically pleasing after pregnancy, and that they had been relatively attractive in the 'golden days' before pregnancy and childbirth. For instance:

> You don't realise at the time before you've had kids, but when you have had them you think, oh, I was Page Three [referring to the

UK's *Sun* newspaper which features a young, slim, partly clothed woman every day on page 3].

(27)

Pregnancy did not result in any positive effects that these women could identify. The main negative effects were stretched skin around the stomach and drooping breasts. For instance:

I've got more stretch marks than I don't know what. I've got millions of them.

(25)

I'd like to get rid of my flabby belly.

(24)

I'd like my bust to be firm again and sit up instead of drooping down.

(27)

All this breast feeding has just ruined my boobs. Yes, I'd change those if I could.

(35)

Interviews with women across a wide age range have shown that most women are dissatisfied with their body size, in particular the lower torso. Many report comparing themselves to models or actresses, and most have a body ideal that is skinny but shapely, epitomised by models such as Claudia Schiffer (who was the model most admired by our respondents across the age range) and actresses such as Demi Moore. Very skinny models (such as Kate Moss) were not so admired, since they were seen as 'too skinny' by some, and an unrealistically slim target shape by others. Being slim was linked with self-confidence for most of the women we spoke to, and most believed that their life would change for the better if they lost weight (irrespective of current body size). One interesting aspect of the interviews was that none of the women we interviewed reported wanting to put on weight (even those who were objectively very thin). And all the women interviewed could identify one body site where they wanted to lose weight. It seemed that many women perceived their body to be heavier than it appeared to the outside observer. Some psychologists have suggested that women tend to overestimate the size of their body (particularly the lower torso). This phenomenon will be investigated next.

Body size estimation techniques

Interest in body size estimation originated in the 1960s when Bruch (1962) suggested that anorexic women showed a marked distortion in their size perception, perceiving themselves as fat even when very thin. We might expect that these women are exceptional and that the majority of women have a pretty good idea of their body size and shape. After all, we are accustomed to looking at ourselves in mirrors, and buying clothes that fit. In fact, research on body size estimation suggests that most women are poor at estimating the size of their body as a whole, and the size of particular body parts, tending to think that they are larger than they really are.

Body size estimation techniques allow women to estimate the size of their bodies, and give a quantitative measure of the degree of distortion. Estimation techniques generally fall into two categories: 'part body' and 'whole body'. Part body methods involve estimating the size of specific parts of the body, usually by adjusting the width of light beams projected onto a wall. Whole body estimation techniques involve looking at an image (usually a photograph of the woman's own body) made either fatter or thinner than actual size, and adjusting the image to match perceived size.

Part body estimation techniques

Part body techniques, which allow the participant to estimate the size of specific body parts in turn, were popular in the 1970s and 1980s but are less so now. The Moveable Calliper Technique (Slade and Russell, 1973) involves asking the participant to adjust two horizontally mounted lights to match the width of a particular body part. This technique was modified in the 1980s by Thompson and Spana (1988) to include a simultaneous presentation of four light beams representing the cheeks, waist, hips and thighs. They call this instrument the Adjustable Light Beam Apparatus. The participant is required to adjust the width of all four light beams to match her own estimate of the width of her cheeks, waist, hips and thighs. An assessment of the participant's actual widths (measured with body callipers) is compared with her estimate; and a ratio of over- or under-estimation is calculated. Kevin Thompson has found that women tend to overestimate the size of all four body parts by about 25 per cent, and that the waist is overestimated to the greatest degree (Thompson *et al.*, 1990). So women tend to perceive cheeks, waist, hips and thighs as 25 per cent larger than they are in reality.

Whole body estimation techniques

These methods involve presenting the participant with real-life images that are objectively thinner or fatter than her actual size. She is asked to select the image that matches her perception of her current size. For example, David Garner, who heads the Eating Disorders Section at Michigan State University in the United States, uses the Distorting Photograph Technique where participants are asked to indicate their size by adjusting a photograph that is distorted in a range from 20 per cent under to 20 per cent over actual size. Degree of distortion in body image (i.e. the extent to which the woman over estimates the size of her body) is measured by the discrepancy between actual size and perceived size. Women show a reliable tendency to overestimate the size of their body, with slimmer women showing more of a distortion tendency than heavier women. Other researchers in Australia (Touyz *et al.*, 1984) and the US (Gardner and Moncrieff, 1988) use the Distorting Video Technique, where participants indicate their perceived size by adjusting a video image that is distorted by from 50 per cent under to 50 per cent over their actual size. Women tend to overestimate their size using this procedure, perceiving themselves as heavier than they actually are. Whole body techniques have been criticised. It has been argued (Thompson *et al.*, 1990) that confrontation with a real-life image that increases in size may be very upsetting to an individual sensitive to appearance (i.e. to many women!). Also, the techniques do not allow the participant to manipulate individual body sites separately. This is important because size estimation may be site-specific and not constant to the whole body (Thompson and Spana, 1988), so that a woman may overestimate size of hips, stomach and thighs, but not the rest of the body. An answer to this second problem may be found in computerised techniques which allow participants to alter specific areas of a visual image on the screen to match their body shape and size.

Combined whole and part body estimation

Emery and his colleagues (1995) from Newcastle and Oxford Universities have produced a sophisticated computerised measure that enables them to 'grab' a frame from a video of the participant in a leotard. The participant then observes the frame-grabbed image on the VDU screen. The participant can use the cursor to modify the shape of different parts of the image to produce what she feels is an accurate representation of her own body shape. The programme can then calculate for each body part the degree of under- or overestimation of size. A study of twenty women between 19 and 32 years of age showed that the women tended to overestimate size of legs, buttocks and abdomen, and underestimate the size of other body parts. The advantages of this method are that it allows study of the particular areas of the body that are over- or underestimated and allows the participant to look at an image that realistically mimics weight loss or gain, rather than just widening or narrowing the image.

Studies using these techniques show that the majority of women tend to perceive their body as heavier than it actually is. Kevin Thompson *et al.* (1990), on the basis of a review of the available literature, argue that anorexic and 'normal' women overestimate to a similar extent. Thinner women overestimate more than heavier women, but if anorexics are matched with women of the same size they overestimate to a similar extent. Stage within the menstrual cycle also has an effect, when the size of the waist is overestimated in the days prior to menstruation (Thompson *et al.*, 1990).

So, to conclude this section, evidence suggests that most women overestimate the size of (at least) parts of the body. It is important to bear this tendency to overestimate body size in mind when assessing the data from studies of body satisfaction, because they need to be understood in the context of the fact that most women have unrealistic images of their body, particularly their waist, hips and thighs. These data also emphasise the importance of focusing on women's perceptions of body size, and discrepancy from the slim ideal, rather than on objective size. In interview work, we have found no relationship between women's actual size and their level of body satisfaction and wish to be slimmer. Perception of size is likely to be a much better predictor of body satisfaction than objectively measured body weight, a prediction borne out in studies that have found that perceived size is a better predictor of body satisfaction than Body Mass Index (e.g. Furnham and Greaves, 1994).

Behavioural indicators of body dissatisfaction

One way to evaluate body shape/weight concern is to look at it indirectly, by monitoring behaviours that would be expected to result from such concern. Interview work has suggested that women engage in dieting and exercise as ways of trying to change body size and shape. This section will investigate body-relevant behaviours in women, including dieting, exercise and plastic surgery.

Dieting

One behavioural indicator of body dissatisfaction is inclination to try to change body shape through diet. Most women have attempted to change weight and shape at some time in their lives by reduction of food intake. Estimates of the frequency of dieting in American and British women show that about 95 per cent of women have dieted at some stage in their lives (Ogden, 1992); and that about 40 per cent of women are dieting at any one time (Horm and Anderson, 1993).

In a study of British women aged 18–35, Furnham and Greaves (1994) found that forty-eight out of fifty-five (87 per cent) had dieted or were currently dieting. When asked their reasons for dieting, women were more likely than men to cite 'to be slim' and 'to increase confidence and self-esteem'.

Most researchers find that diets lead to long-term weight loss in only about 5 per cent of non-obese dieters. The other 95 per cent are likely to feel that they have failed. Nickie Charles and Marion Kerr (1986) found that most of the women they interviewed had dieted as a way to try to lose weight, and most felt that they had failed because they had been unable to keep to the diet.

Most of the women interviewed at Manchester Metropolitan University use dieting to try to lose weight. For instance:

> We know we've got to diet to keep slim.
>
> (43)

> The only way to get rid of it [weight], to feel more comfortable with yourself, is to diet.
>
> (34)

> [If I didn't diet] I'd be fat. If I didn't keep on top of it and keep conscious of it because of my appetite and the amount I eat I would be very fat I think.
>
> (30)

This continuous vigilance over the body was a common feature of women's discourse. Most reported dieting in cycles, losing weight by dieting for between two and six weeks, and then putting on the weight again when they started eating normally. For instance:

> Well, I can't cut down. I have to go to extremes. I have to once I manage it. I keep trying and trying and once I start a diet I can

keep it going for six weeks as long as I don't cheat at all. If I have any cheats that's it. I have to keep to a steady routine, so I'd have branflakes for breakfast, cottage cheese and soup for lunch, and a diet meal for tea, and at weekends I'd probably allow myself to binge. But if I broke that pattern during the week that's it. I'd start eating excessively then. From one extreme to another. When I do it I go over the top really. So I can lose it quick, but that is probably why it goes on so quick.

(35)

My whole life I think is going to be dieting and then non-dieting, then dieting, and I know it's not good for your health.

(43)

Most of the women interviewed distinguished clearly between 'normal' dieting (cutting down on fatty foods, generally eating less, calorie counting) and what most of them referred to as 'fad' (or 'faddy') diets, which were usually liquid protein diets, or all-fruit diets. Liquid protein diets started in the mid-1970s, and involve replacing meals with low-calorie protein drinks (powder mixed with water) which (usually) promise to give you all the protein you need to be healthy whilst reducing calorie intake. There is some evidence that these diets, which were originally designed for people who are obese, may be dangerous for those who are within the normal range but 'feel fat', although, as Jane Ogden (1992) says, these diets are so boring that most people give them up before they can do any real harm. A similar argument can be made for the all-fruit diets, which recommend periods of starvation where only fruit is eaten. These could be dangerous for health. Authors of these diets often encourage the reader to engage in bulimic-type behaviour, bingeing (on off-diet days) and then purging (on diet days), eating fruit which acts as a diuretic to encourage weight loss.

In the interviews, most women said that they were against what they called 'fad dieting', because such diets were seen to be ineffective in the long term (because they were boring and led to cravings for other foods) and bad for health (because they did not contain necessary nutrients). For instance:

I think that fad diets are absolutely stupid. The only way to lose weight is to cut down generally and to exercise.

(46)

> When I go on one of those silly diets I actually feel tired. I'm obviously not getting enough energy.
>
> (30)

Women commonly reported denial of food to look slimmer for a night out. For instance:

> Say you've got something tight on and you don't want it to be so tight, you'd watch what you ate all week so that you could wear it for a night out. You tend to starve yourself till the night then binge after cos it doesn't matter then until the next night out.
>
> (27)

> It's like when I go out on a Friday night I can't eat so I can look slimmer that night when I go out. My belly is flatter if I don't eat.
>
> (25)

This short-term change in behaviour was not usually seen as 'dieting', which was characterised as a more long-term change in behaviour. Restriction of food, even when hungry, to look slimmer was reported by most of the women we spoke to.

Dieting is common amongst women. Many women deny themselves food, especially before a special occasion, to look slimmer. Women diet to look thinner, in the belief that thinness is associated with confidence. Certainly, the slimming industry promotes this association, with images of self-confident-looking thin models, and the rhetoric of a 'new you' after the commercially available diet has helped you to lose weight.

Exercise

There is some evidence that women are exercising more frequently in the 1990s than in the 1980s. In Britain, evidence comes from the two Health and Lifestyle surveys carried out in 1984/5 and 1991/2 on a nationwide sample of adults in England, Scotland and Wales. The 1991/2 survey showed a significant increase in the percentage of women engaging in activities involving physical effort compared to the 1984/5 survey (Cox *et al.*, 1993). As expected, activity levels are highest in the under-40s, and significantly lower in the over-60s. The most frequent activities for women in the 1991/2 survey (across ages) were keep-fit and yoga, followed by dancing, then swimming, then cycling and jogging. Men under 50 did significantly more exercise than women in the same age group, except in keep-fit/yoga and dancing.

It may be that women's motivation for exercise differs from that of men. Furnham and Greaves (1994) found that women were more likely than men to cite exercising for weight control, altering body shape, attractiveness and health. In the interviews with women reported in this chapter, all the women interviewed use (or intend to use) some form of exercise (from walking to aerobics) as a way to lose weight and 'tone' their bodies. The primary motivator to exercise for all the women interviewed was to improve muscle tone and lose weight, rather than for health (e.g. to improve cardiovascular fitness) or other (e.g. social) reasons. For instance:

> [I exercise] entirely for weight. To try to firm up and try to use some calories and I'm always thinking I'm not doing enough. Afterwards, like after I've been swimming, I feel great. I actually feel slimmer.
>
> (32)

> I want to make my legs smaller. I do exercises for that.
>
> (17)

According to the 1991/2 Health and Lifestyle Survey, about 50 per cent of women under 40 engage in some form of exercise. Positive effects are not limited to changes in muscle tone and fitness (although this might be what motivates in the first place). Researchers have argued that women who exercise experience positive changes in body image and self-concept. Snyder and Kivlin (1975) found that women who exercised had a more positive body image than non-exercising women. They present evidence that women exercisers felt more positive towards their bodies, especially in relation to energy level and health, and perceived their participation in sports as satisfying and rewarding.

In a more recent study of exercising and non-exercising British women, exercisers were compared to non-exercisers on body image. Adrian Furnham and colleagues (1994) selected sixty white British women to take part in the study, split into four groups of fifteen. The first group (non-exercisers) were women who did not take part in any regular exercise (most exercised less than once a week). The three groups of exercisers all exercised at least three times per week. The first of these were netball players, the second were rowers and the third were body-builders. Participants were asked to rate nine sketches of naked female shapes (Figure 3.2) ranging from 'anorexic' to

hypertrophic (extremely muscular) on ten attributes (confident, feminine, healthy, masculine, popular, sexy, unattractive, unfriendly,
unhappy, unnatural).

They were also asked to rate their own body on similar measures,
and to identify the sketch closest to the way they would like their body
to look. The researchers found that exercising women tended to
perceive thin shapes more negatively, and more muscular shapes more
positively, than did non-exercising women. Also, the women who exercised had a more positive perception of their own bodies than those
who did not exercise. This may be because exercise contributes to a
slimmer, more toned body. It is also likely that physical mastery
increases self-esteem. Body-builders and rowers viewed the muscular
body shapes more positively than the other two groups, suggesting that
they set less rigid definitions of desirable body shape in women. As
might be expected, the body-builders rated the highly muscular figures

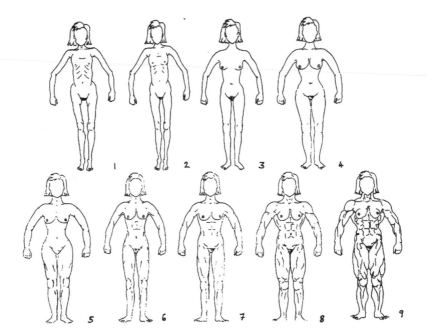

Figure 3.2 Female body shapes

Source: Adapted from Furnham *et al.*, 1994, with permission.

most positively, rating them as more feminine, sexy and attractive, and less unnatural and masculine, than did the other groups.

The body-builders in the Furnham *et al.* (1994) study challenged traditional stereotypes of femininity as represented by the slim, shapely ideal currently in vogue. Body-building is not generally seen as appropriate for women, and women who engage in this sport may face discrimination. In the 1970s, studies showed that men had a negative attitude to women engaging in *any* sport, and particularly those where a traditionally feminine appearance could not be maintained (Fisher *et al.*, 1978; Snyder and Spreitzer, 1974). In Snyder and Kivlin's (1975) study, athletes reported receiving negative comments and experiencing gender-role conflict. It may be that the 1990s have heralded a change in attitudes in relation to women's participation in sports. Certainly, more women engage in sporting activities than they did in the 1980s. However, sports that build muscle are seen as less appropriate for women (Mansfield and McGinn, 1993).

Body-building among women is said to be increasing, although statistical evidence is sketchy. Body-building was not one of the categories of activity studied in the Health and Lifestyle Survey. Surveys of gym membership have tended to find that about one third as many women as men engage in body-building (e.g. Korkia, 1994). Pirkko Korkia's work looks specifically at degree of anabolic steroid use in women using body-building gyms. Twenty-one weight training gyms, in London, Merseyside, Swansea and Glasgow, were surveyed. All women using the gyms over a two-day period, on days when the maximum number of clients could be expected, were asked to complete a questionnaire, and 349 women were surveyed. Of these, eight women (2.3 per cent) had used anabolic steroids at some time, and five (1.4 per cent) were currently using them. In interviews, most women reported that they used oxandrolone, methandrostenolone and stanozolol. In the second part of this study, Korkia interviewed thirteen women who were current users of anabolic steroids. One woman suffered menstrual irregularities through steroid use, and two reported that they had suffered permanent side-effects from steroid use. This study suggests that a significant minority of women are using steroids to help to build muscle mass. United States studies have tended to find slightly higher incidences of steroid use amongst women. Charles Yeselis and Michael Bahrke (1995) place the incidence of use in women at 1–6 per cent, with highest use amongst athletes and body-builders. The main side-effects included menstrual abnormalities, deepening of the voice, shrinkage of breasts, baldness, acne, increased body hair and clitoral enlargement. These side-effects run directly counter to current cultural ideals for women's body image, so could be expected to lead to negative responses from others. It is therefore most interesting that these women are able to reject cultural ideals, and actively strive for a body that is strong and muscular while being socially unacceptable.

Women's body-building has been conceptualised in many different ways by feminist writers. Sandra Lee Bartky (1990) sees it as a direct challenge to the cultural restrictions placed on women in terms of how our bodies should look, and argues that women body-builders represent a radical cutting edge of feminist resistance to cultural ideals. She represents an optimistic view of body-building as a way to challenge dominant ideologies that represent women as physically weak, showing that muscularity (and, by inference, strength) is mostly a product of cultural practices. By showing that women's physical weakness is (mostly) culturally produced, she opens up the possibility that it is surpassable. This view sees body-building as an empowering practice that challenges the cultural association of muscularity (and strength) with masculinity. An alternative view is presented by Susan Bordo (1990), who sees body-building as women's response to cultural pressures to control their bodies into a culturally acceptable, firm, toned, solid form. She links body-building with anorexia, seeing both as attempts to avoid 'the soft, the loose, unsolid, excess flesh' (p. 90). She sees women body-builders as responding to cultural pressures to have a slim, firm body, but doing so in a different way from women who choose to try to attain the ideal through the usual means of restriction of food intake. For Bordo, these women are not challenging cultural ideals, but merely responding to them in a different way.

Leena St Martin and Nicola Gavey (1996) argue that women's competitive body-building in the 1990s does represent a significant challenge to concepts of what is natural for women's bodies, because elite women body-builders are attaining the kind of muscle bulk that is well in excess of what is normative for male bodies – the kind of muscularity that has been traditionally associated with male body-builders. These women's bodies are not merely well-muscled and firm. They are big and bulky and really challenge cultural ideals of how women's bodies should be. However, St Martin and Gavey show that, in competition, body-building women are required to be 'feminine', producing pressures for 'almost hyper-feminine ornamentation, posture and demeanour' (p. 54). They show how women body-builders undergo plastic surgery (such as breast augmentation) to emphasise their femininity, and are expected to ornament themselves as 'feminine' in their posing suits, make-up and hairstyles. Still, they argue that:

While the femininity control institutionalised in competitive body-building cannot be denied, this feminine overlay on a highly muscularized body doesn't automatically prevent it from disrupting the sex/gender system. If we read body-building and bodybuilders' bodies as cultural texts, then it is possible to interpret women's body-building as a challenging and destabilizing cultural practice.

(St Martin and Gavey, 1996: 54)

St Martin and Gavey argue that women's body-building requires bodies that transgress the feminine, and that the requirement for hyper-femininity in competition could be seen as the result of the attempt to bring these women back into the feminine fold, to make them acceptable to the dominant culture. However, ironically, this has the effect of posing more of a challenge to traditional ways of understanding gender than is presented by women engaged in other sports where they are not emphasising their femininity, because the conflict between their bodies and cultural expectations of what their bodies should look like cannot just be explained by denoting them as 'not really women'.

Cosmetic surgery

The 1990s have seen a significant increase in the numbers of women receiving cosmetic surgery in Britain and the United States, especially liposuction and breast augmentation procedures (Gillespie, 1996; Viner, 1997). More and more women are turning to plastic surgery as a way to change the shape of their bodies (Pruzinsky and Edgerton, 1990).

Plastic surgery is not a recent phenomenon. It is possible to trace its history from 1000 BC; the first plastic surgery was reported in India, when rhinoplasty (nose reconstruction) was carried out on individuals whose noses had been cut off as a form of punishment (Davis, 1995). However, it was not until the mid-twentieth century that *cosmetic* surgery (where surgery is performed for the aesthetic improvement of healthy bodies) emerged. Naomi Wolf (1991) traces the beginnings of what she calls the 'Surgical Age', where cosmetic surgery became a mass phenomenon. Today cosmetic surgery accounts for about 40 per cent of plastic surgery, mostly performed on women who are dissatisfied with the way that they look (Davis, 1995).

Why do so many women choose such an extreme method of changing their body shape? The question of why women are willing to undergo unnecessary surgery to make their bodies more pleasing may help us to understand the nature of body dissatisfaction in women.

Kathy Davis (1995) looks at cosmetic surgery from a feminist viewpoint. She argues that understanding why women engage in a practice which is painful and dangerous must take women's explanations as a starting point. She attempts to explore cosmetic surgery as one of the most negative aspects of Western beauty culture without seeing the women who opt for the 'surgical fix' as what she calls 'cultural dopes' (i.e. by taking seriously their reasons for having cosmetic surgery). She carried out her study in The Netherlands, where there had been a general increase in cosmetic surgery in the preceding years (to more than 20,000 cosmetic operations in 1994 – more *per capita* than in the United States). Since cosmetic surgery is freely available to all women in Holland, provided their appearance is classified as falling 'outside the realm of the normal', it was possible to investigate women's decisions without financial considerations being an issue.

She spoke with women who had had a variety of different kinds of cosmetic surgery. She found that women gave accounts that dispelled the notion that they were simply the duped victims of the beauty system. They had histories of long suffering with bodies that they experienced as unacceptable, different or abnormal. She argues that cosmetic surgery is about wanting to be normal rather than wanting to be beautiful. Women she interviewed reported that they experienced the decision to have plastic surgery as a way of taking control of their lives, and that cosmetic surgery was something that they had decided upon for themselves, rather than under pressure from partners or knife-happy surgeons. They were clear that they had made informed choices, based on weighing up the risks and possible benefits of surgery. Davis takes the position that cosmetic surgery may be an informed choice, but it is always made in the context of culturally limited options. She argues fiercely against the idea expressed by many authors, including Kathryn Morgan (1991), that women who opt for cosmetic surgery are victims of male lovers, husbands, or surgeons. She also disagrees that women who opt for cosmetic surgery are the dupes of ideologies which confuse and mystify with the rhetoric of individual choice.

Davis sees women as active and knowledgeable agents who make decisions based on a limited range of available options. She argues that women see through the conditions of oppression even as they comply with them. The women she interviewed reported that they had made free choices, although these 'choices' were limited by cultural definitions of beauty and by the availability of particular surgical techniques. The 'choices' need to be placed within a framework which sees women's bodies as commodities. Davis's arguments echo arguments about surgery in transsexuals when she talks about being 'trapped in a body that does not fit her sense of who she is' (1995: 163), and about 'a way to reinstate a damaged sense of self and become who they really are or should have been' (1995: 169), seeing surgery as a way to re-negotiate identity through changing the appearance of the body. This raises interesting problems for those who object to cosmetic surgery on grounds of political correctness, since there are parallels between the (probably politically correct) right of individuals to have gender reassignment operations because of identity conflict, and the accounts of women who have (probably politically incorrect) plastic surgery for the same reason. She argues against opting for the comfortingly clear politically correct feminist line that sees cosmetic surgery as self-inflicted subordination to the beauty system, and suggests that we should try to understand cosmetic surgery as a dilemma for women, which is desirable and problematic for the women who choose to go down the surgical route. She cautions against closing the debate by accepting the politically correct line, and suggests that:

> As concerned critics of the explosion in surgical technologies for reshaping the female body and of women's continued willingness to partake in them, we simply cannot afford the comfort of the correct line.
>
> (Davis, 1995: 185)

Kathryn Morgan (1991) takes a more mainstream feminist view. She argues that, although women may feel that they are making a free and informed choice, they are not really free to make a genuine choice because of patriarchal cultural pressures on them; that, although women may say that they are creating a new identity for themselves, they are really conforming to traditional (male-dominated) ideologies of how women's bodies should look. She argues that women who believe they are somehow taking control over their bodies (and their lives) by opting for plastic surgery have really been coerced by family, friends, partners and, indirectly, by the medical profession, and she believes that the rhetoric of choice that is found in advertising materials for private plastic surgery is 'ideological camouflage' which hides the real absence of choice. She believes that plastic surgery can never be an acceptable course of action for an individual woman, since to have plastic surgery is to support a system that is oppressive to women.

Morgan's (1991) examples come from women's magazine and

newspaper articles, including personal accounts of experiences of plastic surgery. A random selection of advertisements in women's magazines shows how the advertisers stress improvements in confidence (Transform: 'Years of development in plastic surgery enables women to have beautiful breasts and the confidence to enjoy life to the full'); and in rationality (The Pountney Clinic: '[Liposuction] is the logical way to complete a "trim" figure'); and avoid any mention of pain, stressing instead the virtues of care and reassurance (Transform: 'All treatments are carried out in the caring and reassuring atmosphere of Europe's leading private clinics'). Pictures of conventionally attractive models appear in the advertisements, along with statements such as 'Cosmetic surgery changed my life' (The Belvedere Private Clinic). Also in women's magazines, it is easy to find examples of articles encouraging plastic surgery. For instance, one article headed 'Bigger breasts, cheek implants, nose jobs, tummy tucks . . . You'll be surprised at what's available on the NHS – and how easy it is to get it' (*Company*, February 1995) gives readers 'nine steps to getting plastic surgery on the NHS'. Although the article warns about having unrealistic expectations ('If you're expecting bigger breasts to bring back a straying man, or suddenly give you more confidence in life, you're in for a real disappointment'), telling women how much each operation costs and how to go about getting operations done on the National Health Service suggests general approval of the principle of cosmetic surgery. In conjunction with carrying advertisements for plastic surgery (I have been unable to find any British magazine aimed at young women that does not do so), women's magazines promote the practice.

Social construction of femininity

Susie Orbach (1993) argues that women are taught from an early age to view their bodies as commodities. She shows how women's bodies are used to humanise and sell products in Western consumer culture, and how the fact that women's bodies themselves are objectified creates body image problems for women:

> The receptivity that women show (across class, ethnicity, and through the generations) to the idea that their bodies are like gardens – arenas for constant improvement and resculpting – is rooted in the recognition of their bodies as commodities. A consumer society in which women's bodies perform the crucial function of humanising other products while being presented as the ultimate commodity creates all sorts of body image problems

for women, both at the level of distortion about their own and others' bodies, and in creating a disjuncture from their bodies.

(Orbach, 1993: 17)

Orbach links the objectification and distancing of the body to the rise of *anorexia nervosa*, which she characterises as 'a metaphor for our age', when women use their bodies as statements about their discomfort with their position in the world. This will be examined further in Chapter 7.

Some feminist researchers see women as victims of a society that controls women through their bodies. In the 1980s, several feminist authors suggested that a system of beauty norms set up impossible ideals for women, who were expected to be slender but large breasted. These unrealistic ideals were seen as an ideal way to keep women in a subordinate position, by ensuring that they put their energies into vigilance over their bodies. Women's energies are channelled into the 'fight' for a perfect body. Susan Brownmiller (1984), in *Femininity*, presents a seemingly light-hearted but intelligent and hard-hitting analysis of women's relationships with their bodies. She traces the development of women's concern with the body from childhood into adulthood. She draws on her personal experiences as a woman developing in the United States, and notes how changes in fashions meant that parts of her anatomy that did not change in themselves became more or less problematic depending on current trends. She takes a critical look at the importance of body size in relation to cultural expectations for women, noting that masculinity is tied to concepts of 'powerful' and 'large', whereas femininity is linked to 'small' and 'weak'. She argues that pressure on women to be slight and small is driven by men's desire to dominate:

> When a woman stands taller than a man she has broken a cardinal feminine rule, for her physical stature reminds him that he may be too short – inadequate, insufficient – for the competitive world of men. She has dealt a blow to his masculine image, undermined his footing as aggressor-protector.
>
> (Brownmiller, 1984: 13–14)

Brownmiller notes that, in the majority of species, females are in fact the larger sex, despite the anthropomorphic assumptions made by illustrators of children's books. Nevertheless, the associations of maleness with largeness and femaleness with smallness are firmly embedded in our consciousness, leading to discomfort when these expectations are challenged. She argues that this discomfort extends to fleshiness in women, since fat means additional bulk, a property associated with solidity and power which are not culturally acceptable feminine characteristics. This is despite the fact that women's bodies typically carry 10 per cent more fatty tissue than men's. She shows how women's bodies have been controlled and restricted across civilisations to conform to prevailing aesthetics, and how these practices served to weaken women physically, making them more dependent on men.

Brownmiller traces the history of the prevailing current vogue for extreme slimness, showing how ideals of feminine perfection have changed over the years and pointing to the voluptuous nudes portrayed by Ingres in *The Turkish bath* (Plate 12, p. 91), and the women of the Ziegfeld Follies with their 36–26–38 figures and the accent on their hips.

She notes the importance of the bikini (which looks most pleasing on a skinny body), and of both Jacqueline Kennedy (a determined dieter) and Twiggy, in determining the fashion for slimness in the United States in the 1960s. Slenderness became identified with refinement, will power and chic, and success at dieting became an important form of competition amongst women within a context where women were encouraged to compete in terms of physical appearance:

> How one looks is the chief physical weapon in female-against-female competition.
>
> (Brownmiller, 1984: 33)

She argues forcibly that striving for physical perfection (a physical vulnerability that is reassuring to men) is a constant distraction for women. Women are never free from self-consciousness, and they constantly self-monitor:

> [They are] never quite satisfied, and never secure, for desperate unending absorption in the drive for a perfect appearance – call it feminine vanity – is the ultimate restriction on freedom of mind.
>
> (Brownmiller, 1984: 33)

Wendy Chapkis (1986) argues that women are oppressed by a 'global culture machine' (made up of the advertising industry, communications media, and the cosmetic industry) which promotes a narrow, Westernised ideal of beauty to women all over the world. She looks at the rituals that women go through to try to attain the ideal, and uses these to demonstrate how oppressive these beauty regimes are for women. She argues that women are entrapped in the beauty system, but that there are possibilities for change if women are willing to accept themselves and their bodies as they really are. This would involve a close examination of 'beauty secrets' (the rituals that most women undertake to try to conform to the cultural ideal) and a rejection of these in favour of a celebration of the 'natural' body.

Susan Bordo (1993) argues that preoccupation with fat, diet and slenderness in women is normative. She suggests that Western culture surrounds women with clear messages that overweight (described as 'bulges' and 'bumps') must be 'destroyed', 'eliminated', 'burned'. The ideal is a body completely under control, tight and contained. She argues that the seemingly disparate areas of body-building and compulsive dieting are linked in their rejection of loose, soft flesh:

> The two ideals, though superficially very different, are united in a battle against a common enemy: the soft, the loose, unsolid, excess flesh. It is perfectly permissible in our culture (even for women) to have substantial weight and bulk – so long as it is tightly managed.
> (Bordo, 1993: 191)

Bordo's analysis places women's preoccupation with slimness into a cultural context in order to explain why women are especially susceptible to pressures from the beauty system. She is pessimistic about women's ability really to resist these pressures. She argues that women cannot help but collude with the system because they are submerged in the culture where slimness in women is associated with a specific (positive) set of cultural meanings. She says that feminists should be sceptical about the possibility of developing free, feminine identities that are independent of the mainstream beauty culture, and shows how women's attempts to escape the system may be reabsorbed into negative discourses of femininity.

One of the problems with this analysis is that women end up as 'victims' of a system of oppression. In contrast, Dorothy Smith (1990) sees women in an active role in interpreting cultural messages. She argues that women 'do femininity' in an active way. She represents 'femininity' as a skilled activity. One of the sources of learning the skill of 'being feminine' is to read appropriate materials (especially women's magazines) where information is actively presented on how to be more attractive. The material itself requires prior knowledge in the area to place it into context. She shows how women's magazine articles assume agency in the reader, and how they work by presenting the woman with a specific ideal (in the representation of a 'perfect' model body), and telling her what she needs to do to attain the ideal (diet, exercise, use cellulite creams and make-up). She argues that the creation of dissatisfaction in women leads to active attempts to rectify the perceived deficiency. Women objectify their bodies and are constantly planning and enacting measures to bring them closer to the ideal.

Sandra Bartky (1990) also sees women as actively engaging with the representation of the female body. She argues that what she calls the 'fashion–beauty complex' seeks (on the surface) to provide opportunities for women to indulge themselves, but covertly depreciates women's bodies by constantly presenting messages that women fail to measure up to the current ideals:

> We are presented everywhere with images of perfect female beauty – at the drugstore cosmetics display, the supermarket magazine counter, on television. These images remind us constantly that we fail to measure up. Whose nose is the right shape, after all, whose hips are not too wide – or too narrow? The female body is revealed as a task, an object in need of transformation. . . . The fashion–beauty complex produces in women an estrangement from her bodily being: on the one hand, she is it and is scarcely allowed to be anything else; on the other hand, she must exist perpetually at a distance from her physical self, fixed at this distance in a permanent posture of disapproval.
>
> (Bartky, 1990: 40)

Bartky notes that every aspect of women's bodies is objectified, so that women feel estranged from their bodies. She suggests that the pleasures that women report in body-maintenance procedures result from the creation of 'false needs' by the fashion–beauty complex, which produces the needs themselves (through indoctrination, psychological manipulation and the denial of autonomy), and also controls the conditions through which these needs can be satisfied. She argues that the repressive narcissistic satisfactions promoted by the fashion–beauty complex stand in the way of authentic delight in the body. She suggests a revolutionary aesthetic of the body, which allows an expansion of ideas of beauty and allows body display and play in self-ornamentation. She promotes the release of our capacity to apprehend the beautiful from the narrow limits within which it is currently confined, to produce an aesthetic for the female body controlled by women. She proposes that women should produce a model of feminine beauty that celebrates diversity. This could be an ideal that actually makes women feel better about themselves, rather than one that breeds body insecurity amongst those who do not conform to the slender, well-toned mainstream cultural ideal.

Feminist accounts of women's experience of the body are important in helping to make sense of why women in particular show normative body concern. There can be no doubt that Western culture in the 1990s promotes unrealistic body ideals to women, and that non-conformity to these ideals leads to social disapproval. The question of women's active involvement in restrictive beauty practices (such as dieting and plastic surgery) is more complex, and writers such as Sandra Bartky, Susie Orbach and Dorothy Smith provide useful explanations of women's active involvement in the process of 'doing femininity', seeing women as active agents, making knowledgeable choices about the body within a restricted range of cultural options.

Summary

- Most women are dissatisfied with their bodies, particularly their stomachs, hips and thighs.
- Most would choose to be thinner than they currently are.
- Questionnaires, interviews and body size estimation techniques have found a similar pattern of dissatisfaction in British, American and Australian women.
- Feminist approaches to understanding women's dissatisfaction suggest that social pressure on women to strive for the slender, toned body shape that is associated with youth, control and success encourages the objectification of the body and the disproportionate allocation of energies to body maintenance.
- A positive way forward is indicated by Sandra Bartky (1990), who promotes the development of a new aesthetic of the female body which would allow women to really enjoy bodily display and self-ornamentation through broadening the limits of acceptable body shape and size.

4   Men and body satisfaction

The study of the psychology and sociology of the male body is a recent phenomenon. Until recently, the study of body image was largely restricted to women. Women's bodies are represented more frequently in the media than the male body, and descriptions of women tend to be more embodied than those of men (Morgan, 1993). Over the last decade, psychologists and sociologists have become increasingly interested in men's body satisfaction. This is largely due to the fact that the male body has become more 'visible' in popular culture, producing interest in the effects of this increased visibility on men's body satisfaction. This chapter summarises current research and assesses the effect of increased cultural pressures on men to attain a socially acceptable, muscular, toned body.

There is a general consensus that most men aspire to a muscular mesomorphic shape characterised by average build with well-developed muscles on chest, arms and shoulders, and slim waist and hips, rather than the ectomorphic (thin) or endomorphic (fat) build. Research has shown that there is a general cultural prejudice in favour of the mesomorphic body shape. Men with this shape are assigned a variety of positive personality traits including being strong, happy, helpful and brave (see Kirkpatrick and Sanders, 1978). Given this cultural preference, it is not surprising that many men aspire to resemble the mesomorphic ideal, and report dissatisfaction to the extent that their build differs from this ideal.

It seems likely that the muscular shape is the masculine ideal because it is intimately tied to Western cultural notions of maleness as representing power, strength and aggression. Mansfield and McGinn (1993) argue that 'muscularity and masculinity can be, and often are, conflated' (p. 49). Mishkind and colleagues (1986) cite research that shows that people rate the muscular mesomorphic shape as the most masculine shape, and that they apply stereotypically masculine characteristics such as 'active', 'daring' and 'a fighter' to mesomorphic boys but not to endomorphic or ectomorphic boys. However, although moderate muscularity is rated highly, extreme muscularity (such as seen in male body-builders) is not culturally acceptable, being perceived as unnatural or even repulsive by some (St Martin and Gavey, 1996). The cultural ideal is slender and 'naturally' muscular, without being over-muscled (Mansfield and McGinn, 1993).

Assessment of body satisfaction

A similar array of techniques have been used to assess body shape concern in men as those used for women. These will be considered in turn to evaluate degree and direction of body dissatisfaction in men.

Silhouette studies

Studies using male silhouette figures have produced some interesting findings. April Fallon and Paul Rozin (1985) showed nine male silhouettes (Figure 4.1) to 248 US undergraduate students and asked them to indicate the figures that approximated their current figure, that they would like to look like, and that women would prefer.

There was no significant discrepancy between men's ideal, 'women's ideal', and their current shape. Fallon and Rozin conclude that men's

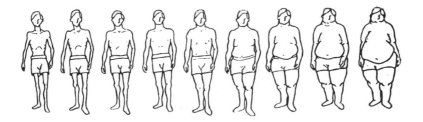

Figure 4.1 Male silhouette figure rating scale

Source: Adapted from Stunckard *et al.*, 1983, with permission.

perceptions serve to keep them satisfied with their figures, and relate the findings to the lower incidences of dieting, anorexia and bulimia in American men compared with American women. These findings have been replicated in more recent American studies (Zellner *et al.*, 1989; Lamb *et al.*, 1993); and by Marika Tiggemann (1992) in an Australian study. However, these studies are flawed, in that the researchers base their conclusions on scores averaged across their samples. Although body dissatisfaction in women usually relates to feeling overweight, body dissatisfaction in men may relate to feeling either overweight or underweight. Averaging has the effect of combining together men who believe they are either overweight or underweight compared to their ideal, so that on average they appear to have no discrepancy between their ideal and current body. Data need to be considered in terms of discrepancies between current and ideal shape for each individual man, to take account of those who are dissatisfied because they feel too thin as well as those who are dissatisfied because they feel too fat.

Marc Mishkind and colleagues (1986) took this methodological problem into account when designing their study. They found that, when shown a similar set of silhouette drawings of male body types ranging from very thin to very fat, 75 per cent of men reported that their ideal was discrepant from their current body size. Roughly half wanted to be bigger than they were and half wanted to be thinner than they were. In this respect there is an important difference between men and women on these silhouette tasks. Women reliably pick a slimmer ideal than their current shape. Men were equally likely to pick a thinner or a fatter ideal. Wanting to be fatter and wanting to be thinner both represent body dissatisfaction. These differences between men are lost when researchers average across groups. Mishkind *et al.*'s data suggest that a significant proportion of men are dissatisfied with their body shape.

Questionnaire studies

Most of the established body satisfaction questionnaires have been designed to look at body dissatisfaction in women, and contain items that are not relevant to men (Thompson *et al.*, 1990). Some are equally appropriate for use with both men and women. An example is Thomas Cash *et al.*'s (1986) Multidimensional Body–Self Relations Questionnaire (MBSRQ), which has a series of Body Area Satisfaction Sub-scales which enable the researcher to identify areas of the body that cause dissatisfaction in men and women. In their 1986 study, Cash *et al.* found that 34 per cent of men were generally dissatisfied with their looks, 41 per cent with their weight, 32 per cent with muscle tone, 28 per cent with upper torso, 50 per cent with mid-torso, and 21 per cent with lower torso. These percentages were higher than those found in a similar study in the 1970s (Berscheid *et al.*, 1973) which had found that only 15 per cent of men reported general dissatisfaction with their looks, 35 per cent with their weight, 25 per cent with muscle tone, 18 per cent with upper torso, 36 per cent with mid-torso, and 12 per cent with lower torso. The difference between these two studies suggests that men in the 1980s may have been less satisfied than men in the 1970s. Marc Mishkind and colleagues (1986) suggested that levels of dissatisfaction amongst men in the 1980s were even more extreme. They found that 95 per cent of the American college men they surveyed expressed dissatisfaction with some aspect of their bodies.

In a recent study, Clare Donaldson (1996) administered body image questionnaires to 100 male students in Manchester, England. They ranged from 18 to 43 years of age, with an average age of 28. The majority (eighty-five) were white. They ranged in height from 5 feet 4 inches to 6 feet 6 inches; and in weight from 7 stone 11 lb (109 lb) to 17 stone 12 lb (250 lb). She found that 27 per cent of the sample were dissatisfied with their weight, showing that men in this sample were, on average, more satisfied than Cash *et al.*'s (1986) American sample. However, 38 per cent were dissatisfied with their muscle tone, 25 per cent were dissatisfied with lower torso, 28 per cent with mid-torso and 37 per cent with upper torso. When asked about general body satisfaction, only 10 per cent of the men reported that they were generally dissatisfied with their body image; and 65 per cent said that they often liked themselves the way they were. However, when asked how often they felt depressed about their body image, only 47 per cent said that they 'never' felt depressed about their looks, with 4 per cent saying they 'often' did, and 1 per cent 'very often'. These data show that these men are clearly more satisfied with their bodies than equivalent groups of women, but nevertheless show some dissatisfaction with body shape and size.

Some studies report much higher estimates of dissatisfaction in British men. For instance, a survey commissioned by *Men's Health* magazine was completed by 1,000 of the magazine's readers. A total of 75 per cent were not happy with their body shape. Most wished their bodies were more muscular. About half were worried about their weight, ageing and going bald (Chaudhary, 1996). Such findings need to be interpreted with caution, since the readers of *Men's Health* may be a group of men who are particularly sensitive to body image issues and whose views are not representative of the general population of British men. However, the findings do demonstrate significant body image concern in men who read magazines which promote a healthy lifestyle and present the slender, muscular male body as the ideal body shape.

In a recent study carried out specifically for this book, body image questionnaires were administered to 100 men in Gainesville, Florida. Questionnaires were distributed by psychology students at Santa Fe Community College (Renee Schert, Melissa Warren, Damien Lavalee, Timothy Ford, Rhonda Blackwell and Harry Hatcher). Respondents ranged in age from 16 to 48 (average age 23), in height from 5 feet to 6 feet 5 inches (average 5 feet 11 inches), and in weight from 8 stone 6 lb (118 lb) to 19 stone 9 lb (275 lb) (average weight 12 stone 5 lb (173 lb)). Only 6.3 per cent reported that they were not generally happy with their body (slightly lower than the 10 per cent estimate from Donaldson's British men). However, 72 per cent would feel better if they became more muscular, and 80 per cent would feel better if they became more toned. Only 22 per cent would feel better if they were thinner. Muscularity and body tone were clearly important to these men, replicating Donaldson's British results. When asked about drugs they had taken to change body shape and size, 3 per cent reported that they had taken anabolic steroids. This is a higher percentage than expected, and suggests significant use of steroids amongst this group of men. Ninety per cent exercised regularly, 55 per cent played team/ball games (mostly basketball and football), 18 per cent did aerobics, 68 per cent did weight training and 36 per cent walked, cycled or roller-bladed. When asked why they exercised, 23 per cent did it for health and fitness, 41 per cent for weight/shape/appearance, 21 per cent for stress relief and 30 per cent for social reasons. These results replicated Donaldson's British findings in showing that a similar group of American men were also primarily concerned with muscularity and body tone, and that they were actively involved in trying to change their body shape and size through exercise (which more men did for cosmetic reasons than for any other reasons), dieting (which usually either entailed more 'healthy' eating, i.e. more fruit and vegetables) or restriction of food intake; and in a small number of cases, taking diet pills, stimulants or anabolic steroids to change body size.

Franzoi and Shields (1984) found three dimensions of body satisfaction in men: physical attractiveness (face and facial features); upper body strength (biceps, shoulder width, arms and chest); and physical conditioning (stamina, weight, energy level). The Franzoi and Shields Body Esteem Scale was administered by Adrian Furnham and Nicola Greaves (1994) to forty-seven British men aged 18–35 (mostly university undergraduates). Participants were asked to rate (on a 10-point scale, from 1 = complete dissatisfaction to 10 = complete satisfaction) how satisfied they were with their nose, lips, waist, thighs, ears, biceps, chin, buttocks, width of shoulders, arms, chest, eyes, cheeks, hips, legs, feet, stomach, body hair, face and weight. They were also asked to rate 'attempt to change' each body part on a similar 10-point scale. Men were least satisfied with biceps, width of shoulders and chest measurement, and were most likely to try to change these aspects of the body. This finding coincides with current ideals of male body shape, where the emphasis is on broad shoulders and well-muscled chest and arms.

There is some evidence that men's self-esteem is tied up with how good they feel about their body shape and size. Mintz and Betz (1986) found that high levels of body satisfaction were associated with high social self-esteem in men and women. Of course, such correlational evidence needs to be interpreted with caution, since any causal link could operate in either direction. It is significant, though, that body satisfaction is related in a similar way in women and men, since the suggestion that body satisfaction may be affected by (or may affect) self-esteem in men is counter to suggestions by some authors (e.g. Ogden, 1992) that, for men, body satisfaction is independent of self-esteem.

Interview studies

One of the limitations of the questionnaire work cited above is that estimates of dissatisfaction fail to tell us why men are dissatisfied, and how this dissatisfaction affects their lives. Jane Ogden (1992) reports interviews with men in which she asked them to talk about their bodies. The results were interesting. She found that the men she interviewed were clear on how the ideal man should look. He should be tall, well-built, with wide shoulders, 'v'-shaped back, firm bottom and flat stomach. Men emphasised fitness and health as being important, and linked the slim, muscular ideal with being confident and in control. There are obvious parallels here with our interviews with women, where being *slim* was equated with being confident and in control.

In a study carried out at Manchester Metropolitan University (Grogan *et al.*, 1997), Clare Donaldson interviewed four men aged 19 to 25 about their body image. These men were in agreement that the ideal male body was toned and muscular. Being muscular was linked with being healthy and fit:

Man 1:   There is a stereotypical man, isn't there? Kind of . . .

Man 2:	There is now.
Man 1:	The shaped jaw and perfect pecs.
Man 2:	Defined stomach muscles.
Interviewer:	None of you have suggested an ideal body shape, but there must be ideals in mind.
Man 3:	Healthy and fit.
Man 2:	Toned definitely.
Man 1:	Height doesn't matter. If you are toned that'd be about as good as you can have.
Man 2:	As long as they look fit and toned and healthy and athletic.

These ideals correspond exactly to the cultural ideal of the well-toned mesomorph.

These men believed that the ideal body was within their reach (through exercise), but were not motivated to exercise to change their body shape since it was not sufficiently important to them. They believed that women were more likely to be motivated to exercise to change body image, but that body shape mattered less to men:

Interviewer:	Do you ever look in magazines and wish you could look like the models inside?
Man 1:	The thing is, most people could. Any of us could look like that if we put the effort and time in.
Man 2:	Go down the gym and sort it out. If we were that bothered we would.
Man 1:	I think we can't be that bothered about it though, otherwise we'd do something about it . . . At the end of the day, it's just me being lazy. I can't be bothered. A lot of girls go to aerobics and the gym but a lot of blokes can't be bothered.

The men agreed that feeling that they were looking good affected their self-esteem. They linked looking good (having a well-toned, muscular body) with feelings of confidence and power in social situations.

Interviewer:	Do your feelings about your body affect your self-esteem?
Man 1:	Yeah, definitely. If you feel like s**t you look really s**t, then you feel really s**t . . . If you're among strangers and you look good it makes you feel more confident.

In another set of focus groups with young men, Helen Richards interviewed two groups of teenage men aged 16–17 who were students at sixth-form colleges in Kent (Grogan *et al.*, 1997). Again, participants were encouraged to talk about body image, with guiding questions from the interviewer. These younger men were clear that the ideal build was muscular. Several of them said that they wished that they were bigger and had more muscle:

Teenager 1:   Well, I'd prefer it [my body] to be slightly larger . . . slightly more weight.
Teenager 2:   I want to put on muscle.
Teenager 3:   I don't want to look small.
Teenager 4:   I don't seem to put on any weight. I want to build up a bit more muscle.

These young men seemed to aspire to the traditional ideal of the muscular physique. The desire to be muscular was clearly differentiated from a fear of being fat. Being big (fat) rather than muscular was related to weakness of will and lack of control.

Teenager 2:   If you've got someone in your family who's quite fat, you see how they are and you think to yourself, I don't want to be like that . . . It's a bit of a turn off if you're fat, so you try not to get like that.
Teenager 1:   The fat thing, it's a point of ridicule. If you think you are fat, you are sort of opening yourself up to it. Having comments made about you.

Two of the young men felt fat (although they were within the normal weight range), and explained how they laughed about excess weight as a way of covering up their embarrassment about feeling fat:

Teenager 5:   Well, I wouldn't mind being a bit slimmer I suppose but . . .
Teenager 6:   Me neither.
Teenager 5:   Most of us are like fat [*laughs*] and we have competitions to see who has got the biggest belly [*laughs*].
Interviewer: What is this competition?
Teenager 6:   I don't know. It's a way of hiding.
Teenager 5:   It's hiding that we're bothered really. I suppose in ourselves we are bothered. If our lifestyles lead us to getting fat we hide it by pretending we like it.

All these young men were concerned with the way that they looked, believing either that they were too thin and needed to put on muscle, or that they were too fat and needed to lose weight. When asked whether they felt external pressure to look a certain way, all felt pressure from others. Mainly pressure came from male peers. Men explained how they felt when their peers criticised their body shape:

Teenager 4:   I'm quite bothered about what people say, to be honest with you. It does affect you. You think, am I like that? Could I change sort of thing.

Teenager 1:   I was quite wound up by [friend who said he was fat]. Quite hurt. So I gave up chocolate.

Competing with peers, and fitting in with the group in terms of size, was given as an explicit reason by some of the interviewees, who wanted to be as big as their friends:

Teenager 4:   Yeah, I need to be a bit bigger because my brothers are like six foot and I'm a couple of inches shorter than all my friends as well and I feel pressure.

Teenager 2:   If you've got friends who are, like, quite big in build you want to be the same as them. Although you might not be able to do anything about it, it's on your conscience all the time. You want to be that sort of size.

We have rarely encountered such explicit competition with peers when talking to women.

These men were clear that they were only willing to put limited resources into trying to attain their ideal body shape:

Teenager 4:   It would be nice to look rather large, but I'm not really bothered if I don't look that big.

Teenager 5:   I wouldn't mind looking like that ['The Chippendales' dance troupe]. But I wouldn't put myself out to look like it you know.

Muscle tone and muscle mass were important to these men, supporting Franzoi and Shields's (1984) suggestion that muscle tone is central to male physical attractiveness. Men seemed to compare themselves with their male friends, and to want to 'fit in' with them in terms of body size. To be smaller or fatter than ideal was seen to be problematic. This coincides with Jane Ogden's (1992) suggestion that most men want to be 'average', to have bodies that are not noticeable. However, the adult interviewees also reported that their self-esteem was tied up with how good they felt about their bodies, conflicting with Jane Ogden's suggestion that:

> Men's weight is separate from their physical attractiveness which is separate from their feelings of self-worth and evaluation of their overall attractiveness.
>
> (Ogden, 1992: 84)

Men interviewed by Clare Donaldson reported that their body image affected their social interactions and self-esteem. However, they were not willing to expend significant effort on trying to change the way they looked. This coincides with Jane Ogden's and Helen Richards's interview data, showing that men may be dissatisfied but did not translate this dissatisfaction into behavioural change. This issue is investigated next.

Behavioural indicators of body dissatisfaction

Dieting

Dieting is significantly less frequent amongst men than amongst women. Most sources estimate that about 25 per cent of men diet at some time in their lives (Rozin and Fallon, 1988), compared with about 95 per cent of women. Only about 2 per cent of members of 'Weight Watchers' are men (Ogden, 1992).

Clare Donaldson (1996) found that 20 per cent of her sample of British male undergraduates had dieted. Eleven per cent of the sample indicated that they 'rarely' dieted, 4 per cent 'sometimes' did, 4 per cent 'often' did and 1 per cent 'very often' dieted. Proportions of male students who diet in the United States may be higher than among British students. When the male Gainesville, Florida, respondents to the survey carried out for this book were asked whether they had ever dieted, 40 per cent replied in the affirmative. However, when asked specifically what they ate when they dieted, only 14 per cent reported reducing food intake generally. The rest reported eating more fruit and vegetables and reducing fat intake, which sounds more like 'healthy eating' than 'dieting'. Certainly, men's style magazines such as *GQ*, *Esquire*, *FHM* and *Men's Health* tend to promote low fat diets rather than calorie counting, and emphasise looking and feeling good rather than slimness. For instance, the May 1997 edition of *Men's Health* features 'The feel-good food manual' focusing on low fat meals, and stressing that low fat meals will result in:

> ... a better body. You can't see your furred arteries but you can see your waistline.
>
> (Cremer, 1997: 49)

In men who are particularly sensitive to health issues, dieting may be more frequent than in the general male population. For instance, in a survey commissioned by *Men's Health* magazine, six out of ten men who responded had reduced food intake to lose weight, and all reported that they were successful in losing weight in the long term (Chaudhary, 1996). However, men who choose to respond to question-naires in magazines may not be representative of the male population, and most estimates are much lower than this.

Dieting is generally seen as a feminine activity (Brownmiller, 1984), and would not be expected to lead directly to the muscular physique that is the cultural ideal for men, so it is perhaps not surprising that men seem less likely to diet than women. Men are more likely to try to eat more healthily (i.e. to reduce the fat in their diets) than to reduce calorie intake in order to try to attain a slender physique.

Cosmetic surgery

Men are increasingly likely to have cosmetic surgery to change the way they look. The Harley Medical Group reports a significant increase in men requesting plastic surgery between 1983 and 1996 (Wilson, 1997). The most popular form of surgery is rhinoplasty, closely followed by breast augmentation to swell the pectoral muscles (the Harley Group perform at least two such operations on men each week) and liposuc-tion on the waist. The Belvedere Clinic reports that, in 1989, only 10 per cent of its clients were male, whereas the proportion had risen to 40 per cent by 1994 (Baker, 1994). Most men at the Belvedere request the insertion of silicone pectorals or the removal of tummy fat by lipo-suction or liposculpture. It is clear that more men are opting for the surgical fix in the 1990s than ever before, although proportions are still significantly lower than for women.

Exercise

In Clare Donaldson's (1996) study, 65 per cent of her respondents reported engaging in sport specifically to improve their body image.

The activity most obviously linked to improvement in body image for men is weight training and body-building, activities that would be expected to lead to development of muscle mass, to bring the male body more into line with the mesomorphic ideal. Peter Baker (1994) reports that 500,000 British men regularly use weights to get into shape, and an increasing number use steroids to accelerate the effects of exercise.

In 1996, Paul Husband and myself carried out a study of body-builders specifically for this book. We administered in-depth questionnaires and interviews to ten male body-builders in their twenties and thirties in Manchester gyms. The men were between 5 feet 7 inches and 6 feet 3 inches tall (mean height 5 feet 10 inches), and ranged in weight from 9 stone (126 lb) to 17 stone (238 lb), with a mean of 12.7 stone (178 lb). They all trained with weights regularly (most days), although one had only recently joined the gym. When asked about activities engaged in specifically to improve body image, four out of ten had dieted, one had cut out meals, five had cut out alcohol, three had played more sport, three had stopped eating take-away foods, three had been running, four had used sunbeds, and one had used fake tan. The percentage of men in this small group who had dieted (40 per cent) is significantly higher than most estimates of dieting in men: Clare Donaldson (1996) found that 20 per cent of her sample of undergraduate students (in the same age range as these body-builders) had dieted; and Fallon and Rozin (1988) set their estimate at 25 per cent. This is not surprising, since diet (and nutrition in general) is as important as weight training in the manipulation of fat-to-muscle ratios. Prior to competition (for instance), professional body-builders reduce body fat to an absolute minimum to reveal muscle definition and detail (Francis, 1989).

They were significantly more satisfied with their lower torso than with any other part of their bodies, in line with other work on men's body satisfaction (Cash *et al.*, 1986; Donaldson, 1996). On average, they were 'somewhat satisfied' with their weight, height, upper, mid- and lower torso, and their overall appearance.

When asked whether they would like to look more like magazine models, on average these men said that they sometimes wished they could look more like the models (with a range from never to always); but when asked how satisfaction with their own appearance was affected by such images, on average these men said they were unaffected, and that such images did not make them feel like improving their physical appearance. It may be important here that we asked about images of male models in general (to which these body-builders may not aspire, since such models may be perceived to be insufficiently muscular). Interview work with these young adult male body-builders has suggested that they may compare themselves unfavourably to other highly muscled men, which may motivate them to train harder. For instance:

> When I was body-building and I saw highly muscled men, like competitive bodybuilders, it made me feel sad, jealous, fed up, depressed, angry with myself because I didn't look like them. It furthered me to go on and get even bigger.

> Before I started being interested in lifting weights, when I saw a competitive body-builder, when I saw the Gladiators on television you know, it made you think, you know, it made you want to be like them.

These results suggest that other highly muscled men become a standard for comparison, against which these men compared themselves unfavourably, prompting the decision to weight train. All our interviewees described how they made unfavourable comparisons with other body-builders seen at the gym, and how these motivated them to try to gain more muscle. For instance:

> I remember one time when I was about seventeen stone, I thought I was getting really good. And a really really big body-builder came to work out at the gym, and he was absolutely enormous and he had a big effect on me, you know, and I really kind of felt rubbish after that. I looked rubbish, felt crap. That kind of spurred me on to get bigger and bigger. In fact, it had that much influence on me, when I actually left the gym kind of looking at him, it was on my mind and I got knocked off my bike on the way home. I was actually on the wrong side of the road. But you know I saw, not him, but you know the muscles, and that's how I wanted to be. It just completely dominated my thoughts.

Reports of other people's reactions when these men started to put on large amounts of muscle were interesting. Other body-builders were generally positive. For instance:

> Other body-builders and bouncers and people like that they kind of painted a picture of me and you know put me on a pedestal

and there was this big guy and he was strong, nothing could bother you, and I started to believe I had nine lives.

My friends and family . . . my friends in body-building, you know in that you meet a lot of, that's the good thing about going to a gym, you meet a lot of friends, so a lot of my friends do also train you know, and some of the friends who don't train have respect in, you know, the way that I've done what I've done, you know, in the short period of time I've achieved it. The family are one hundred percent behind me.

Some body-builders reported generally favourable comments from strangers:

I have noticed it on holiday in that people kind of look and nudge each other. I've not really had nasty comments. I've just had good comments . . . You get the odd comment like 'do you weight train?' or 'do you do weights?'

However, men and women outside the body-building culture tended to react negatively. For instance:

When I was about eighteen and a half around Christmas time or whatever, people were quite different with me then. I was in a pub and one person pushed me, one person tripped me up as, you know, I was going past.

I found men found me threatening on the whole, even though I wasn't. I didn't get eye-contact. I didn't talk to them. But if I was out socialising I got quite a lot of ignorant remarks. I got people saying 'what are you taking?', you know, um. I got people who actually spat at me. I was pushed downstairs in a club. I felt that men were really offended and threatened by how I looked. Women reacted the same really. They felt threatened. They avoided me and just generally assumed that because I was big I was nasty. I was using steroids so therefore I was nasty and aggressive.

These reported negative reactions relate to a general social stigma against body-building men. Doug Aoki (1996) notes how even academics tend to present negative views of body-builders and body-building in general:

Usually circumspect about not denigrating minorities of any type, they nonetheless too often sneer at body-builders for the appearance of their bodies and for their presumed narcissism . . .

(Aoki, 1996: 59)

It is interesting that body-builders attract negative reactions from others. It might be expected that an extreme form of the 'v'-shaped, mesomorphic body would be culturally favoured. Alan Mansfield and Barbara McGinn (1993) note the strong cultural association between muscularity and masculinity. Perhaps there is a ceiling on acceptable levels of muscularity, or perhaps it is the narcissism – closely linked with the bulging muscles of the professional body-builder – that negates the effects of the hyper-masculinity implied by the muscles. Body-builders are defying social expectations on a number of counts. Their behaviour is assumed to be narcissistic, and therefore inappropriate for men (Aoki, 1996), for they are spending time building up their bodies so that they look a certain way. Their bodies are at the same time hyper-masculine (i.e. highly muscled) and feminine (with curves and the development of cleavage). Body-building involves objectifying the body. This is a common phenomenon amongst women, who are taught to partition and objectify the body (Orbach, 1993), so it is seen as essentially feminine behaviour (Aoki, 1996). The bodies of body-builders are seen as unnatural, especially when they are known to use anabolic steroids.

Anabolic steroid use

The use of anabolic steroids to improve athletic performance is well documented (see Ted Epperley, 1993, for a review of this area). Anabolic steroids have long been used by professional body-builders to increase muscle bulk. The earliest documented case was by members of a Soviet weight lifting team in the 1950s (Strauss and Yesalis, 1991). Recent data suggest that they are now being used by a number of young men who want to build up their bodies to a more pleasing muscular shape. Steroids enable the user to build muscle bulk much more quickly than they would be able to do through weight training alone, so they are an attractive option to some young men who wish to become more muscular for cosmetic reasons.

It is not possible to know the extent of non-medical steroid use in Britain. However, it is well-known that steroids are widely available in public gyms and health clubs used by body-builders (Institute for the Study of Drug Dependence, 1993). Recent data from needle exchanges in the United Kingdom show that steroid users constitute over 25 per cent of the group which makes use of the service (Shapiro, 1992). United States figures suggest that usage there may be more widespread. Some studies suggest that almost all professional body-builders, weight lifters and power lifters use anabolic steroids (Hough, 1990). Others put the percentage of body-builders at lower (but still significant) levels. In one US study that investigated steroid use in both male and female body-builders, 54 per cent of the men were regular users of anabolic steroids (Tricker *et al.*, 1989). There has been growing interest and concern about steroid use in adolescents. United States studies suggest that about 7 per cent of adolescent boys may be using steroids (Caitlin and Hatton, 1991), although Vaughn Rickert and colleagues (1992) put the figures higher, at between 5 and 11 per cent of male adolescents, based on their summary of relevant research.

In interviews with male body-builders using anabolic steroids on a regular basis, Paul Husband and myself found that most men start to use steroids because they are frustrated with the slow effects of their weight training programme. For instance, one respondent explains how he went up from ten to thirteen stone in six months through intensive weight training and a high calorie diet, but that he could not get any bigger, despite intensive training:

> I was about ten stone when I first started to put on weight. I think I should have been about twelve to thirteen. Then I went to thirteen within six months. I went every night but I was just putting on bits of fat and I got stuck. So I'd taken about three months after that and I was just completely just kind of levelled out and I couldn't put any more weight on.

Another had been weight training for twelve months, and was frustrated by the fact that other men at the gym were looking bigger than him. He knew they took steroids, and decided after some thought to try them too:

> I was training let's say twelve months, and you know, I'd seen people looking bigger than me, and we got talking, and then I decided you know after a long time to take steroids. Really I needed, I felt I needed to be bigger, and basically I thought steroids would do it. Literally I decided to take them because other people were kind of getting bigger than me and they were taking them, so it was just like a knock-on effect. They do it, so like you do it.

Yet another body-builder was advised by the owner of the gym to take steroids so that he could compete in body-building competitions against men who were using steroids:

> I first started taking steroids when I first started to compete. I'd been training about a year and a half going on for two years and I was thinking of going in for a competition, and one of the owners of the gym where I used to train he advised me to you know go on certain steroids, because if you go in for a competition, there is a line-up of say six other people and they're all taking a certain amount of steroids so to compete on their level really you have to do what they are doing.

All the men we interviewed have cited pressures from images in body-building magazines, and images from films and television, as being influential in their decision to take steroids:

> The more I trained, the more magazines I looked at, the bigger I wanted to be . . . and there was a TV programme and when I watched these people it made me feel really depressed, I didn't look as good as them, and it had a massive effect on my decision to take steroids. In fact it was probably one of the biggest reasons why I did take them, seeing other people bigger than me.

> If I do see somebody you know who looks fantastic on television, it does cross my mind about an extra course [of steroids].

Several respondents cited the body-building gym culture as being influential in their decision to take steroids, because steroids were available and because people talked about them at the gym. For instance:

> In a hard-core body-building gym you are going to see steroids readily available, you know, you are going to hear them talked about. You might see them you know. So yeah, people will talk to you about steroids, you know different things you can take. So yeah, if someone starts off at the gym intending just to train they could be influenced by taking steroids because they can see, you know, they are in an atmosphere where people are taking steroids.

In terms of the effects of steroids on muscularity, reports were generally favourable (as might be expected). These men enjoyed the increased strength and muscularity that resulted from intensive training coupled with steroid intake, linking it with increased self-confidence:

> Obviously it made me look better and it made me feel better.

> It made me look how I wanted to look which was a lot more muscular . . . it made me feel a lot more confident and gave me more reassurance.

> I became more muscular, and, um, stronger, you know, a bigger look. It made me feel more confident in two ways. In the way with me being only quite short it gave me a lot more confidence, you know in general public, it made me feel better in myself.

However, the attention that large muscles attract was not always welcome. One body-builder described how he would hide his muscles when outside the gym:

> I used to wear clothes in the street to make me look smaller, you know like a black baggy jumper just to make me look smaller. It started to bother me after a bit everybody staring at me. When I was twenty stone, people in the street were staring back at me. It started to bother me after a bit.

The men we interviewed were keen to explode the myth that steroids alone would make someone muscular, and stressed the amount of work that goes into creating a well-muscled body, even when steroids are used as a catalyst:

> There's no drug makes a body-builder. People who talk about things like this are often people who have never trained a day in their life. They don't understand the first thing to do with body-building. They just see a body-builder and all they can see in their minds is the drugs that made that body-builder. They don't see how much hard dieting, how much hard training, how much real dedication has gone into it.

This may relate to the general cultural prejudice against artificiality in looks, where the prevailing aesthetic values a 'natural' look. Gaines and Butler (1980) suggest that people do not value the bodies of body-builders because they are perceived as unnatural, so that:

... all those muscles somehow come out of a bottle; that there is something as synthetic, unhealthy, useless and faintly sinful as plastic flowers about what they do and the way they look.

(Gaines and Butler, 1980: 76)

The steroid-taking body-builders we interviewed were keen to show us how much *work* went into their physiques, representing themselves as creating natural muscle and only using the steroids as a catalyst. As such they were emphasising the fact that the muscles gained were not synthetic, not produced by the steroids, but produced through their own hard work. They wanted to take responsibility, to retain ownership of their bodies, resenting the impression of people outside body-building who (they believed) thought of steroids as being a lazy way to achieve a muscular body. This links to Gaines and Butler's suggestion of a cultural belief that their muscles are somehow 'sinful' and 'useless', since they are not the result of hard physical labour (which would not, presumably, be sinful or useless), but the result of pharmacological interventions. It is no surprise, then, that those body-builders who used steroids felt it necessary to explain at length how hard they had to work to attain their body shape and size.

Human growth hormone

Human growth hormone (HGH) is secreted by the pituitary gland. It works by stimulating growth throughout the body. Until 1985, HGH could only be obtained by collecting it from cadavers. In 1985, recombinant DNA synthesis became possible, thus enabling the manufacture of HGH. Human growth hormone stimulates tissue growth and protein synthesis, accelerates linear growth, and increases body weight and mass (Caitlin and Hatton, 1991). It is used medically to treat hormone-deficient conditions in children, such as dwarfism. Administered either orally or by injection, it is also used to treat osteoporosis, and is being investigated for use in speeding the healing of bone fractures (Epperley, 1993). Possible side-effects consist of heart disease, impotence, muscle weakness, and bony enlargement of the forehead, hands, feet and jaw. There is also the risk of contracting HIV/AIDS for those sharing needles. Human growth hormone cannot be detected in the urine of users, and is not on the list of substances banned by the International Olympic Committee.

Anecdotal evidence suggests that human growth hormone (HGH) is being used by young men who wish to increase muscle. It is believed that HGH increases muscle development and strength, prevents the breakdown of muscles when taking a break between steroid cycles, and prevents muscle tearing as a result of strenuous activity (Rickert *et al.*, 1992). Some body-builders and weight lifters have claimed that using HGH has led to increases of 30–40 lb in lean muscle, and there is general agreement that muscle mass increases significantly in users, although strength does not increase significantly because HGH increases the amount of connective tissue rather than contractile elements (Epperley, 1993). It therefore produces cosmetic changes in muscle mass rather than an increase in muscle strength.

Rickert and colleagues (1992) studied HGH use in high-school students in the United States. They were interested in the prevalence of HGH use, the relationship between HGH use and concurrent anabolic steroid use, and knowledge about HGH in users of the drug. Of 208 girls, only one reported use of HGH – for medical reasons. Of 224 boys, 11 (5 per cent) reported past or present use of HGH. Most reported first use between 14 and 15 years of age. Most used anabolic steroids as well as HGH. Sources of information about the drugs were different, with most boys finding out about HGH from persons other than friends or the media (e.g. from sports coaches), whereas those who use anabolic steroids were likely to find out about them from friends or the media. Most HGH users were unaware of side-effects. The authors conclude that HGH use is occurring in significant numbers of young men. They suggest that adolescent boys may be particularly sensitive to influences which promise to improve body appearance because of the importance of body image in early to mid-adolescence.

Social construction of masculinity

Frank Mort (1988) looks at the change in young men's culture that has meant an increased interest in the way that men look. He states that young men are being targeted by the advertising industry, and are becoming more aware than ever before of how they look:

> Young men are being sold images which rupture traditional icons of masculinity. They are stimulated to look at themselves – and other men – as objects of consumer desire.
>
> (Mort, 1988: 194)

Mort argues that this change is significant, and requires a rethinking of the meaning of 'masculinity'. He focuses on the Nick Kamen 'laun-derette' advertisement for Levi's jeans and shows how the film uses the standard technique, current for the past four decades, of the sexual display of women, but points out that the target is now a man. He finds something uncomfortable about this image. Interestingly, the *Sun* newspaper also felt sufficiently uncomfortable about the follow-up Levi's TV commercial, showing James Mardle in the bathtub in his Levi's, to run a story stressing Mardle's heterosexuality. The move of male models from the gay press to the mainstream market obviously presented conflicts for some newspaper editors! Mort argues that changes in the acceptability of the visual display of the male body have prompted men to look differently at themselves and other men, and to be generally more aware of the ways that their bodies look, and of the ways that they dress. However, he notes that this new awareness is not necessarily positive for women. The 'new man' may be more aware of the ways that he looks, but this does not necessarily change the traditional codes of masculinity. Looking at the Levi's advertisements, he shows how the hero is played off against stereotyped images of women (the sweetheart, the fat lady, the harassed mum and the giggling girls). The 'new man' image may just be another version of the old, macho, image of the man going it alone, without/above women.

This theme is taken up by Rowena Chapman (1988), who argues that the 'new man' (nurturant and narcissistic) was largely the result of the style culture of the early 1980s, promoted by the style press (*i-D, The Face, Arena*). The culture legitimised men's concern with their bodies and the consumerism necessary to adopt the role. The 'new man', she argues, is not a major departure from the traditional, John Wayne-style macho man, but is simply an adaptation of the role which is better suited to survival in a culture that now rejects obvious machismo, largely due to the power of feminism.

> This leads me to the conclusion that the new man represents not so much a rebellion but an adaptation in masculinity. Men change, but only to hold on to power, not to relinquish it. The combination of feminism and social change may have produced a fragmentation in male identity by questioning its assumptions, but the effect of the emergence of the new man has been to reinforce the existing power structure, by producing a hybrid masculinity which is better able and more suited to retain control.
>
> (Chapman, 1988: 235)

Chapman notes the historic reticence in Western culture about male nudity, and the recent shift in visibility of the male body. She argues that the dawning recognition of female sexual desire led to an increase in the marketing of the male body on the cards, calendars and posters produced by companies such as Athena. Athena's *L'enfant* poster, featuring a muscular man holding a baby, was their biggest seller in the late 1980s. Such images of men's bodies also sell to the gay community. However, she notes that the images almost never reveal male genitals. Instead, the penis is replaced by a fetishisation of the phallus. Nude men grasp exploding bottles of champagne between their thighs, or play saxophones, or carry whips in phallic poses. So, although there appears to be some democratisation of vision, with the gaze focused on men as well as women, the fact that female genitals are displayed and male genitals are not undermines this, and reduces the power of the viewer of the nude male relative to the viewer of the nude female. She argues that women are still the objects of gaze more frequently and more completely than men, and that the objectification of the male body does nothing to reduce the power of men, and may even increase it in a context where femininity is increasingly prized.

Summary

- The ideal male body shape is slender and moderately muscular.
- Work on men's body satisfaction has suggested that a significant proportion of men are dissatisfied with some aspect of their body shape and weight.
- Men who are dissatisfied with their body shape are equally likely to want to be thinner or heavier (a different pattern from women, who mostly want to be slimmer).
- The main areas that produce dissatisfaction are the mid-torso (stomach, mid-back), biceps, shoulders, chest, and the general muscle tone. Muscle tone and muscle mass were important to British and American men.
- Men tend to use exercise (rather than diet) to try to change body shape. In questionnaire studies, 65 per cent of British and 41 per cent of American college students reported exercising specifically to improve body shape and size.
- Interviews and questionnaires with body-builders demonstrated a strong social comparison effect, where the body-builder compares himself to other men in the gym which encourages him to train harder to try to develop more muscle.
- Some choose to take anabolic steroids to speed up the process of muscle development, despite unwanted side-effects and the negative reactions of people outside the body-building community.

Plate 1 Rembrandt van Rijn, *Bathsheba* (1654)

Source: Musée du Louvre © Photo RMN, Jean Schormans

Plate 2 Gustave Courbet, *The artist's studio* (1855)

Source: Paris, Musée d'Orsay © Photo RMN, Hervé Lewandowski

Plate 3 Auguste Renoir, *Blonde bather* (1881)

Source: © Sterling and Francine Clark Art Institute, Williamstown, Massachusetts, USA

Plate 4 Flapper fashion

Source: Mary Evans Picture Library

Plate 5 Marilyn Monroe

Source: United Artists (courtesy Kobal)

Plate 6 Twiggy

Source: © King Collection (courtesy Retna Pictures Ltd)

Plate 7 Kate Moss

Source: © Robert Fairer (courtesy Retna Pictures Ltd)

Plate 8 Sandro Botticelli, *St Sebastian* (1474)

Source: Gemäldegalerie, Staatliche Museen zu Berlin, Preussischer Kulturbesitz

Plate 9 Michelangelo, *The Battle of Cascina* (1504)

Source: © British Museum

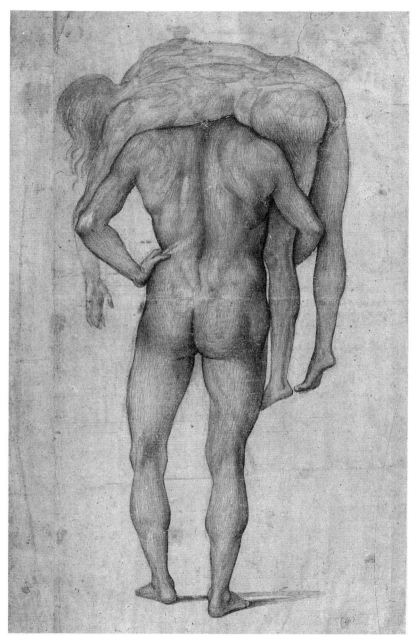

Plate 10 Luca Signorelli, *Study of two nude figures* (1503)

Source: Musée du Louvre © Photo RMN, Michèle Bellot

Plate 11 Dolph Lundgren

Source: Courtesy Kobal

Plate 12 Jean-Auguste-Dominique Ingres, *The Turkish bath* (1863)

Source: Musée du Louvre © Photo RMN, Gérard Blot

Plate 13 Claudia Schiffer

Source: © Robert Fairer (courtesy Retna Pictures Ltd)

Plate 14 Arnold Schwarzenegger

Source: White Mountain Prods (courtesy Kobal)

5 Media effects

This chapter investigates the impact of the media on body image. Many theorists have looked to the media in their efforts to understand the social pressures on men and women to be a particular shape and size. The role of the media in relation to the portrayal of the male and female body is widely debated. Most social commentators agree that the media reflects current social norms. Some have gone one stage further and suggested that media portrayal of slender body shapes can actually affect the ways that women and men feel about their body shape and size. Studying the content of media communications allows us to speculate about the role of the media in moulding and mirroring societal values around body image. Here we will investigate media portrayal of both the female and the male body, followed by an assessment of potential effects on the viewer's body image.

Media portrayal of the body

There is general agreement that pressures on women to be a particular shape and size are more pronounced than pressures on men. Studies that have investigated the portrayal of both genders have found that men and women are portrayed in markedly different ways in relation to body weight. Content Analysis (where the frequency of portrayal of particular images is coded) has reliably revealed that women are portrayed as abnormally slim in the media, whereas men tend to be portrayed as of standard weight. For instance, Silverstein *et al.* (1986) found that, in thirty-three television shows, 69 per cent of female characters were coded as 'thin', compared to only 18 per cent of male characters. Only 5 per cent of female characters were rated as 'heavy', compared to 26 per cent of males. They also found that models in the magazines *Ladies Home Journal* and *Vogue* had become significantly thinner since the 1930s, concluding that:

... present day women who look at the major mass media are exposed to a standard of bodily attractiveness that is slimmer than that presented for men and that is less curvaceous than that presented for women since the 1930s.

(Silverstein *et al.*, 1986: 531)

Magazines aimed at girls and young women tend to present traditional slim images of attractiveness. Eileen Guillen and Susan Barr (1994) investigated body image in *Seventeen* magazine (known as the 'best friend' of high-school girls in the United States) between 1970 and 1990 and concluded that the magazine contributes to the current cultural milieu in which thinness is expected of women, be they adults or adolescents.

Concern has recently been expressed over the representation of such unrealistic images of female beauty in the media. In May 1996, the watch manufacturer Omega made headline news in the United Kingdom by withdrawing its advertising from *Vogue* magazine, complaining that the models used in *Vogue*'s fashion pages (Trish Goff and Annie Morton) were so thin as to appear anorexic. The *Guardian* newspaper of 31 May quotes the brand manager at Omega as saying:

I thought it was irresponsible for a leading magazine which should be setting an example to select models of anorexic proportions. It made every effort to accentuate their skeletal appearance. Since *Vogue* presumably targets an audience which includes young and impressionable females, its creators must surely be aware that they will inevitably be influenced by what laughably passes for fashion in these pages.

(Boseley, 1996: 1)

Although this may have been a publicity 'stunt' on the part of Omega, it brought the question of using very thin models in advertising to mainstream attention.

Some authors have suggested that these images have powerful effects on their readers, serving to foster and maintain a 'cult of femininity' and supplying definitions of what it means to be a woman. Marjorie Ferguson (1985) investigated women's magazines from a sociological perspective. She argued that women's magazines contribute to the wider cultural processes which help to shape a woman's view of herself, and society's view of her. Women's magazines are read by a large proportion of women (about half the adult female population of the United Kingdom) with each copy seen by many women (on average, each copy of *Vogue* is read by sixteen women), since magazines are often shared amongst friends and are widely available in the waiting rooms at doctors' surgeries, dentists and hairdressers. Ferguson used Content Analysis to study a random selection of copies of *Woman's Own*, *Woman* and *Woman's Weekly* between 1949 and 1974, and 1979 and 80, looking for dominant themes, goals and roles. She also interviewed thirty-four female magazine editors about their roles, beliefs and professional practices, and about how they perceived the impact of social change upon their magazines and audiences; and ninety-seven journalists, artists, publishers and managers about their perceptions of the editorial process, publishing organisations and the market context of women's periodical production. She interpreted her data in relation to the writings of Durkheim on the sociology of religion. She argues that there are interesting parallels between the practices promoted by women's magazines and the characteristic elements of the religious cult:

> I have argued that women's magazines collectively comprise a social institution which serves to foster and maintain a cult of femininity. In promoting a cult of femininity these journals are not merely reflecting the female role in society; they are also supplying one source of definitions of, and socialisation into, that role.
>
> (Ferguson, 1985: 184)

She sees the media as doing much more than simply reflecting current values. According to Ferguson, women's magazines may actually change a woman's view of herself by teaching her socially acceptable ways in which to behave.

In the 1980s and 1990s the male body has become more 'visible' in the popular media in both Britain and the United States. Frank Mort (1988) and Rowena Chapman (1988) note the increasing prevalence of the well-muscled male body in British advertising. Marc Mishkind and colleagues (1986) note that examination of US magazines and other media strongly suggests that body image concern is strong for men. They suggest that media images of the young, lean, muscular male body represent changes in society's attitudes towards the male body as a result of which men are under increased pressure to look slender and muscular:

> Advertisements celebrate the young, lean, muscular male body, and men's fashions have undergone significant changes in style

both to accommodate and to accentuate changes in men's
physiques toward a more muscular and trim body.

(Mishkind *et al.*, 1986: 545)

They go on to suggest that the pressures of society to conform to the
mesomorphic male body ideal may be producing an increase in body
dissatisfaction and low self-esteem in men.

Other social commentators have described changes in the exposure
of the male body in the media in the late 1980s and 1990s. Joan
McAlpine (1993) describes the recent trend to portray muscular men in
advertisements, and argues that men are under increased pressure to
attain the muscular mesomorphic shape. Her interviews with male
body-builders tended to confirm this.

Peter Baker (1994) documents social pressures upon men to be
toned and muscular. He notes the current trend to use attractive men
(young, handsome and muscular) in advertisements and films, and the
very recent trend for male dance troupes such as The Chippendales
and The Dreamboys. He argues that this has led to an increase in
men's self-consciousness about their bodies:

Men's self-consciousness about their appearance is probably
greater now than ever before. How could it be otherwise, given the
massive exposure of men's bodies in the media?

(Baker, 1994: 130)

Stuart Elliot (1994) documents this trend in a *Guardian* article of 17
February, describing how *Sports Illustrated* magazine opted to use
male models to advertise swimwear for the first time in 1994. The fact
that the inclusion of men in swimsuits in the magazine was considered
newsworthy shows that the representation of men is still quantitatively
and qualitatively different from that of women.

Mass communication models

Researchers who have analysed media content have generally assumed
that the content has a direct effect on viewers, and that the mass media
affect their audience in a fairly uniform way by 'injecting a dose' of
communication which has a standard effect. This is known as the
'Effects Model' (often referred to as the 'Hypodermic Model') of
media effects. The Effects Model concentrates on the effects of a
specific aspect of media communication on the audience in general –
such as, for instance, the effect of idealised media images of the body

on the viewer. Participants are generally exposed to some media imagery, and effects on their attitudes, beliefs or behaviour are studied. Individual differences between people are usually hidden within group averages. This model does not usually ask people to explain any changes in their behaviour, and is not usually concerned with individual differences in effects; it generally assumes that results obtained in the laboratory can be generalised to real-life situations. However, results obtained in the somewhat sterile laboratory situation may not be generalisable to more realistic viewing situations, for several reasons. Most important of these, experimental research on communications places participants in a strange, unfamiliar situation, in which they are given something specific to observe (rather than choosing it themselves), they are (usually) observed whilst they view, and they are (usually) asked to pay attention to details of the material they view. None of these factors are likely to be common to the participant's everyday life. So those results obtained in the laboratory may be radically different from those that would be obtained if we observed the participants in their everyday environment.

The main alternative to the Effects Model is the 'Uses and Gratifications Model'. This model looks specifically at the function served by different media by asking, for instance, how people use the media to inform body image. It was developed in the 1940s and 1950s by Paul Lazarsfeld and Joseph Klapper (see Lazarsfeld *et al.*, 1948; Klapper, 1960). Using this model, people are asked to account for their own viewing preferences. This means that the viewer produces the theory as to why they consume that medium, and the effects that the medium has on their behaviour. Klapper (1960) proposed that people actively engage with the media, rejecting what they do not want to accept. This model stresses the active involvement of the participants with the material they are shown, and rejects the concept of the passive viewer. Media are conceptualised as fulfilling the viewer's needs in some way (as a diversion, for companionship, etc.). The approach is popular, since it allows the viewer herself to account for a change of attitude or behaviour if it occurs, giving the resulting explanation some validity.

It is not necessary to choose between these two models; instead, it is useful to combine them. Here we will integrate evidence from studies that have used the experimental method (to investigate direct effects of viewing media imagery) with interviews (asking participants to account for any changes in their attitudes, beliefs and behaviour). This approach incorporates the strengths of the Effects Model in terms of control over extraneous variables in the viewing situation, but also allows some investigation of the ecological validity of the research. It also allows us to conceptualise the viewer as being active in the process. Even if viewers are affected by media imagery, this does not necessarily mean that they were passive in the process. Perhaps viewers actively seek out information relevant to body image in the media, in order to evaluate their body shape and size. Indeed, the psychological theories outlined in this chapter have suggested that the viewer is active in using media images to inform body image.

Uses and Gratifications theory would suggest that some images presented in the media may be viewed by women (and men) yet have no significant effect on them, because they actively reject the message. Perhaps viewers are too aware of the unrealistic nature of the images portrayed in the media to allow such images to affect their self-concepts. Recent data suggest that women are becoming critical of media imagery. In a recent British survey of women's attitudes to their portrayal in advertisements, undertaken by Grey Advertising, 68 per cent of British respondents under thirty-five years of age said that they would like advertisements to feature women with stronger personalities; and 72 per cent of US respondents thought that advertising stereotyped women while 69 per cent thought that advertising insulted their intelligence (Armstrong, 1996). In our interviews with women (see Chapter 3) it was clear that they did not uncritically accept the media images offered to them. They were highly critical of the fact that 'skinny' models and actresses were represented as 'normal' body shapes in magazines and on film. They saw fashion models as being too thin, representative of an unrealistic ideal.

Careful consideration of data on the *direct* effects of observing media images is clearly necessary in order to determine whether images of thinness (or muscularity) have a significant effect on women's (or men's) body image. If an effect is seen, an explanation needs to be provided as to how the process operates which takes into account the fact that viewers may actively engage with material presented to them. This must be informed by their accounts of viewing media images. By combining the strengths of these two approaches, it may be possible to investigate media effects without assuming that the viewer is passive in the process, allowing the viewer to account for his or her experiences of observing media imagery. In the sections that follow, the effects of media imagery will be assessed, drawing on two of the most popular psychological theories of media effects on body image. This will be followed by results of interview work which asked respondents to account for their responses to body shape role models in the media.

Effects of media images

Psychologists have suggested that the media can affect men and women's body esteem by becoming a reference point against which unfavourable body shape comparisons are made. For instance, Adrian Furnham and Nicola Greaves (1994) argue that the core of body image dissatisfaction is a discrepancy between a person's perceived body and their ideal (typically slender for women and muscular for men). They argue that a failure to match the ideal leads to self-criticism, guilt and lowered self-worth. This effect is stronger for women than for men, probably because cultural pressures on women to conform to an idealised body shape are more powerful and more widespread than those on men. Women are likely to be exposed more frequently to idealised images of women's bodies, and these images will be more salient.

The most influential psychological theories of media effects are adaptations of Festinger's (1954) Social Comparison Theory and Markus's (1977) Self Schema Theory. These are both examples of the Effects Model, although they are sophisticated variants, since they propose mechanisms to explain observed changes in behaviour, and since neither theory conceptualises the viewer as passive in the process. They will be examined in turn, along with data from authors working within these paradigms.

Social Comparison Theory

In 1954, Leon Festinger published his landmark theory on social comparison processes. According to his Social Comparison Theory, we desire accurate, objective evaluations of our abilities and attitudes. When unable to evaluate ourselves directly, we seek to satisfy this need for self-evaluation through comparisons with other people. Unfavourable comparisons (where the other is judged to score higher in the target attribute than oneself) are known as upward comparisons. Favourable comparisons (where the other is judged as lower on the target attribute) are known as downward comparisons. This social comparison process may be unconscious, and is outside volitional control (Miller, 1984).

Social Comparison Theory would predict that people might use images projected by the media as standards for comparison. Upward comparisons with models' bodies (slim and carefully arranged in the most flattering poses) would be expected to lead to unfavourable evaluation of the body of the perceiver, so long as participants considered models to be similar to them on relevant dimensions and body image to be self-relevant (Major *et al.*, 1991).

Self Schema Theory

An alternative view of media effects is presented by proponents of the Self Schema Theory, which focuses on how individuals process the content of media messages. Of special interest is the way that media messages are incorporated into, and affect, a person's concept of self. Philip Myers and Frank Biocca (1992) have adopted Markus's (1977) Self Schema Theory, and adapted it to explain the effects of social pressure on body image. A self schema is a person's mental representation of those elements that make him/her distinctive from others; those aspects that constitute a sense of 'me'. According to Markus, people develop their sense of self through reflecting on their own behaviours, from observing reactions of others to the self, and through processing social information about which aspects of the self are most valued. Myers and Biocca see a person's body image as one aspect of the mental representation that constitutes the 'self'. As with other aspects of the self, the body image is a mental construction, not an objective evaluation. Hence it is open to change through new information. Myers and Biocca believe that the body image is 'elastic', in that it is unstable and responsive to social cues. They have produced a model of the reference points that they believe a young woman (they do not discuss men or older women) will draw on to construct her mental model of her present body image. These are the 'socially represented ideal body' (ideals represented in the media, and also drawn from other reference groups such as peers and family); the 'internalised ideal body' (a compromise between the objective body shape and the socially represented ideal); and the 'objective body'. They argue that the body image is 'elastic' because its reference points frequently change, and because it depends on mood, the context of the evaluation and the presence of social cues. They suggest that, if the gap between the 'objective body' and the 'internalised ideal body' is too great, self-criticism and lowered self-esteem may result. They argue that the mass media operate to shift the balance between the two, making the 'socially represented ideal body' so slim that the 'internalised ideal body' becomes unrealistically thin.

Relevant empirical evidence

Both Social Comparison Theory and Self Schema Theory predict a significant effect of media images on body satisfaction: Social

Comparison Theory because upward comparisons with the bodies of slender models' will lead to body dissatisfaction; and Self Schema Theory because slender media images would be likely to make the 'ideal body' thinner, increasing the gap between the 'objective body' and the 'possible self' and leading to lowered body esteem. In fact, research investigating direct effects of observation of attractive media models has produced mixed results. Most researchers have measured body satisfaction in women after (and sometimes before and after) observing slim fashion models. Some have found a decrease in body esteem after viewing, some have found no change, and one study even found an increase in satisfaction.

Richins's (1991) female participants were exposed to advertisements showing 'thin, well-proportioned' models, and did not significantly alter their body satisfaction. However, Richins notes that her single-item, seven-point body satisfaction scale may have been insufficiently sensitive to pick up subtle changes in satisfaction.

Lori Irving (1990) looked specifically at the effects of media images on women with 'eating disorders'. She investigated the impact of exposure to slides of thin, average and oversized models on the self-evaluations of 162 women college students who exhibited a significant level of 'bulimic symptoms' on the BULIT test (a test specifically designed to identify such symptoms; Smith and Thelen, 1984). Exposure to the thin models resulted in lowered self-esteem, although not to differences in weight satisfaction. However, the study was flawed in that no pre-exposure measurements of self-evaluation were taken (although the groups were checked for equivalence of bulimic symptoms and age). The post-exposure-test-only design leaves open the alternative hypothesis that the groups may have differed on weight satisfaction prior to exposure to the stimuli, and makes the data difficult to interpret with confidence.

Leslie Heinberg and Kevin Thompson (1995) investigated the effects of televised images on body satisfaction. A ten-minute tape consisting of either appearance-related or non-appearance-related commercials was viewed by 139 women. Pre-test and post-test measures of body dissatisfaction revealed that participants who were high on 'body image disturbance' (rated by Schulman *et al.*'s 1986 Bulimia Cognitive Distortions Scale; Physical Appearance Subscale) and/or high on awareness or acceptance of societal attitudes towards thinness and attractiveness (as measured by Heinberg and Thompson's Societal Attitudes Towards Appearance Questionnaire) were significantly less satisfied after viewing the appearance-related images. Participants below the median on body image disturbance showed no change, or showed improved satisfaction. The authors suggest that, for certain susceptible individuals, media images of thinness are particularly salient; and that this group may use media models as social comparison targets when assessing their own physical attractiveness. Their data suggest that only a specific sub-section of the population – those who agree with statements such as 'being physically fit is a priority in today's society' (awareness of societal attitudes); 'photographs of thin women make me wish that I were thin' (acceptance of societal attitudes); or 'my value as a person is related to my weight' (cognitive distortions related to physical appearance) – are 'at risk' from such images.

Myers and Biocca (1992) ran a fascinating study in which seventy-six female university students aged 18–24 viewed either body-image-oriented or neutral programming. The participants then completed questionnaires measuring mood, and estimated body size using the light-adjustment technique described in Chapter 3. They found that most of the young women overestimated their body size (in agreement with the research cited in Chapter 3). Watching a thirty-minute tape of body-image-oriented advertisements and programming had a significant effect on body size estimation and mood levels. Surprisingly, the body-image-oriented material actually *reduced* body size overestimation and *reduced* depression levels! Myers and Biocca explain these surprising results by suggesting that the young women may have imagined themselves in the ideal body presented in the tape. They may have felt more in control, and may have seen the ideal as more attainable and within reach. They use these findings to suggest a two-stage process of building a distorted body image. In the first stage, young women 'bond' with the models, visualising themselves in the socially represented ideal body. At this stage, the 'elastic' present body image moves towards the internalised ideal body, making the woman feel good about her body. The self-criticism that comes from a realisation of the gap between the objective body and the internalised ideal body comes later. So the short-term effect is to make the woman feel that she is closer to her ideal (through identification with the models, and consequent change to her current body image). However, once the identification has 'worn off', she will make unfavourable comparisons between her objective body and her internalised ideal, leading to dissatisfaction. Unfortunately, Myers and Biocca did not look at the longer-term effects of the images. Their argument on long-term effects would be more convincing if it were accompanied by evidence that this long-…hift does in fact take place. Also, it would have been useful to have measured body dissatisfaction directly, rather than inferring it through body size estimation and depression levels.

Work in this area has tended to focus on women. Few studies have considered the effects on men. The issue of men's body esteem is of particular interest at present because of recent suggestions that Western cultural attitudes to the male body are in a state of change, and that men are becoming more and more concerned with body image (see Chapter 4).

In a recent study, Grogan *et al.* (1996) looked at the effects on both men and women of viewing same-gender, slim, conventionally attractive models. The study was designed to investigate these effects on body esteem. Body esteem scales were completed by 49 men and 45 women (ages 17–32) before and after viewing pictures of same-gender photographic models (experimental group) or landscapes (control group). Women scored significantly lower than men on the body esteem scale, irrespective of whether they were in the experimental or control group, showing that these women were generally less satisfied with their bodies than were the men. There were interesting differences between the experimental and control groups after seeing the photographs. Body esteem scores decreased significantly (and to a similar degree) in men and women after viewing the same-gender photographic models; whereas men and women in the control group (who viewed landscapes) showed no change (see Figure 5.1).

This suggests that these men and women felt significantly less satisfied with their bodies after viewing attractive same-gender models. At least in the short term, these participants felt less good about the way that their bodies looked after comparison with those of well-toned, slender models. The findings would have been predicted by Social Comparison Theory, and also by Self Schema Theory, since the effect could be the result of upward comparisons with the models' bodies (Social Comparison Theory), or of a shift in the 'ideal body shape' to a more slender (women) or muscular (men) ideal (Self Schema Theory). The data are particularly interesting since they show an equivalent shift in satisfaction for both men and women. The effect does not seem to be mediated by problematic relationships with food. Scores on the Eating Attitude Test (a measure of such relationships) did not correlate significantly with body esteem changes in the experimental groups, suggesting that the effect is independent of attitudes to eating. The effect is short-term, and there is no way of knowing how long it will last. It is, none the less, interesting that a relatively brief encounter with pictures of attractive fashion models can have such an

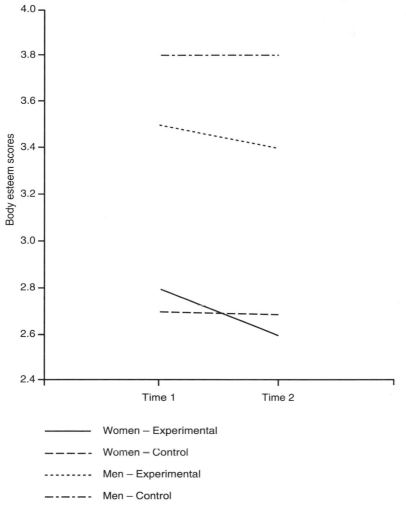

Figure 5.1 Effects of viewing photographic images on body esteem

effect on body satisfaction, suggesting that body image is indeed 'elastic' as suggested by Myers and Biocca (1992).

Body shape role models

Having shown that media images can result in a shift in body satisfaction, it is important to investigate the relative importance of media imagery compared to other sources of social influence. Clearly, the media are only one source of influence on body image, and other sources may be more or less salient at particular times, and to particular individuals.

In Irving's (1990) study with female college students scoring high on bulimic symptoms her participants were asked to rate the importance of different sources of social pressure. When she ordered their responses by rank she found that the most powerful source of perceived social pressure for this group was 'media', followed by 'peers', followed by 'family'. Clearly, these women were aware of media pressure to be slim.

Heinberg and Thompson (1992) looked specifically at this issue of relevant body image comparison groups. They asked 297 women and men to rate the importance of six different groups. These ranged from particularistic (family, friends) to universalistic (celebrities, US citizens). Women and men put the comparison groups in the same order of importance. The most important group was friends. Then came celebrities, classmates and students. Then US citizens and family. So celebrities were rated as equally important as classmates and students. For women, those with 'eating disorders' or body image disturbance were more likely to compare their appearance against celebrities. Heinberg and Thompson used these data to argue that media figures are most likely to be used for body image evaluation in women with body image disturbance.

In 1996, in a study carried out specifically for this book, 200 American college students (and friends of college students) aged 16–48 were asked to nominate their body image role models ('*Who* would you like to look like?'). The sample was made up of equal numbers of men and women. Their responses were Content Analysed and coded into four categories: actor, model, sportsperson and family member. Participants were split into four age groups: 16–19, 20–29, 30–39 and 40–49. Of the men, 23 per cent of 16–19-year-olds had role models who were actors (e.g. Arnold Schwarzenegger, Jean-Claude Van Damme), and 3 per cent had role models who were sportsmen (e.g. Michael Jordan). The rest of the group reported having no role models for body shape. Of the 20–29-year-olds, 13 per cent cited actors, 2 per cent sportsmen and 2 per cent family members (brothers) as role models. In the 30–39-year-olds, 31 per cent cited actors as role models, while the rest reported no body image role models. The older men (40–49) also reported that they had no particular body image role models. Some of the men reported wanting to look like well-muscled Hollywood actors and sportsmen with high media profiles (Arnold

Schwarzenegger and Michael Jordan were those cited most frequently). Men in the 20–29-year-old age group differed from the other groups in proposing family members (usually their older brother, but in some cases their father) as models of how they would like to look.

Of the women, 10 per cent of the 16–19-year-olds cited fashion models as role models (usually Claudia Schiffer, Cindy Crawford, Elle McPherson or Christie Turlington), 5 per cent cited actresses (e.g. Halle Berry, Demi Moore, Alicia Silverstone), 3 per cent cited sportswomen (e.g. Gail Devers), and 3 per cent a family member (usually the mother). Of the women in their twenties, 9 per cent had role models who were fashion models and 9 per cent who were actresses, while 2 per cent cited sportspersons and 2 per cent cited a friend they would like to look like. The actresses, models and sportswomen chosen were the same as those of the younger women. For women in their thirties, actresses (Michelle Pfeiffer, Demi Moore) represented role models for 13 per cent of the group, with 7 per cent citing sportswomen and 7 per cent a family member (mother, sister). Of the women in their forties, 17 per cent cited a family member (mother, sister), and the remaining 83 per cent cited no particular role model.

These results suggest that media figures (fashion models, actors/actresses and sportspersons) provide body image role models for a significant proportion of men and women under forty. Well-muscled Hollywood actors such as Arnold Schwarzenegger and Jean-Claude Van Damme were the chosen model for many men under forty. More men in their thirties cited these actors as role models than in any other age group. For a significant proportion of women in their teens and twenties, fashion models represented how they would like to look. Women in their thirties chose actresses rather than fashion models. As the age of the participants increased, they were more likely to choose a family member, such as a sister or their mother, as their model, rather than a media figure. Clearly, media role models are more important to men and women in the younger age groups. It was also interesting that many participants in each age group did not cite any particular person that they would like to look like. Between 40 and 50 per cent of each group gave 'like myself', or 'no-one in particular' as their response to the question '*Who* would you like to look like?' Perhaps there was some social desirability effect in operation here. It may be that participants wanted to appear satisfied with the way that they looked, with no need of a media role model. Perhaps they were concerned about not being seen to be unduly influenced by anyone else. Or perhaps they really had no particular physical role model to which they compared themselves.

In interview work, this issue was explored further. It is much easier to investigate such issues when you can ask people to detail the reasons for their choices. In interview, girls aged eight and thirteen reported that they thought that fashion models in magazines were too thin to be attractive (Grogan and Wainwright, 1996).

Girl 1:   They look horrible. They're ugly half the time.
Girl 2:   Yeah, they are.
Girl 1:   I think they do sometimes look too thin. They look anorexic.

For the eight-year-olds, members of 'The Gladiators' represented how they would like to look. The women who form the UK TV show's Gladiators are slender and moderately muscled. The eight-year-olds' favourite is 'Jet', although they thought that she was perhaps a bit too muscular. Muscles were seen as inappropriate for women by girls in both age groups.

Adult women expressed similar preferences and concerns to the two groups of girls. Women cited fashion models Naomi Campbell and Claudia Schiffer as how they would like to look, although they said that they were too thin. For instance:

They make me sick. They are too thin. But I would kill for one of their bodies.

In interview, women aged 16 to 60 cited fashion models and actresses as their ideal (see Chapter 3).

Most women we have interviewed at Manchester Metropolitan University present complex views relating to the influence of media models (see Chapter 3). Clearly they aspire to being slim and shapely, like the models Claudia Schiffer (Plate 13, p. 92) and Cindy Crawford, who are often cited as the ideal. However, they generally feel that extreme thinness is inappropriate and unhealthy. Kate Moss and Amber Valetta are often cited as being too thin. In general the women we have interviewed want 'skinny curves', as one woman put it. They want to look slim but curvy. Still, they are pragmatic about the possi-bilities of achieving these 'skinny curves', and some made an effort to explain that, while they would like to look like Cindy Crawford, they accepted that this was not a realistic possibility. For instance, in a discussion group with American women in their twenties carried out by Jacqueline Gardner specifically for this book, one woman talked about Cindy Crawford:

> I don't know anyone who looks like her. I think she comes from another planet somewhere, and they placed her in our society so that we will all feel bad and we'll all go on diets and make the diet industry rich [*laughs*]. She's really a Martian! It doesn't logically make sense, but it makes me feel better.

Models were generally thought to be too skinny, and even Cindy Crawford (who was not considered to be *too* thin) was felt to be unnaturally thin for her height:

Woman 1:	I look at some models and think 'no'.
Woman 2:	I do think that they can be too skinny.
Woman 1:	Cindy Crawford, she's not too thin. She's not sickly thin. She looks quite healthy.
Woman 3:	But she's thin.
Woman 1:	Yeah, and she is 6 foot tall. If I was 6 foot tall and weighed what I do I'd be pretty cool too.

Similarly, talking about how Hollywood has unrealistic standards so that women who are really of average size are perceived as overweight simply because they are not unnaturally skinny:

> They had an interview with, you know, the mother on Home Improvement and they were saying she was 'chunky'. And it's like, her, chunky? I don't think she is chunky, but by Hollywood standards she is chunky.

These women were critical of media portrayal of skinny models, and wanted to see more realistic images of models with average sized bodies in magazines. They were particularly critical of what they saw as double standards promulgated by magazines, where there would be articles saying that all body shapes are fine, but these would be contradicted by images of skinny models on other pages of the magazines:

> This is the image you are trying to attain, in every women's magazine. I get [women's magazine] . . . and every month there is an article saying you should like the way that you look. It is OK. But then on the next page there is someone who weighs 120 pounds and who is 6 feet tall and that is not normal. Actually, they are the

freaks of nature because that is not normal. And every single month they get all these letters and they print a lot of them saying 'why do we never see average sized models?' Every month there is a letter like that.

They were critical of the fact that advertisements for 'plus-size' (large sized) clothes were modelled by average sized women who were at the bottom end of the size range of clothes sold by those companies. There was agreement that these average sized women should be modelling regular clothes instead of the skinny models in the magazines.

Woman 3:   I'll tell you what used to drive me mad. Working for [plus-size clothing company] who were supposed to cater for larger women, 22, 24 . . . They always, on all the billboards they would have size 14 models. They would have models in the smallest size that they carried. I mean, here is a company which is specialising in making clothes for larger women. But what do they do? They still go to size 14. Because to larger women that size 14 looks good. It looks like a size 3.

Woman 1:   The large size models are the same size I am, and I'm a size 9. Christine, she is beautiful, she is a large size model. She's not fat at all. But she is a large size model. She should be modelling regular clothes because she is an average size. I'm not a plus size and she doesn't look like a plus size.

It is striking, when listening to women talking in interview about media representations of the female body, how angry and dissatisfied many women are with the ways that the female body is portrayed in the media. They perceive that the fashion industry tries to manipulate them into feeling insecure about the way that they look. We have found a similar pattern of dissatisfaction in women aged from 16 to 60 in Britain and in the United States. Their experiences challenge conceptions of women as passive 'victims' of a system of oppression. The women we have interviewed are aware that the images presented are unrealistic and unhealthy (although they still aspire to look like fashion models in magazines) and are often angry at what they see as the media manipulating them into feeling bad about the way that they look. In *Beauty secrets* (1986), Wendy Chapkis argued that women need to accept themselves as they really are and reject the unrealistic ideals set up by the advertising industry, communications media and the cosmetic industry. Clearly, women (even the 13-year-olds we have interviewed) are critical of the unrealistic images portrayed to them. However, most women still aspire to a very slim ideal, leaving a wide gap between ideal and current body shape for most women. This ambivalence is clear in our interviews with women of all ages.

Boys aged eight and thirteen reported in interview that they aspired to the bodies of muscular men on television and film – mainly members of The Gladiators, Jean Claude Van Damme and Arnold Schwarzenegger (Plate 14, p. 93).

In interview and questionnaire work with male body-builders (see Chapter 4), we have also found that men often describe making unfavourable comparisons between the media images of highly muscled men on the television and in body-building magazines and their own bodies. In some cases this was cited as a catalyst in the decision to take anabolic steroids:

> The more I trained, the more magazines I looked at, the bigger I wanted to be . . . and there was a TV programme and when I watched these people it made me feel really depressed, I didn't look as good as them, and it had a massive effect on my decision to take steroids.

However, most adult men we have interviewed report a minimal effect of media imagery on their body esteem. Adults and 16-year-olds were more likely to report how they compared themselves with male friends and wanted to match those who were more muscular. An interesting difference between interviews with men and with women is that adult men tended to see media images as realistic goals. There was a general feeling that they could look like the media images if they wanted to, but that they did not care enough about the way they looked to spend time weight training. Spending time trying to look good was generally thought to be feminine – and therefore inappropriate – behaviour (see Chapter 4). A similar pattern emerged from interviews with 16-year-old boys, who reported that they would like to look more muscular (like The Chippendales) but were insufficiently motivated. The implication again is that they could look like them if they chose to do so, but had more important things to do:

> I wouldn't mind looking like that. But I wouldn't put myself out to look like it you know.

Data from interview, when combined with questionnaire data, suggest that men and women do use media images as standards for comparison to evaluate their own body shape and size. However, women (even young girls) are critical of the limited range of images, and (usually) see them as unrealistic. Men may aspire to emulate the muscular form of men who represent their body shape ideal, but are unwilling to admit to putting their energies into trying to build a muscular physique. Body-builders (who are seen as inappropriately narcissistic by many) are exceptional in putting time, energy and money (especially those who take anabolic steroids) into the quest for a well-muscled body that matches more closely the media ideal portrayed on the television and in body-building magazines.

For both men and women, friends and family are also used as body image role models. In interview, they explicitly reported comparing themselves unfavourably against peers. For instance:

> I don't look at movie stars or anything like that. I look at the average person who is smaller than me. Even when I think 'she's really not that pretty', the first thing that hits me is 'she is little', and to me it is like, I would rather look like her. I don't even think she is pretty but I just want to be slender.

> I would never not be friends with someone just because they are smaller than me, but when I am around somebody smaller than I am I feel that everyone is looking at her and then at me and they are thinking 'look how big she is'.

Similar experiences were described by men, although this time they wanted to be at least as big as their friends:

> If you've got friends who are, like, quite big in build you want to be the same as them. Although you might not be able to do anything about it, it's on your conscience all the time. You want to be that sort of size.

Our questionnaire work suggests that media models often become less important standards for comparison, and friends and family more important, as people reach their thirties and forties. Social Comparison Theory would predict that, in order to be effective standards for comparison, people must see the bodies of models and actors/actresses as in some way similar to their own (Major *et al.*, 1991). Since most fashion models are in their teens and twenties, they would be expected to be less influential on other women once those women are out of that age range. This is borne out by our questionnaire data, where actresses (Michelle Pfeiffer, Demi Moore) who are in the thirties age range are seen as role models for women in their thirties. Once in the forties, family role models become more relevant. Similarly for men, actors (Schwarzenegger, Van Damme) who are in the thirties age range are most frequently used as role models by men in their thirties. Above that range, no particular role models for body shape are cited. These data suggest that media models are used as standards for comparison for both men and women, but usually only by those who identify in some way with the person whose body is portrayed.

Recent developments

In the mid-1990s there has been an interesting new trend for media to discuss their use of slender models. This reflects (or, possibly, has created) a cultural awareness of the potential dangers of presenting young women with images of very thin models. Most articles focus on the possibility that 'eating disorders' may result from observing slender models in magazines. More recently there has been a spate of articles suggesting that men make unfavourable comparisons with media images of slender, well-muscled men. Some comments are light-hearted (Taylor, 1997), but some suggest that there may be a link between the increase in portrayal of attractive male bodies in the media and the increase in incidence of anorexia in males (Thomas, 1993). Clearly, the reasons why people suffer 'eating disorders' are complex. Media portrayals of the slender body are a convenient scapegoat. It is unreasonable to propose a direct link between media imagery and 'eating disorders', since 'eating disorders' are clearly not merely the result of dissatisfaction with the way that the body looks, but are the result of a complex of variables (Orbach, 1993). However, the portrayal of such imagery has been shown to reduce body satisfaction, and this is surely sufficient reason for advertisers to opt for the use of models in a range of sizes.

Reducing the effects of media imagery

Recently, psychologists have suggested that people can be made resistant to the negative effects of media imagery by changing the ways that they interpret incoming social information. For instance, Leslie Heinberg and Kevin Thompson (1995) suggest that we should concentrate on investigating the cognitive strategies that some people use when faced with idealised media images, so that these can be taught to other people who find that their body image is affected by images of slender media models. They argue that training in these resistance strategies may reduce distress when faced with media imagery.

If we accept that Social Comparison Theory is a valid explanation of the mechanism through which unfavourable comparisons are made, then some logical suggestions follow. Social Comparison rests on self-relevance and similarity (Major *et al.*, 1991). If people are encouraged to question the self-relevance and similarity to themselves of media images, then it would be unlikely that upward comparisons would be made, since the model would be an inappropriate target.

Researchers working within the cognitive–behavioural paradigm focus on the mental image that we have of our bodies. Rita Freedman (1990) suggests that cognitive–behavioural interventions could be used on an individual level to train people how to resist media pressure, through challenging 'faulty cognitions' and developing new ways of conceptualising incoming information. She argues that the image that we have of our body is not static, but is continually in a state of flux, depending on our recent experiences (including those of media images) and how we make sense of them. She sees body image disturbance as an individual problem caused by faulty cognitions about the body, irrational thoughts, unrealistic and faulty explanations. Using Beck's (1976) taxonomy of cognitive errors, she argues that techniques of cognitive–behavioural therapy can be used to detect such errors, which can generate irrational thoughts about the body, and which lead to body image problems. Freedman's clients are taught how to become aware of their faulty cognitions and are taught techniques to make these thoughts more rational, more self-enhancing and less self-defeating. Although Freedman recognises that social pressures to be slim and physically attractive may exacerbate body dissatisfaction, her main focus is at an individual level, in identifying individuals' 'faulty cognitions and rectifying them'. Her model does not attempt to deal with the social problem of unrealistic media imagery, but tries to give clients a way of countering its effect by training them to question the validity of their interpretation of the incoming information.

These approaches assume that changes need to be made at the level of the individual. An alternative view is taken by many writers who believe that women (as a group) should reject traditional media conceptions of body image completely. Wendy Chapkis (1986) argues that women need to reject traditional cultural ideals and celebrate the 'natural body'. Sandra Bartky (1990) promotes a revolutionary new aesthetic of the body which perceives a range of body shapes to be acceptable, and which challenges traditional conceptions of 'slim as beautiful'. One of the difficulties inherent in these approaches is that they are long-term solutions, and solutions that may not be acceptable to many women because they would involve separation from mainstream culture. An alternative is to challenge the media, and the beauty and fashion industries, to force changes. Our interviews with women suggested that many women (who may not consider themselves radical or feminist) are dissatisfied with the narrow range of images portrayed in the popular media, and are trying to produce change. The media are responding, albeit slowly, and although there is no significant trend towards more realistic photographic models yet, at least magazines are starting to carry stories about the harmfulness of dieting and the importance of accepting a range of body shapes. TV personalities such as Dawn French, Roseanne Barr, Jo Brand and many others have shown how alternative images of beauty can be brought into the mainstream. Activist feminist artists such as the 'Guerrilla Girls' in New York have attacked the traditional position of women within visual culture as objects of male gaze. Other women artists are also challenging accepted notions of how women's bodies are portrayed in the media, often using their own bodies as subjects in their photographs (such as Carolee Schneeman's performance art in the 1970s, and more recently the work of Cindy Sherman, Della Grace and Marianne Muller) to create a counter-aesthetic of the female body (see Muller, 1998). However, it is important not to overestimate the extent of any change. In 1997 the model Sophie Dahl made headlines because she modelled designer fashion and she is a (UK) size 14 – the average size for British women. The fact that this was newsworthy shows that the fashion industry has a long way to go before it regularly uses models that represent realistic images of women's bodies.

Summary

- The media present the male and female body quite differently. Men tend to be portrayed as of standard weight (usually slender and muscular); whereas women tend to be portrayed as underweight.
- Data from studies of the effects of media images have tended to show that both women and men can feel less good about their bodies after viewing these idealised media images.

- Media figures (fashion models, actors, sportspersons) provide role models for a significant proportion of men and women under forty. Young men's body shape role models tended to be well-muscled actors. Women's varied with age, with women in their teens and twenties choosing fashion models, and those in their thirties choosing actresses.
- Women were critical of the narrow range of body shapes presented in the media (which are viewed as unrealistic and unhealthy), and angry at the ways in which they perceive that the media (and in particular the fashion industry) manipulate the ways that they feel about their bodies by setting up unrealistic ideals.
- Most men reported that they would not exercise or diet to try to emulate the bodies of slender, muscular actors. Men who body-build were exceptional, reporting that unfavourable comparisons with media images of highly muscled men often resulted in increases in weight training as they try to become more like their role models.
- Existing data challenge images of the viewer as primarily passive. Viewers engage critically with media imagery, using it to inform body image.

6   Age, social class, ethnicity and sexuality

Previous chapters have identified gender-related differences in body satisfaction. The participants in many of these studies have been groups of white, middle-class college students between the ages of 18 and 25 years, and of unspecified sexuality. Although most psychological research relies on this participant group due to convenience for the academic investigator (Christensen, 1997), results are necessarily limited in generalisability. This chapter focuses on studies that have compared groups differing in age, social class, ethnicity and sexuality. First, we will review evidence for changes in body dissatisfaction throughout the lifespan, to identify critical periods for dissatisfaction and to look at development and change in body dissatisfaction in both women and men. This will be followed by a discussion of the historical links between 'slenderness' and the middle and upper classes, with a review of studies of class differences in body dissatisfaction. Following this, work on the effects of ethnicity on body satisfaction will be evaluated, in particular considering the negative effects of white Western values on body image in black sub-cultures. Finally, the impact of sexuality on body image will be investigated, looking at differential pressures on men and women to be sexually attractive, and establishing links between heterosexual, gay and lesbian sub-cultures and body image.

Body image across the lifespan

Pre-adolescence

When does body dissatisfaction start? At what age do girls and boys begin to criticise and objectify their bodies? Kim Chernin (1983) reports that pre-adolescent girls imitate the discourse of older women, expressing body dissatisfaction and concern over weight gain. Marika

Tiggemann and Barbara Pennington (1990) have also produced evidence that girls as young as nine years of age report body dissatisfaction. In this Australian study, adolescents aged fifteen and children aged nine reliably preferred (age-relevant) body silhouettes that were thinner than their current size as their ideal. Tiggemann and Pennington suggest that body dissatisfaction is the normal experience of girls in Western culture from age nine upwards, and that the imagery surrounding fatness and slimness on television and through other media is very influential in determining children's beliefs concerning correct and incorrect body size.

Andy Hill and colleagues (1992), in a recent British study, have produced similar findings from body satisfaction questionnaires and body figure preferences indicated using line drawings of (age-relevant) female figures. They concluded that girls from the age of nine are dissatisfied with their body shape and size. They argue that children 'consume' adult beliefs, values and prejudices around body shape and size, and adopt them as their own.

In a study carried out in 1995, Nicola Wainwright and myself found that girls as young as eight reported body dissatisfaction (Grogan and Wainwright, 1996). We had been unable to find any study in the published literature where girls and adolescent women had been asked to describe their experiences of (dis)satisfaction with their body shape and size. It seemed to us that this was the most valid way to try to understand how girls and adolescents felt about their bodies. Our experience of talking with adult women had suggested that many women remembered feeling under pressure to be slim from primary school onwards. We wanted to explore the issues around body image and food with young women who could share with us their ongoing experiences, rather than investigating memories of such experiences with adult women. In our study, we carried out two interviews; one with a group of eight-year-olds, and one with a group of thirteen-year-olds. It provided some interesting insights into these young women's experiences and beliefs about their bodies, dieting, exercise and food.

The eight-year-olds agreed that they wanted to be thin, both now and when they grew up. When asked whether they worried about how they looked they said that they worried about getting fat. When they were asked how they would like to look when they were older they were quite clear that they wanted to be thin.

Interviewer: What do you worry about then?
Girl 1:   Being fat mostly.
Girl 2:   Being fat.

Interviewer:	How would you like your body to look when you are older?
All:	Thin!
Girl 3:	Not fat. Really thin.
Girl 2:	Not really thin. Thin like I am now.
Girl 3:	I would like to keep thin like I am now.

All eight-year-olds cited members of 'The Gladiators' as role models, although they said that they did not want to get too muscled. Interestingly, having muscle was seen as being attractive to men, and thus to be avoided because it would lead to an increase in male attention. For instance, when asked whether they would like a lot of muscle like Jet (a female member of The Gladiators):

All:	No.
Girl 1:	No, cos men'd be all around you.
Interviewer:	Do you think men like women with muscles?
Girl 2:	Yeah.
Girl 3:	Yeah.
Girl 1:	Yeah, but I would like to be like Jet though.
Girl 3:	Yes, but I wouldn't want muscles.

Muscles were clearly seen as inappropriate for women (in line with comments from adult women as reported in Chapter 3).

When asked about their satisfaction with their present body shape, two of the eight-year-old girls said that they felt thin (and were satisfied with their weight) and two felt fat (and were dissatisfied). When asked what they would change about their bodies, both the girls who expressed dissatisfaction said they would want to lose weight.

Interviewer:	Is there anything you like to do to change your body shape?
Girl 3:	Lose weight.
Interviewer:	Would you like to lose weight?
Girl 3:	Yeah.
Girl 1:	Lose weight.
Girl 3:	You're thin enough.
Girl 1:	I'm fat.
Girl 2:	Look at your legs.
Girl 1:	They're fat.

The dissatisfaction reported by these young women was similar in kind to that reported by the adult women in the Charles and Kerr (1986) study. The results provided direct evidence that these young women were dissatisfied with their body shape and size, rather than inferring dissatisfaction from the results of comparison of silhouette figures representing self with those representing ideal, or from results of body esteem/satisfaction questionnaires (as in the Australian and British studies cited on p. 118). These accounts show that girls as young as eight years old report dissatisfaction with their body weight and shape and show a preference for a socially acceptably slim body. The young women interviewed presented accounts that suggested that they objectified and criticised their bodies. Their accounts suggest that women from primary-school age onwards are sensitive to cultural pressures to conform to a limited range of acceptable body shapes.

There is a notable lack of research evidence on body satisfaction in boys. Where boys have been studied, they have usually been included as a reference group for a comparison group of girls who are the main focus for the study. It is important to get a picture of how boys experience their bodies, and who or what their influences are when they are evaluating body image and deciding to engage (or not to engage) in activities relating to body image, particularly in the light of recent evidence for a cultural change in the representation of the male body in the media.

Michael Maloney and colleagues (1989) at the University of Ohio carried out an interesting study on a large sample of American boys and girls. Of the boys, they found (based on questionnaire data) that 31 per cent of nine-year-olds, 22 per cent of ten-year-olds, 44 per cent of eleven-year-olds, and 41 per cent of twelve-year-olds wanted to be thinner. They found that 31 per cent of boys had tried to lose weight (36 per cent at the nine year level); 14 per cent had dieted (27 per cent at the nine year level); and 37 per cent had exercised to try to lose weight (44 per cent at the nine year level). They concluded that, for many boys and girls, body shape concerns start before adolescence.

Boys are aware of differences in body shape by about five years old, and tend to show a preference for a mesomorphic (average size, athletic) build from about this age. This is known from studies where children have been asked to indicate which characteristics are associated with different builds. Lerner carried out a number of these personality trait/behaviour attribution tasks in the 1960s and reliably found that boys tended to assign positive characteristics to the mesomorphic build. In a study of five-year-olds in 1972, Lerner and Korn found that favourable traits were associated with the mesomorphic build, and negative with the endomorphic (plump) build, with the ectomorphic (thin) build coming somewhere in between. The boys' own build had no effect on their use of stereotypes. The overweight and normal-weight boys seemed to hold negative stereotypes of the endomorphic physique. A similar pattern of results is reported by Staffieri (1967), who asked boys aged between six and ten to assign personality and behavioural traits to pictures of endomorphic, ectomorphic and mesomorphic body builds. Again, he found that the boys tended to assign negative (aggressive) characteristics to the endomorph (which may relate to the stereotype of fatter boys as being bullies), negative (submissive) characteristics to the ectomorphic, and favourable (personal and social) characteristics to the mesomorphic build. The boys' own body shapes had no influence over their choices.

It is tempting to use these data to suggest that children assign negative characteristics to plump children. However, some shortcomings in the design must be borne in mind when interpreting these results. Children were asked to assign each adjective to one picture. They did not have the choice of assigning the same adjective to more than one picture, or to not assign an adjective. This 'forced choice' procedure may exaggerate differences between the different builds, and may just indicate a general preference for the mesomorphic build which leaves only negative traits/behaviours to be assigned to the other two builds. In other words, it may not indicate prejudice against plump children so much as a preference for the mesomorphic physique. Also, this task is clearly open to a social desirability effect, where children may be demonstrating their knowledge of societal stereotypes rather than their personal attitude. Children are likely to think that they are giving the 'right' answer by assigning stereotypical characteristics to different builds. The findings need to be confirmed using other methods, for instance interviewing children about their preferences, or administering open-ended questionnaires, to allow 'space' for the expression of unexpected preferences.

Recent interview work has allowed us to explain in more detail which aspects of body shape and size provoke most concern. This work has mostly supported the adjective-choice work carried out by researchers such as Lerner in demonstrating that young boys represent adult body shape ideals, and present negative accounts of overweight. In one study, Nicola Wainwright interviewed two groups of boys aged eight and thirteen about their body shape ideals (see Grogan *et al.*, 1997). She found that the eight-year-old boys wanted to be muscular when they grew up, and had role models who were well-muscled:

Interviewer:	When you are in your twenties, how would you like to look?
All:	Muscley!
Interviewer:	Can you think who you would like to look like?
Boy 2:	Hulk Hogan.
Boy 1:	Shadow from The Gladiators.
Boy 3:	Saracen.
Interviewer:	So you would like to be muscley?
All:	Yeah.

None of them had dieted, although they were clear what it meant to diet:

Interviewer:	Do you know what it means to be on a diet?
Boy 4:	Yeah, you don't eat as much.
Boy 2:	And you don't eat any fat.
Interviewer:	Have any of you lot been on a diet?
Boy 3:	No way.
Boy 2:	No.

They all exercised to some extent, and saw exercise as a way to avoid getting fat:

Interviewer:	So do you exercise?
Boy 1:	Erm sometimes.
Boy 3:	A bit.
Boy 4:	I always do it.
Interviewer:	What sort of exercise do you do?
Boy 3:	I do press ups.
Boy 4:	Running, biking.
Interviewer:	So do you think it is important to exercise then?
Boy 1:	Yeah.
Boy 4:	It burns all your fat off.

These results suggest that these eight-year-old boys share body shape ideals with teenagers and young men in their early twenties. They want to be slim (they were fearful of being fat) and muscular (but not too muscular). The interviews supported suggestions that body shape concerns start before adolescence. None of them had dieted, but they would diet or exercise to lose weight should weight become a problem. Body shape role models for these boys were television and film celebrities, rather than their friends (who presumably were still too young to sport the culturally favoured, post-pubertal muscular body).

Taken together, results from pre-adolescent boys and girls suggest that both genders are fearful of becoming fat, and conform to the slender ideal (although girls want to avoid muscularity and boys aspire to a muscular ideal). Accounts from boys and girls are very similar to the accounts from adults reported in Chapters 3 and 4. Body shape ideals are similar, as are role models.

Adolescence

There has been a lot of interest in body satisfaction in adolescence. Betty Carruth and Dena Goldberg (1990) argue that adolescence is a time when body image concern in young women is at its peak due to physical changes in shape that may move girls away from a slender goal or ideal. Adolescence has been conceptualised as a time of change, self-consciousness and identity search (Tiggemann and Pennington, 1990). Studies have reliably shown that most young women between ages thirteen and sixteen are dissatisfied with their body shape and size. Researchers working in this area have tended to infer body satisfaction from surveys of dieting or from judgements of self in relation to silhouette figures. It has been suggested that most adolescent girls say that they feel fat and want to lose weight. Thomas Wadden and colleagues (1991) argue that adolescent girls are at odds with their bodies, and report (on the basis of survey questionnaire data) that body concern is one of the most important worries in the lives of teenage girls.

In interviews with adolescent girls (Grogan and Wainwright, 1996), we found that they expressed a desire to be of average size; neither too thin nor too fat:

Adolescent Girl 3: Not too fat.
Adolescent Girl 4: Not too thin.
Adolescent Girl 2: Normal.

They expressed a dislike for the body shape of models in magazines because they thought they were too thin:

Adolescent Girl 1: They look horrible. They're ugly half the time.
Adolescent Girl 2: Yeah, they are.
Adolescent Girl 1: I think they do sometimes look too thin, they look anorexic.

However, they were envious of those of their friends who were skinny (like the models) and who ate 'fattening' foods like chocolate and did not put on weight. They shared stories about skinny people they knew who could eat anything they liked and about how they envied them:

Adolescent Girl 3:   Well, my friend used to come round all the time but she's a right fussy eater and she's right skinny but she eats a right lot of chocolate bars and everything.

Adolescent Girl 2:   I hate it when really skinny people say 'Oh, I'm fat'. They just do it to annoy you.

The thirteen-year-old girls were dissatisfied with their 'stomachs', which were perceived to be too fat.

Adolescent Girl 1:   I'd maybe change my tummy.
Adolescent Girl 3:   Yeah, I'd like to be a bit thinner.
Adolescent Girl 4:   Yeah, just got a bit of a bulge on my tummy.

These thirteen-year-olds expressed a dislike for muscles which they saw as inappropriate for women because they made women look too masculine:

Adolescent Girl 4:   I don't like women body-builders cos they're right . . .
Adolescent Girl 1:   . . . fat and uhhh.
Adolescent Girl 2:   It's all right for them to have a few muscles but not like . . .
Adolescent Girl 4:   . . . be like a man.
Adolescent Girl 2:   Just looks totally . . .
Adolescent Girl 1:   . . . out of shape.

The findings suggested that these young women have learned about the acceptability of the slim body in Western society (and the unacceptability of the body that does not fit the slim ideal). What struck us most when reading the transcripts was the similarity between the accounts given by these thirteen-year-olds and those given by the adults in the Charles and Kerr (1986) study. Adolescent women and girls may find it particularly difficult to challenge dominant cultural representations of femininity at a time when they are still learning about what it means to be a woman in society, and when they are experiencing changes in body shape and size as they move into womanhood.

There has been very little work on body image in adolescent boys. One exception is a recent study of eleven- and thirteen-year-old boys by Mark Conner and colleagues (1996). The study examined body esteem, current ideal body discrepancy and dieting in 128 eleven-year-olds (61 boys, 67 girls) and 103 twelve- to fourteen-year-olds (52 boys, 51 girls). Although boys were generally more satisfied with their bodies than girls and were less likely to diet, there were significant age differences in body esteem within the boys group. The thirteen-year-old boys were significantly less satisfied with their body shape and weight than the eleven-year-olds. This suggests that boys going through the physical and mental changes associated with puberty are less satisfied with their bodies than are pre-pubertal eleven-year-olds. However, it does not tell us why they are dissatisfied, or what they find unsatisfactory about their bodies.

In interviews with thirteen-year-old boys, we have found that their body shape ideals are very similar to adult men's ideals (Grogan *et al.*, 1997). Thirteen-year-old boys said that their ideal body shape for a man was of average build and fairly muscular, bringing their ideal into line with that of the adult men whose accounts are reported in Chapter 4:

Interviewer:	What is your ideal shape for a man, say when you are in your twenties?
Adolescent Boy 1:	Muscular legs.
Adolescent Boy 2:	Muscular.
Adolescent Boy 3:	Good tan like.
Adolescent Boy 4:	Like a footballer. Just medium build.
Adolescent Boy 1:	Not fat, not right thin, just medium.
Interviewer:	So how would you like to develop?
Adolescent Boy 3:	Body-builder.
Adolescent Boy 1:	Boxer.
Adolescent Boy 2:	Just a bit muscular.
Adolescent Boy 4:	Yeah.
Interviewer:	Where would you like the muscles?
All:	On my arms.
Adolescent Boy 4:	Chest.
Adolescent Boy 3:	Back, biceps and triceps.
Adolescent Boy 4:	All over.
Adolescent Boy 2:	I wouldn't want any of them ones like that though [*illustrates large neck muscles with hands*].

They cited Jean-Claude Van Damme as the person who most resembled their ideal because he was fit rather than really muscular:

Interviewer: So can you think of who you would like to look like when you get older?
Adolescent Boy 1:   Arnie [Arnold Schwarzenegger] but not as much, oh, Van Damme.
Adolescent Boy 2:   Yeah, like Van Damme.
Adolescent Boy 1:   He's not right muscley, he's right fit. He can do like a thousand chin-ups and stuff.
Adolescent Boy 2:   I'd rather be fit than muscley.

They did not want to become too muscular because they believed that this could lead to getting fat in later life:

Adolescent Boy 1:   [Body-builders] will get fat anyway cos when you get older all muscles turn to fat. . . . If you have too much muscle you're gonna be fat when you're older unless you can get rid of it.

They believed that they would be happier if they became closer to their ideal shape:

Interviewer: So if you had this ideal body shape, do you think you would be happier?
Adolescent Boy 1:   Yeah, cos if you were fat you'd be looking at yourself thinking you're right ugly.

Friends with muscular bodies were explicitly mentioned as a relevant comparison group, and unfavourable comparisons were said to lead to unhappiness. This suggests that body image is important for these young men's self-esteem:

Adolescent Boy 3:   And if you're hanging around with a mate who is right muscular and stuff and he's got a right good body shape all women are hanging round him, that would depress you a bit that would.

None of them had tried dieting, although they were knowledgeable about the different diets available, and three of them had family members who had dieted:

Adolescent Boy 1:	My mum does this diet where you can't eat bread and can't eat carbohydrates with protein, summat like that.
Adolescent Boy 3:	Yeah, my mum's been on a hip and thigh diet.
Adolescent Boy 2:	My mum tried Slim-fast.

If they became overweight, though, two of them would diet:

Interviewer:	So would any of you do step-ups?
Adolescent Boy 2:	Not unless I were right fat, about twenty stone.
Adolescent Boy 1:	I wouldn't exercise to lose weight then . . .
Adolescent Boy 2:	I'd just diet.
Adolescent Boy 3:	I wouldn't, I'd exercise.

These data suggest that adolescents present a slender, muscular ideal that is very similar to the adult male ideal. They are fearful of becoming fat, and would diet or exercise to avoid becoming over-weight. Men are socialised from a young age to aspire to the masculine, mesomorphic shape, which is linked with concepts of fitness and health. Looking good was linked with happiness, and adolescents explicitly mentioned making comparisons between their body shapes and those of their friends (who were one of their body shape comparison groups, along with well-muscled actors). Clearly, body image is important to young men as well as young women. These adolescents have a clear ideal that corresponds to the adult male ideal which we have identified in interview work with men.

Adolescent boys and girls share body shape ideals and discourses relating to body image with adults of the same gender. In adolescent girls, the ideal is slenderness (though not too thin), and for boys, slender and muscular (but not too muscular). The boys generally wanted to be more muscular, whereas the girls believed muscularity was inappropriately 'masculine' and wanted to be slender. The area of the body that presented most concern to girls was the 'stomach', whereas the boys wanted to be more muscular in general. Being fat was feared by both boys and girls, in line with adult concerns.

Body image throughout adulthood

Most psychological research on body image in adults has focused on samples of women and men between ages 18 and 25. This is partly because most work has used college students as research participants, and most work has been done in US universities or high schools, where students (who may be co-opted into research as part of a course requirement) are usually young adults and are a convenient participant sample.

Work that has looked at body image concerns in older adults has produced some interesting findings. The idealised slender body shape is generally associated with youth. Women in particular are expected to try to maintain a youthful appearance, since youthfulness for women is valued in Western societies. Many researchers have noted a 'double standard' of ageing, where women are judged more harshly than men in terms of physical attractiveness as they show signs of ageing. Sorell and Nowak (1981) suggest that gender-role expectations interact with age and gender to affect attractiveness judgements. Signs of ageing in men may be seen to make them look 'distinguished', whereas in women (who are often judged in terms of physical attractiveness rather then in terms of abilities or experience) signs of ageing may be seen negatively both by others and by themselves. Deutsch *et al.* (cited in Pliner *et al.*, 1990) found that ratings of physical attractiveness decreased with age for both men and women, but that the decline was steeper for female than for male targets. In another study of participants over 60 years of age, Rodin (cited in Pliner *et al.*, 1990) found that weight was a salient concern for women (second only to memory loss), but that it was rarely mentioned by men.

Adams and Laurikietis (1976) argue that women are often ashamed of ageing because ageing is linked in the public mind with becoming less attractive. Whereas men can become more attractive (in a general sense) with age, women become less attractive by definition, since attractiveness in women is so closely linked with youth in Western society. Jane Ussher (1993) argues that women are culturally defined as useless when they reach the end of their reproductive years. She argues that women of all ages are encouraged to compare themselves to youthful, slender role models, and that the discrepancies between this image and reality become more and more apparent as women age.

> This advent of ageing is experienced as a crisis by many women: a crisis which is not experienced in the same way by men. Within the discourses concerning women, looking young is seen to be one of our main preoccupations: our images of 'ideal women', against whom all women are judged and against which we judge ourselves, are primarily of young, slim, able-bodied, heterosexual, attractive women.
>
> (Ussher, 1993: 116)

Men in their forties and fifties are frequently portrayed on film as attractive and sexual, and as having sexual relationships with much younger women. It is easy to think of examples of Hollywood actors who still play 'love interest' roles in their sixties (Robert Redford, Sean Connery, Jack Nicholson, Clint Eastwood), and it is not uncommon for men to be portrayed as lovers of women twenty years younger than themselves (witness Sean Connery and Michelle Pfeiffer in *The Russia House*). Studies of media portrayal of men over 65 years old have tended to find that they are rarely portrayed on television (on average about 5 per cent of characters on television fall into this age range), although older men are represented significantly more frequently than older women. When they are portrayed, they are often portrayed as incapacitated, incompetent, pathetic and the subject of ridicule. Tony Ward (1983) reports that the old are represented as asexual, feeble and ridiculous, usually as caricatures. Older men's or women's bodies are rarely seen on film, except when they are represented in roles where their bodies might be expected to be exposed (e.g. as hospital patients).

Researchers who have analysed media representations of women have reliably found that the predominant image of 'woman' in the media is of a young, conventionally attractive model. The main concern of this ideal woman from young adulthood is to find a man and marry him, then to become a 'mother' whose main interests are child bearing, child rearing and being attractive to her husband.

In Marjorie Ferguson's (1983) content analysis of representations of women in *Woman*, *Woman's Own* and *Woman's Weekly*, she identified the main themes, goals and roles presented to women in the editorial content of these magazines. Sixty-seven percent of themes were concerned with getting and keeping a man and maintaining a happy family. Other major themes included achieving perfection (17 per cent) and overcoming misfortune (28 per cent). Of the roles represented as gender-appropriate, almost half (46 per cent) were as wives or mothers or as women trying to get married. The major goals held out as desirable for women were personal happiness (23 per cent), having a happy marriage and family (15 per cent), finding and keeping a man (16 per cent), and being beautiful (16 per cent). Ferguson (1983) notes the contradictions implicit in the messages represented to women in these magazines. On the one hand, women should strive for personal happiness, yet on the other hand their first priority should be to be a good wife and mother (p. 189).

Older women are rarely portrayed in films, and when they are they are usually represented as without role (unless that of a doting or senile grandmother), unattractive and boring/bored. Older women are almost never portrayed as sexual, and sexual desire in older women is usually a point of ridicule (Itzin, 1986; Ussher, 1993). When older women are portrayed in sexual roles, they are usually women who have a youthful appearance (e.g. Joan Collins), and the director often avoids exposing the body of the actress by implying sexual activity rather than actually filming the actors naked (Shirley MacLaine and Jack Nicholson in *Terms of Endearment*), or by filming from a distance (Pauline Collins and Tom Conti in *Shirley Valentine*).

Catherine Itzin (1986) notes that older women are less visible than older men in the popular media, and that when they are portrayed they are seen as asexual and dependent on men:

> Rarely are older women portrayed as capable and independent, never as sexually attractive.
>
> (Itzin, 1986: 126)

She shows how older women are exhorted to stay 'young and beautiful', and to wear make-up and clothes that conceal their age. She suggests that the media function to reinforce cultural stereotypes, exerting a negative influence on all women's lives, but particularly on those of older women who are faced with both negative stereotypes associated with women and those associated with old age.

Women over 30 might be expected to suffer from higher levels of body dissatisfaction than younger women, since they may be even further from the youthful, slim ideal than younger women. However, most research has found that there is no change with age in terms of body satisfaction in women, although older men may be less satisfied than younger men.

In our interviews with women (see Chapter 3) we found that women from 16 to 63 represented similar levels of dissatisfaction. Areas of the body that presented cause for concern did not differ in relation to the age of the interviewees. Women reliably reported dissatisfaction with stomach, hips and thighs, irrespective of their age. Most were motivated to lose weight, and represented an ideal that was tall and slim with firm breasts, irrespective of their age. The main motivator for women of all ages was being able to get into favourite clothes. Women of all ages were able to identify part of their body that they would like to change, and almost all wished to be slimmer if possible.

Women in their twenties and early thirties who had recently given birth often felt that the changes associated with pregnancy had brought their body shapes further from their ideals. In particular, having a 'flabby belly' was reported by several women who had recently given birth, and 'droopy breasts' (which they believed had resulted from breast feeding) were mentioned as a specific cause of dissatisfaction. Fox and Yamaguchi (1997) gave questionnaires to seventy-six women who were having their first baby, asking about how they felt about their bodies (all were at least thirty weeks into their pregnancy), both currently and prior to pregnancy. They found that women who were of normal weight prior to pregnancy were likely to experience negative body image changes during pregnancy, whereas those who were overweight prior to pregnancy were likely to have experienced a positive change in body image at thirty weeks gestation. Women's weight prior to pregnancy may also have a significant effect on body image after they have given birth. Women who were of average weight (or below) may experience more negative effects after birth than those who were overweight before (Fox and Yamaguchi, 1997).

Patricia Pliner and colleagues (1990) compared concern with body weight, eating and physical appearance between men and women between ages 10 and 79. Women were more concerned about eating, body weight and physical appearance, and had lower appearance self-esteem (i.e. felt less attractive and less pleased with their appearance). Scores on the 'appearance self-esteem test' did not differ between age groups ranging from age 10 to over 60 years old. Women over 60 were just as concerned as adolescents and young adults. They concluded that social pressures to be slim and attractive impact on women of all ages. This fascinating finding suggests that the body dissatisfaction observed in young adult women may be generalised to women of all ages. Similarly, there were no differences in men's appearance self-esteem across the age range. This suggests that older men are just as satisfied as younger men with their attractiveness, even though they (probably) move further away from the slender, muscled societal ideal as they become older.

Pliner *et al.* did not ask specifically about discrepancy between current and ideal body shapes. More recently, Sue Lamb and colleagues (1993) administered silhouette scales to older and younger women and men. Older women and men (aged about 50) were objectively heavier and considered themselves to be heavier than the younger groups (aged about 20). Younger and older women, and older men, presented body ideals that were much thinner than their perceived size. Only the younger men were satisfied with their bodies. This study suggests that some middle-aged men may be dissatisfied with their bodies, which may relate to the physiological processes associated with ageing, where both men and women become heavier, perhaps taking them further away from their ideal.

Researchers have tended to assume that older people (particularly women) have body shape ideals (derived from the media and other sources of information) that are similar to those of younger groups, producing a larger discrepancy between current and ideal body shapes, and resulting in feelings of inadequacy (see, e.g., Ussher, 1993). However, Lamb *et al.* (1993) argue that older people have a heavier ideal body size, based on a more realistic, age-related body ideal. Since people gain weight as they get older, it is possible that they also modify body shape ideals. Of course, data are difficult to interpret because, in cross-sectional work such as this, the different age groups also differ in terms of their experience of cultural pressures on body image. People in their fifties in the 1990s will have lived through the era of Marilyn Monroe and Jayne Mansfield, where a heavier, fuller body was idealised. Perhaps this result says more about historical changes in stereotypes of body attractiveness than about age differences in body weight ideals. Longitudinal work, where body image is studied in the same group over a period of several decades, would help to answer this question.

In Chapter 5, some data on role models in different cohorts was described. Although these data are beset with the same kinds of problems as the Lamb *et al.* study, they provide some additional insight into the role models of people of different ages. In our samples of one hundred men and women ranging from age 16 to 49, we found that the younger groups (under 30) were most likely to cite actors, actresses and models as body image role models. Older men reported no particular body image role models, and older women were likely to cite a family member, or no particular model. One of the interesting findings of this study was that role models tended to be age-appropriate. Youthful media models became less important standards for comparison as people became older. Each age group tended to cite role models that were similar in age to themselves. Over 40, friends and relations were more likely to be used to make body image comparisons. This is as would be expected from Social Comparison Theory, which would predict that people would choose body image models who were in some way similar to themselves, to draw realistic and relevant body image comparisons. This may in some way explain why Pliner *et al.* and Lamb *et al.* did not find that older women (in particular) were less satisfied with their body shape and size than younger women, as would have been predicted based on Jane Ussher's assumption that women of all ages compare themselves to media images of young, slender models. If women pick age-appropriate role models, then they would not be expected to become less satisfied with age. This raises the question of why men become less satisfied with age (according to Sue Lamb's study). Men over the age of 40 did not cite any role models, although two older men did say, in response to the question '*Who would you like to look like?*', 'Like myself when I was younger'. Perhaps men are more likely to compare themselves against how they used to look when they were younger. If this is the case, then the drop in satisfaction (and the slimmer ideal reported by Lamb *et al.*) would be expected, since most men increase in weight as they age (Cash and Pruzinsky, 1990).

Current data suggest that women are likely to be more dissatisfied than men throughout their lifespan, with no significant changes in satisfaction as they age, despite suggestions that media imagery focuses on the importance of youthful attractiveness. This may be because women choose age-appropriate models for body image comparisons as they age. There is some disagreement as to whether men become more dissatisfied as they age. It is possible that men become less satisfied as they age, wishing to attain a slimmer ideal. Future research in this area needs to look at the process of body change with age in longitudinal studies that follow the same cohort through the various ages, to effectively control for the effects of historical changes in body shape ideals on the development of both men's and women's body image.

Ethnicity and body satisfaction

Variation in attitudes to body size have been documented amongst different ethnic groups in Western countries. Most studies have focused on anti-fat prejudice, body satisfaction and frequency of dieting in different ethnic groups, and most have concentrated on women. There is very little research in the body image literature on ethnic differences in body satisfaction in men. Most research has found that body dissatisfaction is most frequent in British and American white women, and less frequent amongst other comparison groups, including British Asians, Hispanics and African-Americans.

There is some evidence that there are differences in the ways that obesity and overweight are viewed in different ethnic groups. Harris *et al.* (1991) report that African-American participants (both men and women) were more positive about overweight in women than were white Americans. Black American men were more likely than white American men to want to date an overweight woman, and to consider an overweight woman as sexually attractive. Harris *et al.* also found that obese African-American women had a more positive body image than obese white American women, and were less likely to want to lose weight. These findings suggest less negative attitudes towards over-weight in the African-American community.

British and American studies have suggested that Afro-Caribbean, Asian and Hispanic women are likely to report higher desired body weights, larger desired body shapes and fewer weight concerns than white women (Abrams *et al.*, 1993; Harris, 1994). Studies of girls and adolescents have produced similar findings. Studies undertaken in the United States have found that African-American girls report less dieting than white American girls. For instance, Neff *et al.* (1997) looked at body size perceptions and weight management practices in both black and white adolescent women. They selected their sample through a randomised sampling procedure designed to ensure that the sample were statistically representative of high-school students in South Carolina. The resulting sample was made up of 1,824 black and 2,256 white girls aged 14–18. They found that significantly more (41 per cent) white girls than black girls (28 per cent) considered themselves overweight. White girls were six times more likely to use diet pills and vomiting to control weight, and four times more likely to diet or exercise as a way to manage their weight. The authors concluded that white adolescent girls are significantly more likely to consider themselves overweight, and are more likely to engage in unhealthy weight management practices, compared with black girls of the same age.

Similar results have been found in British work. In a British study, Jane Wardle and Louise Marsland (1990) found that fewer Afro-Caribbean and Asian British girls than white girls wanted to lose weight. In a more recent study, Jane Wardle *et al.* (1993) studied body image and dieting concerns in a sample of 274 white and Asian British women aged 14–22. The Asian women were less likely to describe themselves as too fat, less dissatisfied with their body size, less likely to want to lose weight and less likely to diet. Some of these differences were the result of generally lower body weight in the Asian group. However, when the researchers controlled for the effects of body size they found that white women rated their stomach, thighs and bottom as significantly larger than those of Asian women of the same size. The authors concluded that white women felt larger than Asian women of the same size. Wardle *et al.* suggest that these results may demonstrate cultural differences between the two groups, where body shape may be a less emotive issue for the Asian group and/or obesity may not be such a stigma as in the white group.

Very few studies have considered ethnic differences in weight concerns in boys or men. An exception is a recent American study

(Thompson *et al.*, 1997) which looked at ethnic and gender differences in perceptions of ideal body size in nine-year-olds. In a random sample of 817 children, half white and half female, they found that African-American children selected significantly heavier ideal body sizes than white children for the categories of self, male child, female child, adult male and adult female. Black boys selected significantly heavier figures for ideal girl and ideal woman than did the white boys. They concluded that, by age nine, ethnic differences in ideal body sizes are apparent, with black boys and girls selecting significantly heavier figures than white boys and girls.

In another study that looked at ethnic differences in men as well as in women, Gittelson and colleagues (1996) investigated body shape perception in Native Canadians (Ojibway-Cree) living in Northern Ontario, Canada. He found that, while the Ojibway-Cree preferred more slender body shapes than their current shapes (with females choosing significantly thinner ideals than males), the body sizes chosen were significantly larger than those reported for white groups. They concluded that the Ojibway-Cree tend to show a preference for heavier body types than the white population.

It seems likely that these differences in ideals and body concern relate to sub-cultural differences in pressures on both women and men to be slender. In ethnic groups where overweight is not stigmatised, healthier, more satisfied attitudes towards larger body shape and size may develop. The meanings ascribed to images of thinness and fatness have been found to vary between white and non-white ethnic groups. African-American culture has privileged plumpness in women, representing the voluptuous female body as being sexual and powerful. This is displayed in the writings of Alice Walker, Maya Angelou and other black women writers, and in traditional African-American jazz, blues and (more recently) rap music (e.g. the recent work by Missy Elliott) which have represented the full-figured female as a symbol of sexuality and power. This is in marked contrast to the negative images of plumpness in mainstream (white) media.

Sub-cultural pressures may be more important than mainstream media images in influencing the value attached to body size. There are many reasons why black men and women might reject mainstream media images as being offensive or (at best) irrelevant. Positive images of black men's and women's bodies are rare in Western media. Gen Doy (1996) and Linda Nochlin (1991) have both documented the history of the objectification and sensualisation of the black body, which has continued to the present day in mainstream media images of black models and actors, where black women are portrayed as being 'shameless, sensual and available' (Doy, 1996: 19). Chris Shilling (1993) has also argued that the bodies of black men have been constructed as objects of dread and fascination by white men. This is particularly the case in pornographic material, where black men tend to be portrayed as sexual studs or as exotic Orientals, as in *Ajitto* by Robert Mapplethorpe, where the black male body is reduced to a sexual stereotype.

Advertising has also used images of the black body as sensual and dangerous, in order to advertise products aimed at the white consumer. Anoop Nayak (1997) shows how a Haagen Dazs ice-cream advertisement uses a black male model to contrast the 'purity' of the white ice-cream daubed on his back with the sensuality implied by his black skin. The utilisation of the contrast between black skin and white product is also represented in Naomi Campbell's advertisements for milk in the United States, and for Müller yoghurt in Britain. Some authors have suggested that the negative portrayal of black bodies in mainstream media may lead to privileging paler skin colour within the black community (Nayak, 1997), and to dissatisfaction with skin colour and features that do not conform to a Eurocentric ideal (Lewis, 1996).

Not all images of black bodies are negative, but positive images are hard to find in mainstream media. There is a noticeable absence of black models in cosmetic advertisements (Tyra Banks for Cover Girl and Veronica Webb for Revlon are recent exceptions). Naomi Campbell and Iman have been the only really successful black catwalk supermodels to date. The rarity of positive black images in mainstream media would be expected to alienate black viewers. This (along with conflicting values attached to plumpness) may make it likely that black viewers will reject the underlying values implied by mainstream media images. Rejection of white Western values in relation to the idealisation of slenderness may lead to less prejudice against overweight in men and women who identify with other ethnic groups.

Recent work indicates that women from Asian and Hispanic ethnic groups may be becoming less satisfied with their bodies than previously. This has led to the suggestion that we may be experiencing a cultural shift in Hispanic and Asian-American attitudes to thinness in the late 1990s. Thomas Robinson *et al.* (1996) administered questionnaires to almost 1,000 sixth and seventh grade girls (average age 12), which included questions relating to body satisfaction and desired body shape. They found (contrary to other studies) that, of the slimmer girls (the leanest 25 per cent on the BMI), Hispanic and Asian girls reported greater body dissatisfaction than the white girls. They concluded that Hispanic and Asian girls may be at greater risk than had previously been recognised, and suggest that these data may be a reflection of the fact that mainstream socio-cultural pressures towards thinness are starting to spread beyond white women. Identification with mainstream cultural values may lead to a perception of a mismatch between self and the idealised (usually white) images in the media, and may result in increased body dissatisfaction in women and girls from Asian and Hispanic groups. Further research will determine the validity and generalisability of this finding.

Current data suggest that whites (especially white women) are currently at more risk of 'feeling fat', and are more likely to diet, than British Afro-Caribbean and Asian women, or African-American, Asian-American or Hispanic groups. However, there is some evidence that the disparity may be disappearing, leading to more dissatisfaction in Asian-American and Hispanic groups, perhaps as a result of adoption of dominant white socio-cultural values in relation to body image.

Social class and body satisfaction

Differences in body satisfaction in people from different social classes have rarely been addressed in research. Most psychology researchers do not even indicate the social classes of participants in their studies. Those that do indicate the socio-economic status of their participants do not usually analyse for effects of social class, making it difficult to identify any relevant trends in relation to body image.

Researchers who have compared body satisfaction in participants from different social groups have produced mixed results. Some studies have found social class differences in body concern in women. For instance, Wardle and Marsland (1990) interviewed 846 girls aged 11–18 of different socio-economic background about weight and eating. They found higher levels of weight concern in girls from schools catering for higher social class backgrounds. Dieting was also more common in girls from these schools. They concluded that there are social class differences in body concern, with higher levels of concern amongst girls from higher social class backgrounds. Other work with women of differing social classes has also found that those in the higher social class bands are more dissatisfied with their bodies (Striegel-Moore *et al.*, 1986).

However, some studies have failed to find social class differences in body dissatisfaction. In a Spanish study by Josep Toro and colleagues (1989), the authors compared body shape evaluation and eating attitudes in a group of 1,554 adolescent boys and girls aged 12–19. The participants were chosen so as to span upper, middle and lower socio-economic status brackets, based on parental occupation (the authors do not indicate how they determined which occupations fitted into each bracket). Fifty per cent came from the upper classes, 25 per cent from the middle classes and 21 per cent from the working classes, while 4 per cent had parents who were unemployed. They found that social class did not relate to eating attitudes or body shape dissatisfaction. They concluded that the results suggest cultural homogeneity at different socio-economic levels so far as body aesthetics and satisfaction are concerned, for both men and women. This result is supported by Robinson and colleagues (1996) in an American study concentrating on young women. They asked 939 girls aged 12–13 to complete scales including parental education levels (the authors' definition of social-economic status) and body dissatisfaction. They found that parent education level did not correlate significantly with body dissatisfaction, and concluded that there is no link between socio-economic status and body concern amongst young women. They suggest that pressures to be thin are spreading beyond the upper and middle classes, producing increased levels of body concern amongst working-class girls, and that body concern is no longer associated with socio-economic status in women.

Robinson *et al.*'s (1996) suggestion that Western culture is becoming more homogeneous in terms of pressures to be thin, and that this is reflected in evidence of homogeneity in body satisfaction amongst people of different social classes, must be taken seriously. Certainly, many recent social commentators have suggested that the popular media have created more similar cultural pressures on people of different classes. Developments in mass communications in the twentieth century mean that most people have access to the same body shape ideals in magazines, and on film and television. Through this democratisation of vision, people of all social classes are presented with the same kinds of pressures to conform to the idealised images presented in the media. Recent evidence suggests that the democracy of vision produced by the popular media, where people of all classes watch the same television programmes and the same movies, read similar magazines and aspire to the same fashions in clothes (although marketed more cheaply to those in lower income groups), has produced shared body shape ideals that span class divides (Featherstone, 1991).

Psychology studies have tended to find that body shape ideals are very similar in people of different social classes in affluent Western cultures. In one classic study on the effects of social class on body shape ideals, Wells and Siegel (1961) asked 120 adults categorised into three class bands ('lower', 'middle' and 'upper' class) to assign personality traits to adult male silhouettes which were either average, mesomorphic, ectomorphic or endomorphic, using a forced-choice procedure. They found no social class differences in the assignment of traits. Men and women from all social classes rated the mesomorphic trait more positively, and there were no differences between the trait assignments of male and female raters. This early study suggested similar class ideals for men's body shape and size. We have also found similar body shape ideals in women of different class backgrounds in the interviews reported in Chapter 3. Similar ideal slender body shapes were presented by women who were (amongst others) university students, waitresses, managers of shops, schoolteachers, nurses, solicitors, gym owners and office cleaners.

In one recent study (Hodkinson, 1997), ten men and ten women from Occupational Class 2 (Intermediate: Teachers, Nurses, Managers) and Class 3 (Shop Assistants) on the Registrar General's scale were asked about body shape beliefs in relation to work. Participants (irrespective of their own occupational group) believed that overweight people were slow workers, that slim people got most work done, that employers preferred slim staff, that you had a better chance of getting a job if you were slim, that slim people were more successful at work and that they would be more successful in their jobs if they were slimmer. These responses support suggestions that cultural prejudice against overweight leads to fewer college and job opportunities in overweight people (Crandall, 1995; Averett and Korenman, 1996). All groups associated positive characteristics (self-discipline, health, fitness and being energetic) with slenderness, and all agreed that overweight people were kind and caring. Slimness was also associated with youthfulness by all occupational groups, and all groups (on average) believed that they would look younger if they became slimmer. Obviously these data only come from a limited range of occupational groups. Nevertheless, they are interesting in demonstrating similarities in beliefs and preferences in people within these groups.

In the past, body shape ideals varied between social classes. The expectation of class differences in body concern is probably based on the historical fact that, until the twentieth century, body concern was mostly limited to the middle and upper classes, those who had the time and money to follow 'fashion' in clothes, and the body shape required to show off the clothes to full advantage (Orbach, 1993). People with economic power have always set the standards for what is fashionable. This usually means that only the wealthy can afford to buy into the ideal. When resources are scarce, wealth may be reflected in plumpness and clothes that show plumpness to best advantage (seen, for instance, in Britain in the mid-nineteenth century). When resources are plentiful, and there is little fear of starvation, the wealthy may aim for a slender ideal. The wealthier classes have also tended to set styles in clothes, which often require a particular body shape and size for them to look as the designer intended.

Susan Bordo (1993) notes how, until the nineteenth century, body size was an indication of social class: the middle classes opted to display their wealth ostentatiously by eating enough to attain a corpulent form, whereas the upper classes attempted to attain a slender form, rejecting the need for an outward show of wealth. Bordo shows how corpulence went out of fashion for the middle classes at the turn of the century, when social power became linked with the ability to control and manage the labour of others. A slender ideal in men and women started to be associated with success and will power, and overweight with lack of self-control. Bordo argues that slenderness has retained some of its high-class associations, although the link has become weaker over the years. Overweight and being working-class are often associated characteristics in the media (witness *Roseanne* in the United States and the Dingle family in *Emmerdale* in Britain) and often the overweight person is represented as lazy and without those managerial qualities that (according to popular ideology) confer upward mobility. Popular Western culture is also full of symbols of upward mobility through mastery (and control) of the body (e.g. the *Rocky* films in which Sylvester Stallone is shown to be enduring pain to build up his strength and become successful, and – of course – to become wealthy and attain the trappings of the middle classes).

Susie Orbach (1993) shows how fashion trendsetters have generally come from the middle and upper social classes, because they had the economic means to experiment with different kinds of fashion images. This was particularly the case in 1960s Britain. Jean Shrimpton, the first model to be represented as angular and thin, came from the upper-middle class, and was photographed in magazines catering for the upper classes (*Vogue, Harper's Bazaar*) wearing clothes designed by upper-middle-class designers whose message was that women should break out from the confines of convention. The so-called 'Jet Set', the wealthy young, produced a trend representing freedom and adventure. Tied in with this new image was the idea of thinness, which came to signify freedom and the rejection of convention. Thinness was seen as the key to enable working-class women to transcend the barriers of class, and to emulate the 'Jet Set' life. The emergence of Twiggy, a working-class model who did not attempt to hide her background, signalled to other young women that freedom and elegance could be achieved through thinness. In the United States, thinness became part of the 'American Dream', apparently achievable by anyone.

This apparent democracy is an illusion because, as we have seen, for most people the attainment of a fashionable body image requires economic power. Fashion designers and those in the slimming and cosmetics industries ensure that the fashionable 'look' is constantly changing, and that to achieve it requires time and money. It is often costly to attain a fashionably slender but muscular body. Sufficient resources are not equally available to everyone (Whitehead, 1988; Cox *et al.*, 1993), thus effectively keeping the ideal at arm's length for most people. There are well-documented social class differences in the incidence of obesity in women. Working-class women are more likely to fall into the 'obese' category than those in the dominant classes (Sobal and Stunckard, 1989). The current slender, toned and muscular Western ideal requires time and resources for most people (unless they have a job which requires heavy manual labour). April Fallon (1990) argues that this ideal is easier to attain for the rich, who have the resources to spend time in the gym (or to have plastic surgery) to become fashionably lean and fit. She proposes that the body itself (with or without clothes) has become a way to conspicuously distinguish between the lower and the upper classes.

In addition to differences in the availability of resources for body maintenance, there may also be social class differences in motivation to treat the body as a 'project' in need of change. Pierre Bourdieu (1984) argues that different social classes develop clearly identifiable relations to the body, resulting in physical differences. He suggests that the working classes tend to develop an instrumental, functional (rather than aesthetic) relation to the body. When sporting activities are engaged in, these are seen as a means to an end (weight training to build strength, soccer for excitement/socialising). On the other hand, the dominant classes are more likely to treat the body as a project for improvement in its own right, which can either be conceptualised as making the body more healthy, or as making it more aesthetically pleasing. According to Bourdieu, the dominant social classes choose sporting activities with the aim of improving health and/or with improving the 'look' of the body. Elsewhere, Bourdieu conceptualises class differences in sport as a result of the ways in which the body is viewed, as well as being due to constraints on the amount of time and money available to invest in body maintenance, which he also views as important (Bourdieu, 1986).

Research linking social class to body image suggests that social class is not related to body shape ideals, since people from different social classes present similar ideals. Studies relating body satisfaction to social class have produced inconclusive and sometimes conflicting results, casting doubt on the assumption of many researchers that body dissatisfaction is a middle-class phenomenon. Social theorists have suggested that social class relates to the ways in which the body is conceptualised, with the dominant classes being more likely to view the body on aesthetic (rather than functional) dimensions, and being more likely than the working classes to invest time and energy in sports activities as a means of changing the way the body looks. Much more work is needed in this area, looking specifically at income and class differentials in body image, to extend the current literature and to develop work on body satisfaction beyond the traditional middle-class student group which is usually chosen for study by psychologists.

Body shape, sexual attractiveness and sexuality

Most of this text has considered body image in terms of aesthetics rather than sexual attractiveness. Body shape and size have important implications for sexual attraction. Some researchers have focused on the relationship between body shape and size and perceived sexual attractiveness, and have produced some interesting findings. There is some debate in the literature as to the basis for opposite-sex attraction in terms of body shape and size. Social psychologists and sociologists have generally argued that sexual preferences in body shape and size are largely learned, and are affected by the value that a particular culture attaches to that kind of body shape. They have stressed the cultural relativity of body shape features that signal sexual attractiveness, and have focused on same-sex as well as opposite-sex attraction. On the other hand, evolutionary psychologists have argued that people have an inherent preference for sexual partners who are biologically 'fit' (healthy and able to reproduce), and that body shape features such as being of normal weight and having a pronounced waist (in women), or no pronounced waist (in men), serve as biological indicators of 'mate value' to the opposite sex. Here we will consider arguments from these two perspectives, evaluating the usefulness of each approach in explaining available data in relation to body shape ideals and body satisfaction. For convenience, this section is divided into four sections, looking separately at the specific social pressures on heterosexual women, lesbians, gay men and heterosexual men.

Heterosexual women

Many researchers, particularly within the feminist tradition, have focused on the social pressures experienced by women to conform to a particular body shape in order to be attractive to men. Nickie Charles and Marilyn Kerr (1986), in their interviews with 200 British women, found that sexual attractiveness was cited as one of the major reasons why women desired to conform to the slim ideal. For most of the women they spoke to, this was phrased in terms of the necessity of staying (or getting) slim to maintain their current (heterosexual) sexual relationship. Many women reported that their sexual partners monitored their 'fatness' and told them when they needed to lose weight. Charles and Kerr concluded that body image is closely linked with sexual attractiveness, and that, particularly after childbirth, women feel pressure from their sexual partners to regain their figures and to be slender, in order to maintain their sexual relationship. They concluded that the unnaturally thin feminine ideal leads women to be constantly dissatisfied with their bodies, and that perceived pressure from sexual partners is a key factor in this dissatisfaction.

In our interviews with women (reported in Chapter 3), some women reported that they felt their sexual relationships had suffered because they were self-conscious about their bodies, usually feeling too fat. They were clear that they had more desire to be sexually active when they felt good about themselves (including good about their bodies). Ironically, many women reported that their sexual partners thought they were attractive, and had not commented negatively on their bodies, yet they still felt fat. For instance, one 23-year-old woman said:

> I'm off [on vacation] for a week, and I want to wear little sexy things and all that, and my sex life is suffering because of my body image. There are a lot of times that I would like to and he would like to, but I just can't bring myself to undress. I don't want him to see how fat I am.

The relationship between body image and satisfaction with sexual relationships is well documented (see, e.g., Weiderman and Pryor, 1997). Werlinger *et al.* (1997) reported a significant increase in sexual desire amongst US women who had lost weight and developed a more positive body image as a result. However, the reasons why such a relationship exists are complex, relating to self-confidence (which may result from, or produce, body satisfaction).

Many of the women we interviewed felt that it was important that their male sexual partner should be heavier and generally bigger than them, and they cited occasions where they were made to feel really good because they felt that their partner was much larger than them. For instance:

> I have to look for someone with a certain body image that will make me feel better, feel small. I had this boyfriend in college who was huge, he was 6 feet 4 and he was a tanker. And I would put his jacket on and the sleeves would fall over my hand and I loved it. I mean, I loved it.

> [My partner tried to get my jeans on] the other day and he said 'oh, I am going to have to lose some weight' and I'm like . . . it was funny but it made me feel so good that he couldn't wear my jeans.

These experiences may be most relevant to women with traditional views of male–female relationships in terms of dependence–independence, who tend to be more concerned with body image than those with less traditional views (Cash *et al.*, 1997).

Some interesting work has compared women's perceptions of men's ideal body size for women with men's actual preferences. April Fallon and Paul Rozin (1985) asked a group of 248 men and 227 women to indicate their current figure, their ideal figure, the figure that they felt would be most attractive to the opposite sex and the opposite sex figure to which they were most attracted, using Stunckard *et al.*'s (1980) body size line drawings. The authors did not ask the participants to indicate whether they were heterosexual. For women, the current figure was heavier than the ideal figure, with the figure expected to be most attractive to men coming in between. For men, all three figures were almost identical across the group. Interestingly, it was found that both men and women erred in estimating what the opposite sex would find attractive. Men think that women prefer a heavier figure than they actually choose, and women think that men would like a thinner figure than they choose in reality. The authors concluded that men's perceptions serve to keep them satisfied with their bodies, whereas women's serve to keep them dissatisfied. Men's ideal was generally thinner than women's perceived current figure, showing that men generally prefer a more slender figure than women's perceived current size.

These findings were supported by another American study in which Sue Lamb and colleagues (1993) found that women tended to believe that men preferred much thinner body shapes than the men themselves actually chose. They found that women's ideal is actually thinner than the size that they think men prefer, and it seems likely that women are sensitive to pressure from men to be thin, but also that they are sensitive to more general cultural pressures, from the dieting industry for instance, which may set up an even slimmer ideal, and pressure from other women to conform to a thin ideal.

Fallon and Rozin's (1985) results were replicated by Gail Huon and colleagues (1990) on a group of Australian men and women. Forty men and 40 women in the first year of a psychology course at the University of New South Wales were asked to select a photograph showing their ideal female figure, their actual size (or for men the size of their best female friend), the one they thought most men would prefer and the one that most women would prefer. The choice was from twelve projected photographs of two female models, adjusted to different sizes by a device that systematically varied the images about the vertical axis. Men were accurate in predicting women's preferred size. Women's preferred female size was the thinnest, followed by what they believe to be men's preferred female size, followed by their own ideal, followed by their actual size. The authors concluded that the data suggest that women's body image is affected by general social pressure, from women as well as from men.

Most evolutionary psychologists suggest that there are biological reasons for body shape and size preferences in potential sexual partners. According to Buss (1989), a woman's physical attractiveness is largely a reflection of her potential reproductive success. Reproductive success is defined as the optimum (for the environment) number of children surviving to reach sexual maturity and to become parents themselves. Buss believes that men (irrespective of culture) place more significance on body shape and size in women than women place on men. He suggests that there are cultural universals in desired body shape and size for man–woman sexual attraction, and that these derive from the division of labour between men and women during the course of evolution, where males specialised in hunting activities and women in food gathering and child rearing. Natural selection is believed to have operated so that men and women whose bodies were best suited for these roles (normal weight, muscles for men, fat layers around hips for women) were more attractive to potential mates and so were more likely to reproduce. According to evolutionary theorists (Buss, 1987; Kenrick, 1989), women's physical attractiveness is important because it gives male sexual partners reliable cues to their health and potential reproductive success.

Devendra Singh (1993) suggests that men's preferences for women's shapes are determined by the woman being of normal weight and having a waist-to-hip ratio (WHR) that signals fertility. At puberty, women typically gain weight around the waist and hips. Singh suggests that the curves created by this 'reproductive fat' provide men with a gauge of reproductive potential. According to Singh, healthy fertile women typically have waist-to-hip ratios of 0.6 to 0.8, meaning that their waists are 60–80 per cent the size of their hips, whatever their weight. When women go through the menopause, they generally become heavier in the waist, so that WHR becomes similar to the male range of 0.85 to 0.95. He suggests that women with higher WHR report having their first child at a later age than women with lower WHR. He also argues that low WHR relates to better general health, as defined by the absence of major diseases such as diabetes, heart attack and stroke, which are all less common when people carry more fat in the lower body (Singh, 1993: 295). He concluded that WHR reliably signals degree of sexual maturity, reproductive potential and good health.

In a study of *Playboy* centrefolds and 'Miss America' contest winners, Singh found that women whose bodies were considered appropriate in the 1980s were measurably leaner than the women who were chosen in previous decades, yet their WHRs stayed around 0.7. When he asked male volunteers to rate line drawings of female figures for attractiveness, sexiness, health and fertility, the preferred figure (irrespective of the culture or age of the participants) was the figure with the 0.7 waist-to-hip ratio (which was the figure with the lowest WHR that he presented; see Figure 6.1). Singh concluded that the distribution of body fat plays a crucial role in judgements of women's physical attractiveness, health, youth and reproductive potential; and that, to be perceived as attractive by male judges, women must be of normal weight *and* have a low WHR – neither factor alone is sufficient to predict attractiveness since being either underweight or overweight reduces perceived attractiveness and also perceived healthiness.

Singh suggests that WHR may be involved in the initial stages of physical attraction, where men may be more likely to initiate contact with women with low WHR, so that this would lead to a filtering-out of women with high WHR. Then a second filter would take account of culturally defined standards of attractiveness for that particular culture (for instance, overall plumpness or slenderness, facial features, etc.). However, all societies (whether they generally preferred plumpness or slenderness) would favour women of low WHR, because of its association with fertility and health.

It is a shame that Singh did not offer his participants the choice of

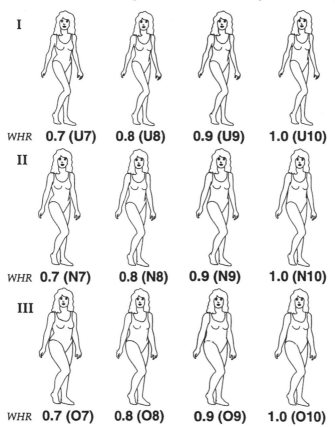

I
WHR 0.7 (U7)   0.8 (U8)   0.9 (U9)   1.0 (U10)

II
WHR 0.7 (N7)   0.8 (N8)   0.9 (N9)   1.0 (N10)

III
WHR 0.7 (O7)   0.8 (O8)   0.9 (O9)   1.0 (O10)

Figure 6.1 Female stimulus figures varying in WHR

Source: Adapted from Singh (1993). Copyright © 1993 by the American Psychological
Association. Adapted with permission.

Note: Figures represent underweight (I), normal weight (II) and overweight (III), with
waist-to-hip ratios (WHRs) shown under each figure in each weight category,
along with a letter and number in brackets which identifies body weight category
WHR.

the full range of WHRs (i.e. including WHRs of less than 0.7). The
range of figures that he used (0.7 to 1.0) gave participants a restricted
choice, and did not allow an assessment of the effects of very low
WRH on perceived sexual attractiveness. Presumably there may be an
optimum WHR below which men no longer find the figure attractive.
Although very few women have WHR below 0.5, it would nevertheless
have been interesting to see how attractive figures of 0.6 and 0.5 were

rated. Following Singh's logic, these should be perceived as more sexually attractive than the 0.7 figure which was the lowest he presented. Indeed, the corset and bustle combination that he mentions (Singh, 1993: 296) would have produced a WHR below 0.7 in many women, through constricting the ribcage to give a tiny waist in relation to the hips (see Brownmiller, 1984). Although Singh assumes that the female body with low WHR is more sexually attractive to men than one with higher WHR, it would have been informative to have investigated the limits on this effect, in order to try to identify an optimum WHR (as he has done for women's judgements of men).

Most evolutionary theorists (e.g. Buss, 1987) assume that attractiveness is intrinsically related to 'mate value'. However, Singh found that rankings of 'reproductive ability' were independent of rankings of 'health, youth, attractiveness and sexiness'. These findings suggest that Singh's respondents rated women's attractiveness independent of their 'mate value', probably on an aesthetic (rather than reproductive potential) dimension.

Although Singh investigates consistency of the WHR effect in men of different ages, his biological argument would be more convincing if it were based on cross-cultural data. His participants were all American (White and Hispanic) males, so were all likely to be experiencing similar cultural influences (television, magazines, etc.). It could be that he is observing a learned preference for a 'slender but curvy' shape. Sixty-five per cent of men rated normal weight figures most attractive, and 35 per cent underweight. The 'overweight' woman (irrespective of WHR) was not found 'most attractive' by any man, despite the fact that she was not sufficiently overweight to represent a threat to reproductive status or health (the figure is designed to represent a 5 foot 5 inch tall woman weighing 150 lb, who is not obese as judged on the Metropolitan Life Insurance Tables). What strikes the reader is the fact that the 0.7 and 0.8 WHR bodies look familiar (i.e., they are similar to body shapes represented in the media), whereas the others do not. If, as Singh says, models tend to conform to the 0.7 WHR, then perhaps the findings reflect a familiarity effect; a learned preference for this kind of body shape. It would be interesting to show his line drawings to heterosexual women (or gay men), and to see which pictures are chosen as 'most attractive'. If the preferences he observed reflect learned social preferences rather than biological mate value, we would predict the same pattern of preferences in women as those seen in Singh's male participants. In fact, Singh did not ask his respondents to indicate their sexuality, which is a serious oversight when discussing female sexual attractiveness to men.

In Chapter 3 we saw that the area of the body that presents most concern for women is the very area (hips and thighs) where women store the reproductive fat that is supposed to make them attractive to men. Nearly all the women we have interviewed, whatever their body type and weight, wanted to lose weight around their hips (i.e., to increase their WHR). This would not be predicted from Singh's model. Also, women generally want to be slim (rather than of normal weight). There is clearly a conflict between the factors identified here as being high in 'mate value' and women's desire to attain the slender, slim-hipped ideal. It seems likely that there may be a difference between heterosexual men's body shape preferences for women, and women's own preferences, which (according to interview data in Chapter 3) may relate more to fashion for a particular body type than to being sexually attractive to men, although this may be a secondary concern.

Social psychologists and evolutionary psychologists have generally been reticent about discussing the inter-sexual significance of breasts, even though there is no doubt that breast size and firmness is intimately tied to Western notions of heterosexual attractiveness in women. Evolutionary psychologists have generally argued that breast size is largely irrelevant to sexual attractiveness, since breast development does not reliably signal fertility. Women with adrenal tumours, and true hermaphrodites, have fully formed breasts, but they are infertile. Singh argues that these women have male-like WHR, making WHR a more reliable indicator of fertility. Desmond Morris (1985) even argues that the breasts evolved to mimic buttocks (to make women's front view more attractive to men!), and have no sexual significance of their own. However, most social psychologists would agree that moderate-to-large breasts on a slender frame are men's cultural ideal in Western societies. A cursory perusal of men's magazines such as *GQ*, *Esquire* and *Playboy* leaves the viewer in no doubt that the magazines' editors expect their readers will prefer women with firm, moderate-to-large breasts. In a study of *Playboy* centrefolds, Mazur (1986) notes that, although the women portrayed there have become thinner over the years, their breasts have remained relatively large.

In a study of men's preferences for women's bodies, Wiggins *et al.* (1968) produced 105 silhouette figures with systematically varied shapes of legs, breasts and buttocks. In general, men showed a preference for medium-to-small buttocks, medium sized legs, and slightly oversized breasts. This result has been replicated in more recent studies (see Hatfield and Sprecher, 1986).

Kevin Thompson and Stacey Tantleff (1992) ran an interesting study in which they asked US men and women to select schematic male and female figures differing in breast (see Figure 6.2) or chest size as current, ideal, and the size that they thought was the opposite sex's and their own sex's ideal. Overall, results indicated a preference for large breast/chest sizes. Both sexes rated their own current size as smaller than ideal. Men's conception of ideal breast size was larger than women's. It was concluded that the findings explain the societal preoccupation with breasts, overall dissatisfaction with this area of the body in women, and the decision to seek cosmetic surgery for breast enlargement. Positive adjectives were associated with large breasts (particularly confidence, popularity and being likely to succeed) for both men and women judges. The only positive characteristics associated with small breasts were athleticism and intelligence.

Susan Brownmiller (1984) is interested in the paradox for women of possession of breasts that are intensely private (usually hidden from view), yet very public (evaluated socially by men and by women themselves). She is particularly interested in the ways that men fetishise, and claim ownership of, women's breasts, leading women to be self-conscious about perceived inadequacies (too large, too small, not firm enough).

> No other part of the anatomy has such semi-public, intensely private status, and no other part of the body has such vaguely defined custodial rights. One learns to be selectively generous with breasts – this is the girl child's lesson – and through the breast iconography she sees all around her, she comes to understand that

Figure 6.2 Female stimulus figures varying in breast size

Source: Adapted from Thompson and Tantleff (1992) with permission.

breasts belong to everybody, but especially to men. It is they who invent and refine their myths, who discuss breasts publicly, who criticise their failings as they extol their wonders, and who claim to have more need and intimate knowledge of them than a woman herself.

(Brownmiller, 1984: 24)

If men tend to prefer slenderness with largish breasts, this presents a conflict for women who wish to be attractive to men. Slenderness may be achieved through restriction of food intake. However, weight loss will also lead to breast shrinkage. Media images of women's bodies aimed at a male audience often present an unusual, slim-hipped, long-legged, large-breasted ideal (Pamela Anderson from the TV series *Baywatch* is a good example). This ideal is only possible for most women through a mixture of diet and exercise (to slenderise hips and thighs) and plastic surgery (to swell the breasts).

The popularity of plastic surgery to augment the breasts is increasing every year. It is estimated that the number of such operations doubles every five years (Wolf, 1991). Breast augmentations were first carried out in the 1950s in Japan, and by the 1960s silicone implants were being used more and more frequently to increase breast size, despite problems with rejection of the implants by the body's immune system (Meredith, 1988). In the 1990s, concern over silicone leakage has led to a preference for saline implants which, if they leak, cause less damage. Despite wide publicity about health risks, it is estimated that over a million women in the United States have had breast implants, and six thousand implant operations are carried out every year in Britain (Davis, 1994). According to Kathy Davis, women tend to report that they have the operation for themselves, to rectify perceived inadequacies, to 'take control of their lives', rather than being coerced by their partners. Kathryn Morgan (1991) takes a more mainstream feminist view, arguing that, although women may feel that they are making a free choice, such freedom is not really possible in a culture where women's bodies are objectified, and where the cultural ideal is set up by men. It has recently become popular to talk about plastic surgery as a feminist gesture. Katherine Viner (1997) critiques the current fashion to argue that plastic surgery allows women to gain control over their bodies and their lives, showing that defending a woman's right to do what she wants with her body allows the potential for harm through (for instance) anorexia, bulimia, 'cutting' and plastic surgery. She notes that plastic surgery reduces women to the sum of their parts, and is the result of a defeatist, 'quick fix' mentality.

Gillespie (1996) also argues that collusion with restricted models of femininity may be a rational choice for some women at the individual level. However, at the social level, such action goes against women's collective interests, and perpetuates social inequalities.

Heterosexual women are clearly under pressure to conform to a very slender ideal. Most studies have shown that women prefer a thinner ideal than men do. Social and evolutionary psychologists have suggested than individual Western men report preferences for 'normal weight' (rather than very slender) women's bodies. However, women operate within a cultural context where a very thin ideal is promoted by the beauty industry, and these pressures (which Naomi Wolf, 1991, argues are controlled by male-dominated institutions) contribute to women's thin ideal. The recent increase in breast augmentations may reflect perceived pressure from men, although women tend to report that the decision to have plastic surgery was taken independent of pressures from sexual partners. It is difficult (or impossible) to separate women's choice in this matter from cultural influences (which include pressures from men), although women's accounts that they are making a free choice by taking control of their lives through plastic surgery obviously reflect the felt experience of many women who opt for the 'surgical fix'.

Lesbians

There is very little research in the literature on the degree of pressure exerted on women who choose female sexual partners, although most authors tend to assume that lesbians are under significantly less pressure from sexual partners than are heterosexual women. Brown (1987) argues that lesbian culture downplays the importance of conventional physical attractiveness, leading to higher levels of body satisfaction amongst lesbians compared with heterosexual women, and lower levels of anorexia and bulimia. However, Andrea Dworkin (1988) argues that lesbians are socialised to conform to the same societal standards of physical attractiveness as heterosexual women, and must comply with socially accepted standards to be accepted within the lesbian community.

In an American study based on a small number of lesbian and heterosexual women, the authors concluded that the two groups did not differ in degree of body dissatisfaction, although the lesbian group showed a lower frequency of dieting (Striegel-Moore *et al.*, 1990). Similarly, Brand *et al.* (1992) found no differences in body satisfaction between lesbians and heterosexual women, concluding that gender was a better predictor of body dissatisfaction than sexuality.

Michael Siever (1994) compared the importance placed on physical attractiveness in fifty-three lesbians, sixty-two heterosexual women, fifty-nine gay men and sixty-three heterosexual men. He found that the lesbians who took part in his study placed significantly less importance on physical attractiveness in their sexual partners than did heterosexual women, and reported that their partners placed significantly less importance on physical attractiveness than did all other groups. Lesbians were also more satisfied with their bodies than were heterosexual women (although this difference was not statistically significant on most measures). Some of the lesbian group indicated that they had suffered with body dissatisfaction and disordered eating before they 'came out'. Siever suggests that the lesbian sub-culture may have a protective function in relation to body dissatisfaction, in that lesbians may become more satisfied with their bodies as they become assimilated into the sub-culture. He proposes that the lesbian sub-culture places less emphasis on youth and beauty, and does not promote the unrealistic ideals seen in mainstream heterosexual culture, leading to less objectification and higher body satisfaction.

Siever's work is suggestive of differences in body satisfaction in lesbians and heterosexual women, but his results are not conclusive. Research where lesbians are asked to give accounts of body image would be useful in developing some of the ideas suggested in Siever's article. Members of his group of lesbians were significantly heavier than his heterosexual women, making valid comparisons between the two groups difficult. In particular, Siever does not look at the impact of gender role orientation of the women who took part in his study. Studies on lesbianism need to take into account butch/femme gender stylisation (Butler, 1991; Tyler, 1991). This is particularly important for studies of body image, where it could be expected that style of presentation could be salient in determining satisfaction with the body. It is possible that there is more social pressure for women presenting as 'femme' to conform to prevailing social mores on slenderness (from their sexual partners, from lesbian sub-culture, and/or from mainstream culture). This is a question that could be addressed through in-depth interviews with lesbians presenting as butch/femme.

The political climate within which lesbianism exists is also important in understanding lesbian body image. There is widespread cultural prejudice amongst the heterosexual population against homosexuality in general and lesbianism in particular (Kitzinger, 1987). Judith Butler (1991) argues that lesbians are oppressed through non-recognition:

Lesbianism is not explicitly prohibited in part because it has not even made its way into the thinkable, the imaginable, that grid of cultural intelligibility that regulates the real and the nameable. How then to 'be' a lesbian in a political context in which the lesbian does not exist? That is, in a political discourse that wages its violence against lesbianism in part by excluding lesbianism from discourse itself?

(Butler, 1991: 20)

Celia Kitzinger reiterates Butler's experiences of oppression, conceptualising lesbianism as a political movement (see Kitzinger, 1987). In this context, rejection of male-dominated, mainstream cultural representations of how women should look, and the forging of a woman-centred aesthetic amongst lesbians, might be predicted. Prejudice from mainstream culture may strengthen group identification and social support from within radical feminist sub-culture. A woman-centred philosophy will enable lesbians to forge more positive body images than heterosexual women. Certainly feminist writers (e.g. Wolf, 1991) would predict that a woman-loving philosophy (amongst straight women and lesbians) would promote more positive and accepting images of the female body. Some lesbians present accounts that reject lesbianism as a political decision (Kitzinger, 1987). It might be expected that these women might be more affected by mainstream cultural pressures to be slender than other lesbians who are more politically motivated (and better supported through radical feminist sub-culture). Future research needs to address this issue through asking women for accounts of social support, political beliefs and body image.

Researchers working within the socio-cultural perspective present a convincing account of the role of sexuality in determining the kinds of social pressures faced by individual women in relation to body image. In particular, the work of Michael Siever suggests that women who choose to have sexual relationships with other women may suffer less body dissatisfaction. Further work is needed to investigate sources of social support, and the effects of gender-style presentation and political orientation on body image in women.

Gay men

Gay men may be under more extreme social pressure than heterosexual men in relation to body image, in a context in which they are the objects of male gaze. It is generally agreed that gay male sub-culture places an elevated importance on body shape (Lakoff and Scherr, 1984). Jamie Gough (1989) notes a significant change in gay male culture that took place between the 1970s and the end of the 1980s, whereby having a male athletic body became important in developing the fashionable muscular, toned look. He notes that this change is most marked among gay men whose social life is centred on the 'gay scene' (clubbing, drinking in 'gay' venues, etc.), and in big cities more than in small towns. He is interested in this shift because it challenges traditional ideologies of gay men as effeminate (see Marshall, 1981). He argues that the masculinisation of the 'gay scene', where the body must be toned and muscular, is oppressive to men (Gough, 1989: 120).

> Masculinity as a sexual fetish is, therefore, oppressive not simply for dictating a certain norm, but for demanding something that cannot be achieved. The new style of sexual attractiveness is all the more tyrannous in that, as we have seen, it prescribes not only social behaviour but also physiology.
>
> (Gough, 1989: 121–2)

Studies of body satisfaction in gay men have generally suggested that they tend to show higher levels of body concern than heterosexual men. Marc Mishkind *et al.* (1986) found that, in a sample of both heterosexual and gay men, the gay men expressed greater dissatisfaction with body shape, waist, biceps, arms and stomach. They also indicated a greater discrepancy between their actual and ideal body shapes than did straight men, and were more preoccupied with their weight and diet. The study was flawed, in that the sample of 'heterosexual' men was drawn from a group of undergraduate men in an Introductory Psychology class who were assumed to be heterosexual. However, the study presents some interesting findings in relation to differences in pressures from the gay male sub-culture to conform to the male body ideal.

Mishkind *et al.*'s findings were replicated by a recent study with Yale University undergraduate students. Beren *et al.* (1996) found that their sample of fifty-eight gay men reported significantly higher levels of body dissatisfaction than fifty-eight heterosexual men. Using self-report measures, they were able to measure level of affiliation with the gay community. They expected that those who were more strongly affiliated with the gay community would indicate more body dissatisfaction, due to the emphasis placed on body appearance in the gay community. They supported this hypothesis, finding that those who identified most strongly with the gay community were least satisfied with their bodies. They concluded that aspects of the gay community increase vulnerability to body dissatisfaction. Perhaps these data needed to be interpreted more cautiously, since what they have actually demonstrated is merely an association between the two variables, meaning that the causal link may run in the opposite direction (so that men who are more satisfied with the way they look feel a closer link with the body-conscious gay culture). Still, the demonstration of a link is interesting and suggestive of social pressure within this community to have a 'good' body.

Michael Siever (1994) notes that many researchers have proposed that the gay male sub-culture imposes pressure on gay men to be physically attractive, and that empirical data suggest that gay men generally value physical appearance more than heterosexual men do. In a study at the University of Washington, Siever asked both men and women to complete a packet of self-report questionnaires, including the Franzoi and Shields (1984) Body Esteem Scale, the Cooper *et al.* (1987) Body Shape Questionnaire, and the Stunckard *et al.* silhouette drawings (see Chapters 3 and 4). He found that gay men and heterosexual women showed the highest levels of body dissatisfaction. Gay men were significantly more dissatisfied with their bodies than heterosexual men. In fact in this study gay men were less satisfied with their bodies than were heterosexual women. Siever suggests that this may be because gay men have the potential to be dissatisfied with their bodies on two dimensions. Like heterosexual men, they may worry that their bodies are inadequate in terms of athletic prowess and, like heterosexual women, they may rate themselves on an aesthetic dimension. Siever concludes that sexual objectification results in increased emphasis on physical attractiveness and body dissatisfaction in the recipients of the objectification, be they men or women. He argues that assimilation into the gay sub-culture may lead to gay men becoming less satisfied with their bodies, within a context where slenderness and muscularity are prized.

It is important to place pressure from the gay community in its social context. Body-image-related pressures from the gay 'scene' do not exist in a vacuum. They exist within a culture where young men generally have significant spending power, making them an attractive market for consumer goods (Mort, 1988). The 1980s and 1990s have seen an opening-up of young men's markets generally, and particularly that of young gay men (O'Kelly, 1994). It is clearly in the interests of purveyors of clothes, cosmetics and other body-related consumer goods to encourage body consciousness in the gay community and to capitalise on the resulting demand, and the spending power of those gay men who are affluent. In the late 1980s, Frank Mort noted that gay men were taking up a variety of different styles (high camp, biker imagery, retro) which all involved consumerism, which acted to the advantage of advertisers and marketers (Mort, 1988). Cultural pressure from the 'gay scene' to be physically attractive is actively encouraged and supported by advertisers and others with a financial interest in gay men's spending power, who promote aspirational images of the muscular, attractive gay man through the media to encourage consumerism (O'Kelly, 1994).

In addition to pressures from within the gay community to be attractive, gay men are also faced with the cultural stereotype that 'gay men look after their bodies' and are 'physically fit'. Mainstream media are full of examples where gay men's bodies are represented as attractive and 'fit'. For instance, in an *Independent on Sunday* article discussing the reasons why women were not buying the new soft-pornography magazines aimed at women, one of the 'problems' identified by the journalist was that magazines aimed at heterosexual women tended to use gay male models, since 'gay men are the ones who tend to look after their bodies' (Forna, 1996: 3). Even feminist writers fall into the trap of objectifying gay men and expecting them to conform to the 'fit gay' stereotype:

> Many gay men, as straight women often observe, are very attractive. There's a lot to be said for tight pants on a good body in excellent condition.
>
> (Brownmiller, 1984: 71)

As when women's and black men's bodies are objectified, the objectification of gay men's bodies is a way of disempowering the group. In a culture where the quest for beauty has been used for hundreds of years to control women's energies (Wolf, 1991), the expectation that gay men should be attractive can be conceptualised as a form of social control. Diana Fuss (1989) argues that gay men (and lesbians) are seen as a threat to public safety, and believes that gay men are persecuted by the state apparatus. The 'gay man as fit body' stereotype is a potential source of social control, especially in the context where 'heterosexism' is validated by the supposed risk of the spread of AIDS. Many authors have documented the rampant heterosexism that has emerged with the AIDS epidemic in both Britain (Kitzinger, 1987; Ellis and Heritage, 1989) and the United States (Watney, 1995; Yingling, 1991). External 'fitness' can reassure the fearful both within and without the gay community that the gay man (and his behaviour) does not represent a risk.

Most studies have found that gay men are less satisfied with their bodies than are heterosexual men. This may relate to pressures from the gay community to have an acceptably muscular body, within a mainstream cultural context where gay men are more 'embodied' than heterosexual men, and where there is a cultural expectation of body consciousness in gay men from within and without the gay community. More work is needed in this area to compare men of different ages (since most work has focused on men under 30), and to compare men involved in the 'gay scene' with others who are not. Choosing samples from venues attended by gay men (as most researchers have done) may overestimate the extent of body dissatisfaction by producing a sample who identify most strongly with the 'scene'. As Beren *et al.* (1996) have shown, men who are more highly involved in the 'scene' may show higher levels of concern than those who have gay relationships but would not identify themselves with that sub-culture. At present it seems likely that men who are subject to male 'gaze' are more concerned about their bodies than are heterosexual men.

Heterosexual men

Despite recent media interest in the social pressure on heterosexual men to conform to the well-muscled slender ideal, there is little evidence that men are responding to pressure from women by trying to attain a well-muscled look. In the Fallon and Rozin studies (Fallon and Rozin, 1985; Rozin and Fallon, 1988), men's current and ideal sizes, and the size that they believed was attractive to women, were very similar, leading the authors to conclude that men's perceptions serve to keep them satisfied with their bodies.

Interview work (Chapter 4) suggests that men believe that women prefer them to be toned and muscular, but are not motivated to try to achieve this look through exercise or diet. Most pressure came from male peers (rather than women) who criticised body shape and size, in particular if a man was considered to be overweight. Some of the body-builders we interviewed have commented that the primary motivation to start to body-build was to be more sexually attractive to women. However, after that, competition with other men became a more important motivator. None of the men who were using steroids cited pressure from female partners as a motivator. Pressure from media models and other men training at the gym was a more significant factor here (see Chapter 4).

Michael Siever (1994) found that gay men and heterosexual men did not differ significantly on beliefs as to the degree to which their body mattered to potential sexual partners. If gay men feel significantly more objectified than straight men, then a difference would have been expected here. Also, there were no significant differences in perceptions of importance of attractiveness to potential partners between heterosexual men and heterosexual women. The difference was in the (assumed) result of this. In heterosexual men it did not translate into body dissatisfaction. So body dissatisfaction is not a necessary effect of perceived objectification. Similarly, when asked about the importance of physical appearance in potential sexual partners, there were no significant differences between heterosexual women, heterosexual men and gay men. These data are important since they show that (according to their own reports) heterosexual men and gay men do not place a higher premium on physical attractiveness in their partners than heterosexual women.

The most parsimonious interpretation of these findings, taken together with the interview work detailed in Chapter 4, is that heterosexual men receive, and perceive, pressure from women to look slender and muscular, but that this is not sufficiently important to them to result in body dissatisfaction, probably because the pressure is to some extent counterbalanced by a general cultural attitude that values attributes other than physical attractiveness in men. Increased cultural pressures on heterosexual men to attain a well-muscled physique (identified by Mishkind *et al.*, 1986) do not seem to have resulted in significant body dissatisfaction.

Evolutionary psychologists have generally failed to consider what women find attractive in men, largely because of their assumption that what women are looking for in a man is his ability to defend and support her! However, even Charles Darwin argued that women would choose men for the ways that they looked (rather than for their abilities to support her financially, or for personality factors):

> Both sexes, if the females as well as the males were permitted to exert any choice, would choose their partners not for mental charms, or property, or social position, but almost solely from external appearance.
>
> (Darwin, 1871, cited in Singh, 1995: 1089)

Devendra Singh (1995) has recently suggested that body shape may be important in determining how attractive women rate men to be. He suggests that body fat distribution is important in determining which men are judged sexually attractive by women. After puberty, men tend to lose fat from lower body parts, and deposit fat on upper body parts (shoulders, nape of neck, abdomen). From an analysis of data from the National Aeronautics and Space Administration, sampling from European, Asian, African and Latin American men, Singh argues that most men, irrespective of culture, have a WHR of between 0.8 and 0.87. He argues that men with WHRs in this range are healthier than other men, and are likely to be of reproductive age. In a series of studies, he found that white and Hispanic women of different ages found men with WHR in the average range most attractive when presented with male body shapes varying in WHR (see Figure 6.3). This effect was maximised if the males were of higher financial status. Singh suggests that physical appearance is important in determining women's choice of sexual partner because it relates to health:

> Women may select mates who are healthy to ensure that their offspring inherit a predisposition for good health and that the man would be able to provide good quality parental care.
>
> (Singh, 1995: 1099)

There are similar problems associated with these arguments to those relating to the data on men's preferences for women's body types. Singh cannot show that these preferences are biologically determined. They are as likely to be the result of learned preferences. Again, data come from American (white and Hispanic) women who share similar cultural influences. The results would be more convincing if they came from different cultures. He shows that women tend to prefer men who fall into the average (i.e. most familiar) range. He does not examine waist-to-shoulder ratios, or waist-to-chest ratios, which may be more telling in terms of women's preferences for male body types.

Kevin Thompson and Stacey Tantleff (1992) found that women showed a preference for large chest sizes for men when presented with male figures varying in chest size (Figure 6.4). Most men rated their current chest size as smaller than ideal on this scale. Women associated adjectives such as assertive, athletic, sexually active, confident and popular with large chest sizes for men. Thompson and Tantleff concluded that women (and the men themselves) show a distinct preference for large chest sizes.

Evolutionary psychologists have also argued that body symmetry is important in inter-sex attraction. Randy Thornhill and Steven Gangestad (1994) have suggested that having a symmetrical body may be extremely important in inter-sex physical attraction. Thornhill is a biologist, who became interested in the effects of symmetry when he found that scorpion flies which had more symmetrical wings fared

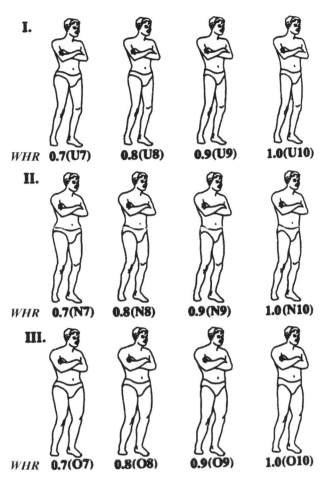

I.

WHR **0.7(U7)**   **0.8(U8)**   **0.9(U9)**   **1.0(U10)**

II.

WHR **0.7(N7)**   **0.8(N8)**   **0.9(N9)**   **1.0(N10)**

III.

WHR **0.7(O7)**   **0.8(O8)**   **0.9(O9)**   **1.0(O10)**

Figure 6.3 Male stimulus figures varying in WHR

Source: Adapted from Singh (1995). Copyright © 1995 by the American Psychological Association. Adapted with permission.

Note: Figures represent underweight (I), normal weight (II) and overweight (III), with waist-to-hip ratios (WHRs) shown under each figure in each weight category, along with a letter and number in brackets which identifies body weight category WHR.

better in the competition for food and mates. Working with psychologist Gangestad he started to look at symmetry in humans. They measured body symmetry in hundreds of male and female college students. Through adding up the right–left differences in seven measurements

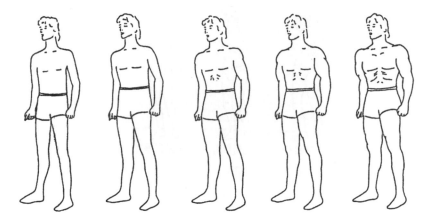

Figure 6.4 Male stimulus figures varying in chest size

Source: Adapted from Thompson and Tantleff (1992) with permission.

(breadth of feet, ankles, hands, wrists, elbows, and breadth and length of ears) they were able to produce a score indicating degree of asymmetry for each person. For men and women, greater symmetry predicted larger numbers of sexual partners. Thornhill and Gangestad suggest that symmetry predicts other features with 'mate value' including muscularity, health and athleticism. Although symmetry may relate to health, it is also possible that it is a culturally determined preference. The data presented by Thornhill and Gangestad (1994) show that such a preference may exist, but do not present a convincing argument that this preference has any biological basis.

One of the problems with evolutionary arguments is that they are mostly *post hoc* explanations of existing social effects based on parallels with data derived from animals. Although they may be valid, they do not allow us to reject alternative, cultural explanations. Bob Connell (1987) argues that socio-biological arguments are really pseudo-biological, as they do not rest on serious biological investigation of human social life. He suggests that, despite their claim to scientific explanation, they cannot adequately substantiate the mechanisms through which sexual selection is supposed to operate. He suggests that socio-biology starts with an interpretation of social behaviour (which may be factually incorrect, as it is often sexist and ethnocentric) and projects this back upon a mythical history of human society, using this to posit processes of natural selection which justify the current social arrangements. This argument is supported by Chris

Shilling (1993), who sees socio-biology as providing an incomplete view of human mating behaviour since it focuses on strategies for maximising the chances that genes will be passed on to future generations, to the exclusion of social factors:

> Individuals are like robots controlled by forces beyond their reach. Human behaviour and social interaction is explained in terms of the costs, benefits, and even strategies of genes engaged in a competitive struggle for survival. Put simply, there is no need to look to social structures as determinants of human behaviour as there is no such thing as emergent social structures.
>
> (Shilling, 1993: 50)

Other critics agree that the search for a biology of physical attractiveness is a thinly veiled attempt to justify existing gender divisions in society. Geoffrey Cowley (1996) cites Kartha Pollitt as saying:

> It's the fantasy life of American men being translated in to genetics. You can look at any feature of modern life and make up a story as to why it is genetic.
>
> (Cowley, 1996: 66)

Similarly, quoting Micaela di Leonardo, he writes:

> People make decisions about sexual and marital partners inside complex networks of friends and relatives. Human beings cannot be reduced to DNA packets.
>
> (Cowley, 1996: 66)

April Fallon (1990) also argues against the biological determinist view. She demonstrates that some biological characteristics associated with reproduction, such as menstruation, pregnancy and lactation, are rarely valued in terms of attractiveness. Similarly, features in males representing maturity and social dominance (for instance baldness) are rarely considered attractive. She suggests that cultural diversity demonstrates that cultural influences are important in determining what is considered attractive, pointing to the fact that many cultures consider obesity attractive, and citing examples where plump women are considered to have greater sex-appeal and to be more sexually satisfying that thin women.

Data on sexual attractiveness suggest that heterosexual women and gay men perceive most pressure from actual or potential sexual partners to conform to a particular body shape and size, although heterosexual women are likely to perceive the male ideal as slimmer than it is according to men's reports. Heterosexual men perceive some pressure from sexual partners, but expect that their current body shape and size are close to ideal, leading to body confidence. Lesbians are likely to perceive little pressure, and to be significantly more satisfied with their bodies than are heterosexual women. Arguments from evolutionary psychologists suggest that women and men in heterosexual relationships look for characteristics in their partners indicating 'fitness' (low WHR in women, average WHR and body symmetry in men). However, these effects are open to alternative, socio-cultural interpretations. Evolutionary psychologists have failed to demonstrate convincingly that preferences for particular body shapes are biologically based, and their work has many critics. Demonstration of cross-cultural similarities in effects of WHR would lend more credibility to arguments presented by researchers working within this paradigm. Current data suggest that body satisfaction is largely determined by social factors, and is intimately tied to sexuality.

Summary

- This chapter has reviewed data from a variety of sources looking at the mediating effects of age, ethnicity, social class and sexuality on body image.
- Body dissatisfaction is evident from eight years of age. Boys and girls express similar concerns to those voiced by adults in relation to their 'fear of fat', and describe similar body shape ideals to those described by adults (slender for girls and slender but muscular for boys). Looking at body satisfaction throughout the lifespan, studies have found that women of all ages are less satisfied than men. Women do not appear to become less satisfied with age, and there is some indication that women's ideals may become heavier (in line with actual body size) as they become older. There is some evidence that men become less satisfied as they become older, although the gender differential is maintained throughout the lifespan.
- Data in relation to ethnicity show that African-Americans and Afro-Caribbean British participants have heavier body shape ideals, and are less dissatisfied than white Americans or white Britons. There is some evidence that Asian and Hispanic men and women living in Western cultures also have heavier ideals and are

more satisfied with their body image. However, recent work suggests that women from these groups may be becoming less satisfied as a result of the spread of mainstream white cultural prejudice against overweight beyond the white community.

- Studies of the effects of sexuality on body image have shown that heterosexual women and gay men may be most dissatisfied with their bodies, and lesbians most satisfied, due in part to differences in cultural pressures in relation to body shape and size, and differences in perceived objectification by potential sexual partners.

- Data in relation to body image in people of differing age, class, ethnic group and sexuality emphasise the crucial importance of understanding socio-cultural pressures on group members in order to make sense of variations in body image.

7 Conclusions and implications

The preceding chapters have summarised existing work on men's and women's body image, and have painted a picture of degree of body dissatisfaction in the average Western man or woman. From what we know about the impact of the effects of membership of particular cultural groups (gender, class, ethnicity, sexuality and age), being white and being heterosexual are likely to predict body dissatisfaction in women. Age or class are unlikely to have a significant impact. Men are likely to be more satisfied in general, although older, white and gay men may be expected to be most dissatisfied. The average woman could be expected to have dieted to try to lose weight, and the average man is probably not highly motivated to diet or exercise even if he perceives a mismatch between his current body and his ideal body image. If he does change his behaviour he will probably exercise. Women are likely to feel dissatisfaction with hips, thighs, 'stomachs' and breasts; men are more likely to be dissatisfied with 'stomachs' and general muscle tone. Most women want to lose weight, whereas men are equally likely to want to be heavier or lighter.

Dissatisfaction exists in a context where body image is subjective and socially determined. The social relativity of body satisfaction has been demonstrated by illustrating how satisfaction varies by social group. Data from different social groups have shown that the same body shape may be perceived more or less positively depending on the gender and social group of the person doing the perceiving. A person's body image is not determined by the actual shape and size of that body, but by that person's subjective evaluation of what it means to have that kind of body within their particular culture. Work has shown conclusively that body dissatisfaction is not related in any logical way to actual body size, as determined by Body Mass Index (BMI; see Chapter 2). In Marika Tiggemann's (1992) study of the silhouette choices of young and mature Australian women and men (described in

Chapter 6) she found that there was no relationship between BMI and body dissatisfaction in men or women of either age group. Actual body weight (relative to height) did not predict how satisfied people were with their body size. Also, BMI was not associated with self-esteem, so people who were thinner (or fatter) did not feel better about themselves generally.

In another study carried out on British men and women, Adrian Furnham and Nicola Greaves (1994) reported the same pattern of findings. Body dissatisfaction showed absolutely no association with BMI, although it was highly correlated with self-esteem and perceptions of control. These findings are replicated in countless studies in the psychology literature, leading psychologists to agree overwhelmingly that body satisfaction does not relate to actual body shape and size (even for people living in the same culture). Clearly, perceptions of body size and shape are not determined by actual body size. This has led researchers to argue that body image is subjective, and open to change through social influences. The factors that seem to predict body satisfaction most accurately are social experiences, self-esteem and perceptions of control over one's life (including perceived control over the body).

The preceding chapters have focused almost exclusively on the effects of social experiences on people's body image. In Chapter 5 we looked at ways of resisting social pressure (especially media pressure) through encouraging people to challenge potentially damaging imagery (Chapkis, 1986), reconceptualising the meanings of incoming information (Freedman, 1990), and by rejecting traditional images of the body and replacing them with a revolutionary new aesthetic of the body that perceives the 'natural' range of body types to be acceptable (Bartky, 1990).

This chapter will go one stage further to review work on individual differences, in an effort to identify individual psychological factors that predict body dissatisfaction. To do this, we need to look at those who have been found to have a high level of body concern, to identify psychological factors that predict dissatisfaction (and satisfaction). By looking at those who may be unusually dissatisfied with the way they look, and by identifying psychological factors that predict extreme dissatisfaction, we may be able to produce some useful ideas for encouraging a more positive image of the body.

Groups with low body satisfaction

Psychological and sociological evidence suggests that there is a small number of people who have more pronounced body concerns than the remainder of the population. Here we will review some of the available evidence relating to some of these groups: women and men classified anorexic and bulimic; frequent exercisers (including body-builders); and chronic dieters.

People experiencing 'eating disorders'

One group of individuals who could be expected to be unusually dissatisfied with their bodies are those with 'eating disorders'. Here we will review studies of the relationship between problematic relationships with food and body dissatisfaction, weight concern, and a drive for thinness. We will then investigate additional psychological factors that seem to predict 'eating disorders'.

The term 'eating disorder' is generally used to describe eating patterns that fall outside the normal range, usually involving severe restriction of food intake (*anorexia nervosa*), and regular binge eating followed by 'purging' usually characterised by deliberate vomiting but sometimes using laxatives or vigorous exercise (*bulimia nervosa*). Although there is some disagreement in the literature on 'eating disorders' as to whether people with problematic relationships with food should be seen as a specific clinical group (Orbach, 1993; Rosen, 1990), or conceptualised simply as the extreme end of the continuum of body concern (Rodin *et al.*, 1985; Chesters, 1994; Dewberry and Ussher, 1995), there is general agreement that some women and men have more problematic relationships with food than the rest of the population (Raudenbush and Zellner, 1997). Several researchers have suggested that culture plays an important role in the development of 'eating disorders'. It is generally accepted that anorexia and bulimia are more common in countries that value slimness, and that when people move from cultures that value plumpness to those where slenderness is valued they become more likely to develop problematic relationships with food (Rosen, 1990). However, many women are exposed to the 'culture of slenderness' and only a few become anorexic or bulimic, so clearly other factors are involved. There is general agreement that anorexia and bulimia are determined by multiple factors, and that they are most common in women (Orbach, 1993).

Much of the research in the literature on 'eating disorders' has focused on groups of women from the general population (usually groups of college students) rather than from women classified as 'anorexic' or 'bulimic', often because it is easier for researchers to gain access to groups of students than to women with 'eating disorders'. It is generally found that women students with the most problematic attitudes to food have thinner body size ideals than those with less problematic attitudes (Rosen, 1990). For instance, Debra Zellner and colleagues (1989) carried out a replication of the Fallon and Rozin silhouette study (1985) described in Chapter 3, controlling for the effects of 'eating disorders' by testing participants on the Eating Attitudes Test (EAT). This test identifies people who have abnormal eating behaviours by measuring dieting, food preoccupation and self-control. The authors identified nine women and one man who scored above the criterion indicating 'eating disorders' from a group of thirty-three men and fifty-seven women. All participants were asked to choose the silhouette that represented their current and ideal size, that most attractive to the opposite sex, and the opposite sex figure that they found most attractive. They found that men chose similar figures for current, ideal, and most attractive to opposite sex, as suggested by Fallon and Rozin. Women scoring high on the EAT test also showed the same pattern as that reported by Fallon and Rozin (current being larger than the figure believed attractive to men, which in turn was larger than ideal). Women scoring low on the EAT test showed ideal and figure attractive to men to be very similar, and thinner than ideal. So, all women desired to be thinner, but the 'high EAT score' group had an ideal that was significantly thinner than the 'low EAT score' group. The authors suggest that women with more abnormal eating behaviours have a thinner ideal than other women, demonstrating a higher drive for thinness in this group.

Studies that have looked at the relationship between body dissatisfaction and eating attitudes in the general population of college women and high-school students have reliably found a significant relationship between body dissatisfaction and problematic relationships with food (Rosen, 1990). Those with the most problematic relationships with food are likely to be most dissatisfied with their bodies, usually perceiving them to be too heavy.

Very few studies have actually looked at body dissatisfaction in women classified as having 'eating disorders'. Studies that have done this have tended to find that women with anorexia or bulimia do not differ significantly on body satisfaction from other women (Garner *et al.*, 1983; Wilson and Smith, 1989). The observed lack of difference probably reflects the generally high levels of food preoccupation and low body esteem in women in the general population (Charles and Kerr, 1986: Chesters, 1994). Any group of women sampled from the general population is likely to include women with problematic relationships with food (Zellner *et al.*, 1989). Many women have extremely problematic relationships with food, even though they have never been referred for medical attention with 'eating disorders' (Charles and Kerr, 1986; Chesters, 1994; Zellner *et al.*, 1989). Liz Chesters (1994), interviewing British women with and without anorexia, found that the discourses used by the two groups were very similar, being constructed from dissatisfaction concerning their bodies, and seeing weight loss as an attempt to gain control over their lives. She argues that women both with and without anorexia share body dissatisfaction and food preoccupation.

Although clinical groups do not differ from 'normals' on general measures of body satisfaction, there is some evidence that they do differ on specific indicators of weight concern. Garfinkel (1992) reports that 93 per cent of a group of women classified as bulimic evidenced over-concern for weight. Cooper *et al.* (1987) compared anorexics and bulimics with women with no history of 'eating disorder' and found that women with anorexia and bulimia exhibited significantly greater levels of weight concern than the 'normal' groups. It is well established that 'eating disorders' usually begin with an episode of dieting (Rosen, 1990). Wilson and Smith (1989) compared women who dieted regularly with women classified bulimic to see whether there was any difference in degree of weight concern between the clinical sample and women who restricted food intake on a regular basis but had not been classified as having an 'eating disorder'. They found that the bulimic women showed significantly greater weight concerns than women who dieted regularly. These findings suggest that women classified as having 'eating disorders' show significantly greater weight concern than those who are merely dieting.

The popular tendency to suggest that body dissatisfaction leads to 'eating disorders' is not borne out by the available evidence. Body dissatisfaction may be an important element in 'eating disorders', but clearly other factors have to be present for an individual woman to develop problematic relationships with food. Most women are dissatisfied with their bodies, and most diet, yet most do not develop 'eating disorders'. Body dissatisfaction may be a necessary condition, but it is certainly not a sufficient condition for the development of 'eating disorders'. Many other factors have also been implicated in the development and maintenance of 'eating disorders', including family relationships and genetic factors (see Orbach, 1993). Here we will focus on psychological factors: perceptual distortions of body size, low self-esteem, and perceptions of lack of control.

One commonly held belief about anorexia is that anorexic women overestimate the size of their bodies. This idea originated in the work of Bruch (1962), who suggested that body image disturbance was a pathological feature of *anorexia nervosa*. Other authors have also suggested that anorexics' self-perceptions of body size are faulty, mainly from clinical experience. For instance, in a quote from an anorexic woman who weighed 33 kg and was 168 cm in height:

> I look in a full length mirror at least four or five times daily and I really cannot see myself as too thin. Sometimes after several days of strict dieting, I feel that my shape is tolerable, but most of the time, odd as it may seem, I look in the mirror and believe that I am too fat.
>
> (Garner and Garfinkel, 1981: 265)

Although anorexic women overestimate the size of their bodies (Smeets, Smit, Panhuysen, and Ingleby, 1997), they do not do so more than 'normal' women. As shown in Chapter 3, most women overestimate the size of their bodies (usually hips, thighs, stomach). Current data show that if 'anorexics' are matched with 'normal' women of the same size, they overestimate to the same extent (Thompson *et al.*, 1990). Clearly, anorexia is unlikely to be the result of a perceptual deficit.

Low self-esteem may also be an important trigger for 'eating disorders'. Studies that have focused on self-esteem in anorexic women have shown that women with 'eating disorders' generally have very low self-esteem relative to the rest of the female population. Eric Button (1993) argued that low self-esteem is an important precursor to the development of 'eating disorders'. However, his data were derived from people who already had 'eating disorders', leaving open the question of which factor comes first, or whether a third factor could be producing the observed relationship.

To counter these criticisms, Button and colleagues (1996) carried out a prospective study of the relationship between self-esteem and 'eating disorders' (Button *et al.*, 1996). The researchers measured self-esteem in 594 schoolgirls aged 11 using the Rosenberg Self-Esteem Scale. They re-tested 397 of the girls at age 15 using a 'health questionnaire' that included items measuring feelings of fatness, use of weight control mechanisms, all items from Garner *et al.*'s EAT (1982), and Zigmond and Snaith's Anxiety and Depression Scale (1983). They found that EAT-26 scores at age 15 were predicted significantly by self-esteem scores at age 11. Whereas only 3 per cent of girls in the high self-esteem group went on to have high EAT scores, 28 per cent of those in the low self-esteem group went on to have high EAT scores at age 15. Button *et al.* use the data to suggest that girls who are low in self-esteem at age 11 are at significantly greater risk for developing the more severe signs of 'eating disorders' at age 15. Fatness concern at age 11 was also predictive of high scores on the EAT-26. Those who scored higher on fatness concern at age 11 tended to have higher EAT scores at age 15. It is not possible to be sure that self-esteem at age 11 pre-dated eating problems. To be sure of this, the authors should have administered the EAT-26 with the Rosenberg scale at age 11. It could be that some of these girls were already experiencing food-related problems at that age. Nevertheless, the study is interesting in clearly linking self-esteem and eating problems in young women.

This study is also interesting in that it produces percentage estimates of weight control strategies in these 15-year-olds. Of these young women, 57 per cent 'felt too fat', 46 per cent had dieted in the past, and 19 per cent were currently dieting. Exercise had been used at some time by 38 per cent as a means to control weight, and 22 per cent were currently exercising to lose weight. Surprisingly, 9 per cent reported vomiting to control weight, and thirty-five were currently using this weight control strategy. Laxatives had been used by 4 per cent, and fifteen were currently using laxatives. Diuretics had been used by 2 per cent, and 3 per cent were currently using them. The fact that 9 per cent had vomited, and 4 per cent had used laxatives, to control weight is cause for concern.

Perceptions of lack of control may be important in determining the time when 'eating disorders' develop. Bruch (1973) argues that young women who develop 'eating disorders' often come from families with domineering, over-protective parents, who make it difficult for the young woman to exert her independence. Pursuit of thinness may be an effort to exert control. Losing weight (which is within the woman's control) may lead to the perception of increased effectiveness. Slade (1982) has suggested that young women at risk for anorexia attempt to deal with stress and feelings of lack of control by striving to attain control over the body through starvation.

In a psychoanalytic analysis of the basis of 'eating disorders' in women, Susie Orbach (1993) describes them as 'a metaphor for our age'. She likens anorexia to a hunger strike, where women are protesting against the conflicting demands placed on them by a society that expects women to be 'Superwomen':

> The myth of Superwoman – baby on the hip, briefcase in one hand, and exercise schedule, credit cards, and flash cards offering quick routes to designer lives clutched in the other – has been developed by unconscious co-conspirators to ridicule the aims of

thousands and thousands of women who've striven to extend their lives and their conceptions of self and other women and men.

(Orbach, 1993: xxii)

She argues that anorexia is an attempt at empowerment, since not eating when you are starving is an act of courage and desperation. In order to understand why the protest takes the form of starvation, she places anorexia within a social context. She believes societal pressures (including the media) prompt women to objectify, and become disassociated from, their bodies. Some women develop an anorexic response to these pressures by denying themselves food. She believes that anorexia is only tangentially about slimness. What is important is that thinness signals to a culture that values denial that the woman herself is able to deny and control her own needs. The societal promotion of slimness may legitimise the restriction of food intake. She shows how the denial of food raises self-esteem (at least in the short term) and erects a kind of psychological barrier around the woman, making her feel more in control. Orbach sees the anorexic as quite separate from other women who diet to excess, because the primary purpose of the dieter is slimness as a goal in its own right, whereas the anorexic's main goal is self-control and denial.

Very few men are classified anorexic or bulimic. Most researchers estimate that between 5 and 10 per cent of people classified as having 'eating disorders' are men, although some researchers suggest that doctors and clinical psychologists may fail to recognise 'eating disorders' in men because of the expectation that these are problems only found in women (Hsu, 1990). The usual explanation of the lower incidence of male anorexics is that social pressure on men works against extreme thinness (the mesomorphic body type is the most valued for men) so that men getting thin are likely to face negative social responses, whereas women may face encouragement and praise in the early stages of anorexia, as being effective dieters (Orbach, 1993). Men who become thin will not have this social reinforcement. There has been much media interest in the increased incidence of anorexia amongst men recently. In an article for the *Independent on Sunday* entitled 'Anorexia – now it's Nineties man who suffers' (Dobson, 1996), Roger Dobson suggests that the increased exposure of the male body in the media is a trigger for anorexia in men, in tandem with low self-esteem and role conflict. This is supported by experiential accounts of anorexia in men (see, e.g., Krasnow, 1997).

In some ways, anorexia in men presents more of a challenge to social theorists than anorexia in women, because it is unlikely that men receive social support for thinness, so their starvation is not explicable in terms of social reinforcement. Clearly, other factors (such as low self-esteem, perceptions of lack of control) must be important in producing 'eating disorders' in men. The increased exposure and objectification of the male body may perhaps have focused men's attention on their bodies as objects to signal their psychological distress, as suggested by Orbach (1993) in relation to women. This explanation seems to make more sense than the suggestion that men use the images in the media as role models and seek to aspire to them. Getting thinner would bring the body away from the muscular ideal currently fashionable for heterosexual and gay men.

Research on 'eating disorders' suggests that body dissatisfaction is not sufficient to trigger an anorexic or bulimic response. Other factors are involved. 'Eating disorders' can be prompted by feelings of lack of control of bodily needs, low self-esteem and extreme weight and shape concerns. Body dissatisfaction may be a necessary condition, and cultural preferences for slimness may also be important (which may explain the low incidence of 'eating disorders' in cultures where thinness is not valued), but they are not sufficient to explain why some women (and a few men) starve themselves or become bulimic. Feelings of lack of control of bodily needs, low self-esteem and extreme weight and shape concerns seem to be predictive of 'eating disorders'.

Chronic dieters

Dieting is a frequent result of body dissatisfaction, particularly in women (see Chapter 3), and chronic dieters can reasonably be expected to be a group of individuals who are low in body satisfaction when they start to diet (Charles and Kerr, 1986). In fact, dieting may have unforeseen effects for the dieter's body image, self-esteem and perceptions of control. Data presented in Chapter 2 showed how dieting has been linked with weight increase and health problems. In Chapter 3, the guilt provoked by dieting failures was discussed. There is some evidence that dieting can also lead to overeating, low self-esteem, feelings of lack of control, feelings of fatness, and increased body dissatisfaction in the absence of any physical change in body size.

Christopher Dewberry and Jane Ussher (1995) found that chronic dieters showed a significant tendency to overestimate their body weight when asked whether they thought that they were very overweight, a little overweight, about right, a little underweight or very underweight for their age and height. This finding supports others that have demonstrated that women who are frequent dieters tend to overestimate their weight (Garner *et al.*, 1984), but does not tell us whether weight over-estimation is a cause or an effect of dieting, or whether there is a more complex relationship between the two variables.

Marika Tiggemann (1996), on the basis of questionnaire responses and silhouette figure choices in a group of 178 young Australian women, argues that repeated dieting causes women to 'feel fat'. This is distinct from 'thinking' they are fat, and reflects emotional/affective responses rather than cognitions. She suggests that the chain of events is that a person thinks she is fat and then diets to try to reduce weight; and that constant dieting, and the well-documented lack of success, lead the person to feel fat (perhaps due to lowered self-esteem). This is supported by other work showing that 'feeling fat' is related to frequency of dieting (e.g. Striegel-Moore *et al.*, 1986). Tiggemann notes that only a longitudinal study could separate out these variables and determine the direction of the relationship.

This is an area that presents particular problems for the researcher. Clearly, a randomly chosen group of dieters and non-dieters would be expected to differ in body satisfaction, since the dieters would not be expected to be dieting unless they were in some way dissatisfied with their bodies. Similarly, non-interventionist longitudinal work faces the problem that there may be differences (such as body weight) in groups who opt to diet and those who do not that would make comparisons between groups difficult. Any interventionist work, where groups are persuaded to diet, presents ethical problems (particularly given what we know about the negative health effects of dieting). Nevertheless, Tiggemann's data (added to the work on cognitive effects of dieting reported above, and reports from interviews where women report guilt and lowered self-esteem after dieting failure) suggest that dieting may lead to increased body preoccupation and dissatisfaction. Future work is needed to identify any causal links.

Some researchers have proposed that chronic dieting leads to feelings of being out of control in relation to food, and sometimes to a cycle of bingeing and starving that leaves the dieter feeling dissatisfied, guilty and low in self-esteem. In some interesting work on externally imposed food restriction, researchers have reliably found that restriction of food leads to overeating as soon as the restriction is lifted, and to feelings of being out of control. For instance, in a classic study by Keys *et al.* (1950), thirty-six men were only allowed to eat half the calories that they usually ingested for a period of twelve weeks. They showed increased preoccupation with food during the study, and lost about 25 per cent of their body weight on average. At the end of the study they were allowed to eat freely. They reported bingeing, and a lack of control in relation to food. In a replication of this study in the 1980s, using women as well as men, Warren and Cooper (1988) placed participants on calorie-restricted diets and observed the effects over a two-week period. They also found reports of lack of control in relation to food, and food preoccupation.

These experimental results are interesting because they agree almost completely with reports from dieters who have imposed their own diets (see Charles and Kerr, 1986; Chapter 3). Both groups report becoming obsessed with food, and feeling out of control in relation to food. In people who choose to diet (rather than having the diet imposed on them) the overeating that follows dieting usually leads to lowered self-esteem.

These results suggest that chronic dieting may lead to a vicious circle of dieting and bingeing, where body dissatisfaction results in dieting, which leads to bingeing and feelings of being out of control in relation to food, which lead to guilt and decreased self-esteem, which (taking into account potential weight increases) may exacerbate body dissatisfaction – and so on. Clearly there is a complex and dynamic relationship between chronic dieting and body dissatisfaction, which may be exacerbated by low self-esteem and low perception of control.

Frequent exercisers

It has recently become fashionable to exercise (rather than to diet) to try to attain the slim ideal and to reduce body dissatisfaction (see Chapter 2). Some authors have suggested that frequent exercise can actually increase body dissatisfaction rather than reducing it.

Research has suggested that frequent exercisers are at risk for body dissatisfaction, body preoccupation and 'eating disorders', particularly in the case of women. It has long been known that professional sportswomen in sports where thinness confers a performance or aesthetic advantage (such as dancers and gymnasts) tend to be highly preoccupied with their weight (see, e.g., Brownell *et al.*, 1992). Katz (1988) proposes that a high level of physical exercise may be a predisposing factor for 'eating disorders' in women who have other predisposing factors (for instance, doubts about their self-control). This proposition is supported by Davis and Dionne (1990), who suggest that regular exercise may foster excessive body concern in susceptible individuals. Since the well-publicised withdrawal of Lucy Hasell and Alison Outram from British athletics in 1995 and 1996 as a result of 'eating disorders', there has recently been some concern that professional women athletes are developing 'eating disorders' (Bee, 1997).

Many studies have shown that women who exercise frequently are more preoccupied with their weight than non-exercising women (Katz, 1986). Studies by Caroline Davis and colleagues have shown positive correlations between weight and diet concern and physical activity levels in groups of women who frequently engage in exercise (see, e.g., Davis and Dionne, 1990), leading the authors to argue that frequent exercise may cause body dissatisfaction. This argument is problematic, since they have no way of knowing whether women who are frequent exercisers started off (before exercise) feeling satisfied and have become less satisfied; or whether they were dissatisfied before the exercise regime (which could have been the motivation for taking up exercise in the first place). The only way to disentangle this complex relationship would be to take non-exercisers and randomly allocate them to 'exercise' and 'non-exercise' conditions, observing subsequent effects on body satisfaction. At present it is not possible to be sure which direction any causal link follows, and it seems likely that the relationship between these two variables is more complex and dynamic than is suggested by those who believe that exercise produces weight concerns.

One group of frequent exercisers which has attracted particular attention are women and men body-builders. Although some authors suggest that body-building is empowering for women in allowing them to adopt alternative body shape ideals and to value a larger shape (Furnham *et al.*, 1994; see Chapter 3), others have proposed that body-building may lead to decreased body satisfaction when the desire to lose fat and gain muscle becomes a compulsion. Jean Mitchell (1989) proposes that body-building is not empowering for women. She argues that women body-builders are simply setting up an alternative (muscular) ideal instead of the slender image of mainstream culture, and that this is just as damaging to women. She believes that body-building can become an obsession similar to the anorexic's denial of food, where women cannot imagine living without a muscular body and will spend significant proportions of their lives lifting weights, denying their bodies' needs by enduring pain on a day-to-day basis, and by eating a diet carefully calculated to build muscle mass:

> Just as the anorexic is driven almost mad with hunger, the body-builder mercilessly pumps iron, trying to push her body beyond the pain barrier, to lift yet heavier weights, day in, day out. Like the anorexic, when she achieves her goal and successfully 'masters' her body, she gains a feeling of 'strength', of moral superiority, of being 'good'.
>
> (Mitchell, 1989: 163)

Mitchell argues that there are strong parallels between women experiencing anorexic phases and women who body-build, since both groups are trying to do battle with their bodies and to keep them under control. She argues that women who exercise compulsively are trying to develop a feeling of controlling their lives through controlling their bodies, and that their body dissatisfaction is just as real as that of other women, despite the fact that they have quite different ideals. She suggests that body-building reflects perceived lack of control, and that body-building women are as dissatisfied with their bodies as the rest of the female population.

Other work on body-builders has focused on body dissatisfaction in body-building men. Harrison Pope and colleagues (1993) have recently suggested that some body-building men develop a negative body image which they call 'reverse anorexia'. This is specific to men who lift weights, and is characterised by a fear of being too small, and by perceiving oneself as small and weak even when one is large and muscular. Pope *et al.* interviewed 108 American men, of which about half used anabolic steroids. To be classified as having 'reverse anorexia' the subject had to display a persistent and unrealistic belief that he looked too small or too weak, to the extent that his day-to-day activities were affected (for instance by covering his body in public to disguise his 'smallness'). Participants were asked whether they had used anabolic steroids, and whether the belief that they were too small had prompted them to try steroids. The authors found that nine of the fifty-five steroid users fell into the 'reverse anorexic' group, and none of the non-users. Four of them reported that their use of steroids was prompted by the idea that they looked small, and four others had started to feel too small once they started taking steroids. Pope *et al.* suggest that body-builders may be at particular risk for body dissatisfaction, due to the pressure placed on them by the body-building culture (other body-builders and body-building magazines). They suggest that 'reverse anorexia' may precipitate or perpetuate the use of anabolic steroids. Although it seems possible that the body-building culture (and social comparison with other body-builders) exacerbates feelings of 'smallness', it seems most likely that these are men who felt inadequate and 'small' before they started body-building. Indeed, 'feeling small' was the most frequent reason given for starting to body-build in the accounts from body-builders cited in Chapter 4. There is likely to be a complex, two-way relationship between body dissatisfaction (in this case 'feeling small') and body-building.

It is tempting to generalise from the results of these studies to suggest that exercise has negative effects on body image. However, the negative effects reviewed here have only been shown to affect a minority of exercisers, and it is likely that examples cited by theorists relate to those who were dissatisfied with their bodies before they started exercising. Results show that, for some individuals, frequent exercise may exacerbate body shape concerns. However, this must be placed in a broader context. Very few people become obsessed with exercise. In fact, most people find it difficult to start and maintain any form of exercise (see pp. 185–6). This raises the question of whether the observed link (on the basis of the available evidence) is sufficiently compelling to lead to suggestions that we should be discouraging people from undertaking exercise, and clearly it is not. Data show that only very few exercisers become sufficiently preoccupied with their weight to affect the rest of their lives (Furnham *et al.*, 1994). Also, there is evidence in the literature that exercise improves psychological and physical health, and even that it may protect against 'eating disorders' by *improving* body satisfaction (Crago *et al.*, 1985). Evidence that exercise is beneficial to mental and physical health currently overwhelms evidence of negative effects. The most parsimonious interpretation of the available data is that exercise has predominantly positive effects, and that women (and men) should be encouraged to take moderate exercise. Those who have predisposing factors, such as doubts about their self-control, may develop exaggerated body concerns as a result of frequent exercise, but these are likely to be a minority of the exercising population.

Development of a positive body image

Studies of people with particularly low body satisfaction help us to understand the factors involved in predicting positive images of the body. Research with women and men who are prone to have episodes of anorexia or bulimia, to over-exercise, or to diet repeatedly, shows that low self-esteem and perceptions of lack of control tend to go hand in hand with body dissatisfaction. Chronic dieting is likely to lead to lowered self-esteem when the diet fails to have the expected effect. Although the person may feel that they are taking control over their life (and body) by restricting food intake and/or eating diet foods, the temporary feeling of mastery is likely to be replaced by low self-esteem when the promised reduction in weight is not maintained. In fact, a common advertising ploy when selling diet foods is to talk about 'taking control', playing on the cultural associations between overweight, self-indulgence and loss of control (Orbach, 1993). An anorexic episode is most likely to occur at a time when the person feels out of control (e.g. in adolescence: Pennycook, 1989; or when feeling conflict or anger: Epstein, 1989) or when self-esteem is low (Orbach, 1993). Perceptions of lack of control and low self-esteem can be temporarily relieved by gaining control over the body which produces (in the short term) increased self-control due to mastery over bodily needs. The same can be said of frequent exercise. Both starvation and extreme exercise give a 'high' that can make people feel (temporarily) better about themselves (and their bodies).

Psychologists have suggested various psychological factors that predict positive body image. Most important of these are self-esteem, and beliefs about personal control. Here we will examine the proposed link between these psychological variables and body satisfaction, and look specifically at how this psychological knowledge can be useful in trying to improve body satisfaction in women and men.

Self-esteem

It has generally been found that self-esteem correlates highly with body satisfaction for both women and men. People with high self-esteem also tend to feel good about their bodies. Mintz and Betz (1986) found a significant positive relationship between body satisfaction and self-esteem in both men and women, showing that in both genders feeling generally good about the self is linked with positive feelings about the body. Berscheid *et al.* (1973) put a questionnaire in the magazine *Psychology Today*, read by psychologists and other professionals, asking about satisfaction with the body in general, and with specific body parts. They found that body satisfaction was related to feelings of personal happiness for both men and women.

Furnham and Greaves (1994) measured self-esteem (using the Rosenberg self-esteem scale) and body satisfaction (using a modified version of the Body Cathexis Scale described in Chapter 3) as part of a study of the relationship between self-esteem, perceived control and body satisfaction. Their participants numbered about 100 undergraduates, about half of which were male and half female. They found that high self-esteem was correlated with high body satisfaction, and that women scored significantly lower on both variables compared to men. Self-esteem was more closely linked to body satisfaction in women than in men. They conclude that body image is more crucial to women's self-esteem than to men's, due to the higher importance placed on physical appearance for women in Western cultures.

In a recent study with Mexican-American female adolescents, Guinn *et al.* (1997) measured body image, self-esteem, body fat levels and activity levels. They found that self-esteem was the most powerful predictor of body satisfaction scores (more than body fat levels). They suggest that self-esteem-building activities should be carried out with adolescent women, and that this would impact positively on their body satisfaction.

Interview work has also supported the link between self-esteem and body image in both women and men. In interviews with women carried out by Charles and Kerr (1986), and by others on women and men of different ages (Grogan and Wainwright, 1986; Grogan *et al.*, 1997), positive body-image is reliably linked with positive feelings about the self, and feelings of self-confidence and power in social situations.

Marika Tiggemann (1996) has shown that people who score high on self-esteem tend not to 'feel fat'. In a group of women undergraduate students, she found that low self-esteem predicted 'feeling fat' (as judged by silhouette figure choices). She concluded that high self-esteem is a significant predictor of body satisfaction in young women.

Findings in this area are very consistent. Of course, the evidence we have to date only shows that the two variables are linked, and does not tell us whether high self-esteem leads to higher body image (feeling good about oneself, generally, leads to feeling good about one's body) or whether feeling good about the body leads to higher self-esteem, or whether some other factor is involved. It seems likely that self-esteem and body satisfaction are linked such that each impacts on the other. Future research should look at the effects on body image of attempts to build self-esteem.

Personal control beliefs

The importance of perceptions of control in women with 'eating disorders' is well documented (see pp. 172–3), and many authors have proposed that perceptions of lack of control are the primary trigger in the development of *anorexia nervosa* (Orbach, 1993). Work with people who have no history of 'eating disorders' has suggested that perception of control has a more general effect on people's body image. Those who feel greater personal control are likely to be more satisfied with their bodies, and are likely to feel hopeful and positive about attaining their ideal body shape (Furnham and Greaves, 1994).

Furnham and Greaves administered a Locus of Control test to a group of British men and women in relation to body satisfaction (1994). The Body Shape Beliefs (BSB) scale covers items regarding changing body shape through exercise and dieting, and also more general beliefs about body shape. One third of items related to internal control ('a perfect body shape can only be achieved through self-control'); one third to fatalistic control ('the body shape you have is the one you have inherited'); and the other third to external control ('only strong peer pressure leads one to do something to change their body shape').

Furnham and Greaves found that different beliefs about perceived control resulted in different self-perceptions and associated behaviours. People with high internal locus of control on the BSB scale placed high emphasis on body shape, and used exercise specifically to achieve this aim. They concluded that people high on 'internality' believe that they can alter their body shape, and are willing to engage in behaviours to bring about such a change; while people with external locus of control are likely to feel that there is nothing they can do to alter their body shape, resulting in low self-esteem and depression. They argue that in order to improve body satisfaction, strategies for increasing perceived control should be used.

Psychological techniques for improving body image

In Chapter 5, some techniques for avoiding social pressure were described in relation to body image. Here we will investigate some alternative techniques for developing positive body image that focus on developing self-esteem and perceptions of control.

There is some evidence that increasing perception of control through group discussions may be an effective way of improving body image. Gail Huon (1994) investigated the extent to which it was possible to change young women's attitudes to their body and their reported intentions to diet. Twenty-four women aged 18 to 25 were assigned to four discussion groups. Discussions focused on ideas for helping others to give up dieting, and to develop a more positive body image. She found that participation in the discussion groups, relating to strategies for development of a more positive body image and for giving up dieting, was sufficient to produce highly significant changes in the women's body satisfaction scores. Discussions of barriers to developing a positive body image produced no significant effects. Informal conversation after the interviews revealed that the women experienced the two kinds of discussion quite differently. Discussion of strategies (taking up sport, identifying goals, learning to value individuality) was experienced as positive and motivating, because the women felt that they had some control over these things. Discussion of factors over which they felt that they had no control (barriers such as media promotion of the thin image, social attitudes about weight and shape) was experienced as demotivating because of low perceptions of control over these factors. Huon suggests that engagement in group discussion about practical strategies for changing body image (stressing 'taking control') may lead to improved body satisfaction.

Other work has suggested that training in self-efficacy (perceived competence) in relation to body image may improve perceptions of control along with self-esteem, and reduce body dissatisfaction (Lewis *et al.*, 1992). In order to improve perceived self-efficacy, group discussions (and the resulting social support) may be necessary. In a study of the effect of written materials, Blair *et al.* (1992) sent leaflets to fifty women. The leaflets were designed to facilitate improvements in self-efficacy and self-esteem, and to enable success at weight loss for those who wanted to lose weight. The 'Personal Effectiveness' leaflet addressed general assertiveness and also assertiveness in response to offers of food and comments regarding body shape. The 'Social Pressure on Women' leaflet focused on societal attitudes that influence women's self-value, particularly as they relate to physical appearance, in an attempt to persuade women to reconsider their level of satisfaction with their present body size. They found significant reductions in emotional eating, and non-significant improvements in perceptions of body size, self-esteem and self-efficacy. They concluded that group interaction is important in producing significant changes in self-esteem and self-efficacy, and suggest that it would be productive to use the leaflets in discussion with others concerned about body shape, with or without a psychologist to act as facilitator.

Work on self-esteem and self-efficacy suggests that low self-esteem and low perceptions of personal control may be related to body dissatisfaction. Raising self-esteem and self-efficacy through assertiveness training may help to improve body satisfaction. For women, information about social pressures to achieve an unrealistically slender body shape may help to improve body image. Gail Huon's work suggests that merely engaging in discussion of strategies for developing a more positive body image may be sufficient to improve body satisfaction, so long as participants feel that the issues they are discussing are within their control.

Anne Kearney-Cooke (in DeAngelis, 1997) believes that clients should identify times when they feel out of control (through writing a body image log), so that this can be used to identify environmental triggers leading to lowered self-efficacy and body dissatisfaction. She believes that many people use the body as a screen upon which they project their feelings of ineffectiveness. She argues that, when people find ways of dealing with the situations (or other people) that make them feel ineffective in a direct way, the feelings of body dissatisfaction become less extreme. Thomas Cash (in DeAngelis, 1997) uses a similar technique, encouraging perceptions of control, and using relaxation techniques and exercise to make people feel better about their bodies. He suggests that the 'high' produced by exercise makes it easy to persuade clients to take up exercise and maintain an exercise regime that focuses on how the body feels rather than how the body looks.

Therapeutic effects of moderate exercise

Despite evidence that compulsive exercise can lead to body dissatisfaction, there is a growing body of evidence that shows that moderate exercise, focusing on mastery rather than aesthetics, can improve perceptions of control, self-esteem and satisfaction with the body, as well as improvements in health and fitness. Obviously, engagement in moderate exercise (such as walking, cycling) is not appropriate or practical for some people. However, it is important to consider the effects of exercise here, since several researchers have suggested that exercise improves mood, well-being and perception of control, at least in the short term (Brown and Lawton, 1986), and there is a large body of evidence suggesting that exercise improves body satisfaction.

Snyder and Kivlin (1975) have shown that female exercisers have higher body satisfaction than do controls. Other work has found positive effects on self-esteem and body image as a function of exercise in both men and women; Adrian Furnham and colleagues (1994) looked at self-perception in women classified as 'exercisers' (netball players, body-builders, rowers) and non-exercisers (those who exercise less than three times a week). They found that the exercisers rated themselves as more attractive, confident, healthy and popular, and had significantly higher body satisfaction scores, than non-exercisers, despite being significantly heavier (average 11.5 lb) than the non-exercising group.

In a recent Canadian study by Caroline Davis and colleagues (1991), 103 male students in the 18–34 age range (college males) and eighty-eight regularly exercising men aged 16–64 (exercising men) completed self-report surveys, including the Eysenck Personality Inventory (EPI), physical activity, body dissatisfaction and weight satisfaction scales. Exercisers engaged in more than double the physical activity engaged in by the college sample. The exercisers were also significantly more satisfied with their bodies. In regression analysis, physical activity predicted about 11 per cent of the variance in body dissatisfaction, showing that frequency and duration of exercise is a significant predictor of satisfaction with the body. The authors concluded that men who are physically active are more satisfied with their bodies, suggesting that men's body satisfaction may be influenced by the extent that they perceive themselves to be physically fit rather than by the extent that they conform to a subjective weight ideal.

Few studies have looked at differences in satisfaction with the body between women who take moderate exercise and those who do not, although most data suggest that exercising women are more satisfied. In a recent United States study (Koff and Bauman, 1997), 140 college women participating in one of three types of physical education classes (wellness, fitness, sports skills) responded to questions about body image, body–self relations, and lifestyle behaviours at the onset and conclusion of a six-week programme. The wellness and fitness classes both produced increased satisfaction with the body and physical appearance, although there was no change on these variables in the sports skills classes. The authors suggested that participation in wellness and fitness classes empowers participants, making them feel more positive towards their health and general well-being, including their body image. These results are convincing, because they study changes within individuals before and after exercise, rather than comparing exercisers with non-exercisers (who may differ on other psychological variables).

It seems likely that exercise enhances self-esteem and body image by producing a firmer and stronger body, by giving the person a sense of competence, and by focusing on performance of the body rather than on aesthetics. These positive effects of exercise on mental health and well-being, and especially on body satisfaction, suggest that people should be encouraged to undertake exercise as a way of improving self-esteem and body image.

Work on frequency of exercise has tended to find that relatively small numbers of people in Britain (particularly in older age groups) undertake regular exercise, despite physical and mental health effects. According to the 1991/92 Health and Lifestyle Survey in Britain, about 50 per cent of women under 40 engage in some form of exercise. Activity levels are much lower in women over 40, with a significant reduction in women over 60 to about 20 per cent (see Figure 7.1). Most frequent activities at all age levels are keep-fit, yoga, dancing and swimming. More men engage in exercise at all age levels. About 60 per cent of men under 40 engage in some form of exercise, dropping with age down to around 30 per cent under 60 (see Figure 7.1). Most popular activities for men at all age levels are cycling, dancing, swimming and keep-fit/yoga. There were age differences in activity in the male sample. The most popular forms of exercise amongst younger men (age 18–40) were football and jogging, which reached negligible levels in men over 50.

In the Health Behaviour of School-Aged Children survey (Turtle *et al.*, 1997), the authors randomly sampled pupils aged 11, 13 and 15 from each of seventy-five schools in England, producing a final sample size of 6,372 who completed all parts of the questionnaire. One in five young people played games or sports that made them out of breath or sweaty in their free time every day. One-third of the group only engaged in strenuous exercise once a week or less. Boys were more likely to engage in strenuous exercise than girls (one in four boys

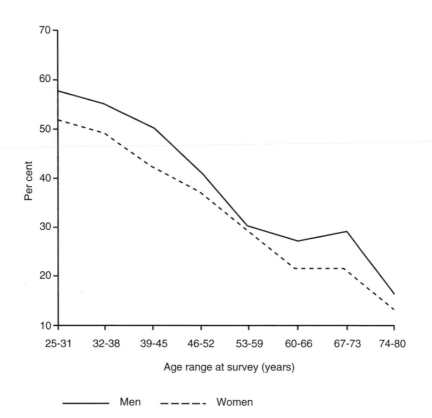

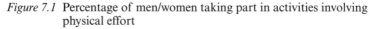

Figure 7.1 Percentage of men/women taking part in activities involving physical effort

Source: Adapted from Cox *et al.* (1993) with permission.

reported aerobic exercise once a day compared to one in ten girls). As children became older they engaged in less and less exercise. By age 15, one in ten never got out of breath playing sports in their free time (see Figure 7.2).

Given the relatively low levels of exercise being currently undertaken by adults and children, it is important to know what barriers to exercise are perceived by men and women. In another study recently undertaken in the United States, Myers and Roth (1997) administered questionnaires to 432 college students, asking them about current exercise, perceived benefits and barriers to exercise, and intentions to become more active. Participants perceived many benefits of exercise (including benefits to body image), but found it hard to motivate

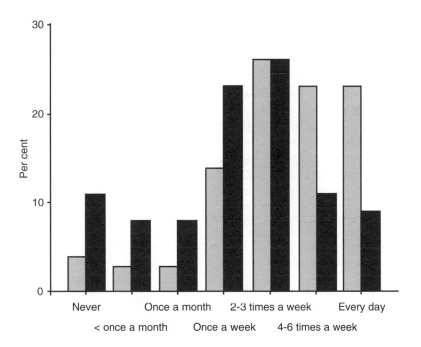

Figure 7.2 Frequency of children getting out of breath and sweaty playing games or sports in free time

Source: Adapted from Turtle *et al.* (1997). Copyright © Health Education Authority. Reproduced with permission.

Note: Base: boys 3396; girls 2976.

themselves to take exercise due to perceived lack of time and social responsibilities. Whitehead (1988) notes that another major barrier to taking exercise is cost. Making exercise cheaper (e.g. available at community sports centres) may be one way to encourage people to exercise more.

Shifting the focus of exercise from competition to enjoyment (as the recent 'Sport for All' initiative in Britain tried to do) may encourage those who were alienated from sport through team games at school. This is particularly important for groups who may feel alienated from the competitive 'sports culture', including women and people of either sex over 40 (Cox *et al.*, 1993). A group which may feel particularly alienated is overweight people (or those who 'feel fat'). Shelley Bovey, in *Being fat is not a sin* (1989), says that exercise is made difficult for people who are overweight by other people's reaction to them. Compliance with exercise regimes depends on enjoyment, which is difficult for obese people who may be ridiculed, and may find that equipment and sports clothes are not suitable for their weight. Encouragement of enjoyment (rather than competition) in sports may make it easier to feel comfortable for people who are alienated by the competitive exercise culture, and hence improve motivation to exercise. There is now sufficient evidence for the potentially beneficial effects of sport to encourage a regular regime of exercise in everyone, to improve self-esteem and body image and to counteract stress. When Gail Huon (1988) asked young women to identify strategies for developing a more positive body image, one of their suggestions was that girls and young women should be encouraged to take up enjoyable sporting activities in their leisure time. Studies reviewed in this chapter suggest that moderate exercise, along with improvement in self-esteem and perceptions of control, are likely to be the most effective ways to improve body image.

General conclusions

This book has been an attempt to present a balanced account of current research on body image in men, women and children. It has been necessarily selective. Most of the research that is cited comes from the realm of psychology, since most empirical work on body image has been carried out by psychologists. Where possible, data from other social sciences are presented. The result is a comprehensive review of the variety of influences on men's and women's body image, and the behavioural effects of these influences. People most at risk for body dissatisfaction are those who belong to identified at-risk groups (white heterosexual women, and gay men), who have low self-esteem, and who perceive a lack of control over body image. Media representations of the slender ideal (slender and muscular for men) may lead to unfavourable social comparisons, and may result in dissatisfaction. However, interview work suggests that women in particular are cynical about media portrayal of the 'ideal body', and want to see more realistic images of women in the media. Media role models may differ depending on the age of the viewer, with viewers making active choices as to comparison groups. Older women are not more dissatisfied with their bodies than young women, in spite of media preferences for very young models, probably because they choose age-relevant targets for body image comparisons. There is some evidence that older men are more dissatisfied than younger men (although still more satisfied than women of all ages), probably because they compare body size with themselves at a younger (and usually more slender) age. Children from age eight present similar discourses of body shape, and similar levels of body concern, to adults. It seems that some body dissatisfaction is the common experience of most people raised in Western culture.

There are still many questions to be answered through further research. We need to know more about the effects of building self-esteem on body image. We need to know much more about the development of body dissatisfaction, especially in children under eight years of age. We also need to know whether cultural homogenisation in body satisfaction, in relation to social class and ethnic group as described by Thomas Robinson *et al.* (1996), is a reliable trend. More research with non-white, non-middle-class groups would help to answer this question. Also, we need to know more about the strategies used by those who are satisfied with their bodies to maintain a positive body image and to resist cultural pressure. Clearly, there is scope for future investigation.

Based on what we do know about men's and women's body image, we can conclude that the way forward in terms of developing positive body images must be a reduction in the objectification of the body (both male and female) and the development of body ideals based on function as well as aesthetics. In particular, the cultural acceptance of the wide variety of body shapes and sizes that represent the normal range, and the de-stigmatisation of overweight, may help to reduce dissatisfaction. Cultural factors are hugely important in determining people's experience of their bodies, and current evidence from cultural groups that do not stigmatise obesity suggests that acceptance of diversity may be expected to lead to a reduction in body dissatisfaction.

A recurrent theme in the literature is the importance of gender in determining body satisfaction. Irrespective of age, ethnicity and class, women (in general) are more dissatisfied with their bodies than are men. Clearly, future work needs to do more to clarify this gender imbalance, and to present potential solutions for improving women's body image.

Feminist authors, such as Sandra Bartky (1990) and Naomi Wolf (1991), have suggested ways forward in terms of reclaiming the ways that 'beauty' for women is represented in the popular media and in the culture as a whole. Wolf suggests that women need to regain control of their own bodies, to resist the objectification of the female body, and to build a model of female beauty that allows individual women freedom for adornment, expressed sexuality and time spent grooming their bodies, within a context that does not judge women on the basis of the extent to which they conform to a (male-determined) ideal:

> Costumes and disguises will be light-hearted and fun when women are granted rock-solid identities. Clothing that highlights women's sexuality will be casual wear when women's sexuality is under our own control. . . . Women will be able thoughtlessly to adorn ourselves with pretty objects when there is no question that we are not objects. Women will be free of the beauty myth when we can choose to use our faces and our clothes as simply one form of self-expression out of a full range of others.
>
> (Wolf, 1991: 273–4)

Wolf argues that Western culture (through the media in particular) sets up women in competition with each other in relation to their bodies, and that this harms all women. In our interviews with women and girls (Chapters 3 and 6) we found that women compared their bodies explicitly with those of other women (models, friends, family members) in their accounts, and (often) found their bodies wanting, leading to lowered body satisfaction. Naomi Wolf argues that competition between women on the basis of their bodies is actively encouraged by the beauty industry, who have a vested interest in women's dissatisfaction. She says that women need to resist cultural pressures to compete on the basis of their bodies, and to support each other's beauty choices and 'look', to build women's body satisfaction. She sees male-dominated institutions (rather than individual men) as the biggest challenge to the development of a radical new approach to beauty for women. She argues that women must reject models of beauty promoted by self-interested, male-dominated institutions, and develop a women-oriented ideal to put in their place which allows women to experiment and play with images of the body, and to accept the variations in bodies of women of different ages as acceptable and beautiful, rather than trying to conform to the unrealistic ideals promoted by advertisers and the fashion and diet industries. In her vision of the 'new women's beauty', she suggests:

> A woman loving definition of beauty supplants desperation with play, narcissism with self-love, dismemberment with wholeness, absence with presence, stillness with animation.
>
> (Wolf, 1991: 291)

Wolf's ideas are constructive and inspirational and present a cultural perspective on improving women's body image. This approach does not conflict with suggestions made earlier in this chapter in relation to raising self-esteem and perceptions of control. These are strategies that individual women may find useful in raising body satisfaction, in tandem with trying to develop a new women-centred aesthetic of the body.

The recent move towards the objectification of the male body was discussed in Chapter 4. This must be resisted strongly. Although it is tempting to see this cultural shift as in some way 'levelling the playing field', such that men will be placed under the pressures that women have experienced previously, it cannot be in the interests of women if cultural objectification of the body is expanded to include men's bodies as well as women's. We need to resist the objectification of the body in general, and in particular the cultural expectation that women's bodies should conform to an ideal that is unattainable to most women.

The end of the twentieth century is doubtless a time of increased concern with the body. Scientific developments in fields such as plastic surgery, diets and drugs (e.g. anabolic steroids) have given people in Western culture the potential to change the ways that their bodies look. The representation of a narrow range of body shapes in the mass media leaves the viewer in no doubt as to how they are expected to look. The cultural homogeneity of the ideal body shape for men and women, added to the fact that people now feel that they have the power to change their bodies (if only they had the will power or were willing to spend the time on diet or exercise – see Chapters 3 and 4), leads to social comparison, body dissatisfaction, lowered self-esteem, perceptions of lack of control, and guilt, in many people. A reduction in the objectification of the body, a shift in body aesthetics to encompass a variety of body shapes and sizes (in the long term), and social support for alternative body types to the prevailing aesthetic (in the short term), may lead to increased body satisfaction and increased quality of life for a significant proportion of the population, and particularly for women.

Summary

- The social relativity of body satisfaction has been demonstrated by illustrating how satisfaction varies by social group. Data from different social groups have shown that the same body shape may be perceived more or less positively depending on the gender and social group of the person doing the perceiving. Being white and being heterosexual are likely to predict body dissatisfaction in women. Men are likely to be more satisfied in general, although older, white and gay men may be expected to be most dissatisfied.
- The average woman could be expected to have dieted to try to lose weight, and the average man is probably not highly motivated to diet or exercise even if he perceives a mismatch between current body image and ideal body image. If he does change his behaviour he will probably exercise.
- Personal control beliefs and self-esteem are closely linked to body satisfaction.
- As a short-term solution to improve body satisfaction, research suggests that assertiveness training (to raise self-esteem and perceptions of control), and discussion of strategies for improving body image, may increase body satisfaction.
- In the long term, cultural changes in the objectification of the female body, and the discouragement of dieting, would be likely to impact positively on the experiences of all women, and women prone to 'eating disorders' and chronic dieting in particular.

Appendix
What causes overweight?

There is a popular myth that overweight people are fat because they are out of control, lazy and lacking in will power. The reality is that researchers are unsure about what causes some people to become fatter than others. It is clear that people become overweight when they take in more calories than they expend. Common sense suggests that people become overweight because they eat more than those who are thin or of normal weight, or expend fewer calories (by exercising less), or both. Research evidence suggests that other factors may also be important.

It is generally assumed that people who are overweight (particularly those who are obese) eat more than their normal-weight peers. Although overweight people obviously have to eat a certain amount to maintain their weight, there is a large amount of evidence from psychology and sociology sources that they do not eat more than other people. For instance, in eighteen out of nineteen studies of the amount that people ate, overweight people ate less than, or the same amount as, people who were of normal weight or thin (Wooley et al., 1979). Data came from a variety of sources, including self-report of eating habits, observations of eating in natural settings, and laboratory studies where researchers saw how much people ate when food was made freely available and they were engaged in a task designed to distract them.

An alternative hypothesis relates to energy expenditure in over-weight people. Do fat people get fat because of lack of exercise? Certainly, many researchers believe that lack of exercise contributes to overweight. Kelly Brownell and Thomas Wadden (1992) argue that energy expenditure has decreased significantly over the last 200 years, as fewer and fewer people do jobs involving strenuous physical labour. They argue that, even since the 1960s, Americans have become less active, and have also become fatter.

> Automobiles, remote control devices for televisions and garage
> doors, and a host of electrical appliances conspire to reduce
> energy expenditure . . .
>
> (Brownell and Wadden, 1992: 506)

Andrew Prentice, head of human calorimetry at the Dunn Clinical
Nutrition Centre in Cambridge, echoes these sentiments in relation to
Britons. He argues that most people lead sedentary lives that involve
the lowest expenditure of energy in living memory, and believes that
the lifestyle changes in the 1980s and 1990s have contributed to the
increase in weight of British people in the 1990s (Prentice and Jebb,
1995).

There is some evidence that fat people are less active than thin
people. For example, fewer obese people (1.5 per cent) chose to use the
stairs rather than the escalator than did non-obese people (6.7 per
cent) (Wooley *et al.*, 1979). Low levels of activity in obese people may
be primarily the result of, rather than the cause of, their overweight.
There is a well-documented social stigma attached to exercise in overweight people in Western society which makes it less likely that fat
people (and even those who 'feel fat') will exercise. Shelley Bovey
(1989) says that exercise is made difficult for people who are overweight by other people's reaction to them. Compliance with exercise
regimes depends on enjoyment, which is difficult for obese people who
may be ridiculed, and who may find that equipment and sports clothes
are not suitable for their weight.

One way to investigate the direction of any cause–effect link is to
look at the results of controlled studies of the effects of exercise on
people who are overweight. Studies have shown that, compared with
changes in diet, exercise is not a very effective way to reduce weight,
because few calories are burned by even quite vigorous exercise
(Epstein and Wing, 1980). George Bray (1986) notes that, even under
heavy exertion (such as running), most people only expend around 7.5
calories per minute. The average lunch consists of around 500 calories,
which at that rate would take over an hour's running to 'burn off'. It
seems unlikely that lack of exercise is the most important factor in
making people overweight, although it may interact with other factors
to maintain weight gain. In fact, most people (fat and thin) engage in
very little exercise. For instance, the Health and Lifestyle Survey (Cox
et al., 1993) showed that the majority of Britons over 40 do not take
part in any active (sports) pursuits. Yet only a small percentage of the
population become obese. Clearly, lack of exercise is not sufficient to
produce overweight.

Some researchers have argued that obesity is genetic. This is based on research comparing metabolic differences in the obese and the non-obese. Nisbett's (1972) Set Point Theory suggests that each individual has a natural set point (or range) for body weight, and that the metabolism changes to maintain this specific range of weights irrespective of the amount eaten. According to Nisbett, set points vary markedly between individuals, although the socially acceptable range is quite narrow. This means that a proportion of the population will always be heavier than is socially acceptable unless they engage in chronic food deprivation. Ironically, self-starvation can lead to the body lowering its metabolic rate, and storing fat in case it is needed, leading to increased weight gain. Nisbett argues that many people are in states of starvation even though they have weights in the obese range.

Andrew Prentice (1995) argues that the relationship between genetics and weight is complex; and that there is good evidence that overeating is the key to understanding obesity. He reports a study where he persuaded groups of lean and overweight men to live for seven months in a long-stay volunteer facility, allowing careful monitoring of their diet. During part of the stay, the men were overfed by 50 per cent compared with their baseline energy requirements. Measures of energy expenditure revealed no differences between overweight and lean men, and lean men put on about the same amount of weight as the overweight men. Prentice argues that this shows that lean men do not differ in metabolism compared with the overweight men. He puts the blame for obesity on a high fat diet and a sedentary lifestyle; and argues that genetics contributes only about 25 per cent to the cause of overweight.

However, other researchers contend that body weight has a substantial genetic component. It was found that identical twins brought up by different families tended to be similar in terms of body weight (Stunckard *et al.*, 1990). Both low metabolic rate and increased numbers of fat cells may be influenced by genetics. Obviously all that can be inherited is a tendency to become overweight, which can be significantly affected by environmental factors such as diet and exercise (Brownell and Wadden, 1992). Current evidence suggests that genetics plays a part in tendency to put on weight.

Bibliography

Abrams, K., Allen, L. and Gray, J. (1993) 'Disordered eating attitudes and behaviors, psychological adjustment, and ethnic identity: a comparison of black and white female college students', *International Journal of Eating Disorders*, 14, 49–57.

Adams, C. and Laurikietis, R. (1976) *The gender trap: a closer look at sex roles*, London: Virago.

Alley, T. and Scully, K. (1994) 'The impact of actual and perceived changes in body weight on women's physical attractiveness', *Basic and Applied Social Psychology*, 15, 4, 535–42.

Andres, R., Muller, D. and Sorkin, J. (1993) 'Long-term effects of change in body weight on all-cause mortality: a review', *Annals of Internal Medicine*, 119, 737–43.

Aoki, D. (1996) 'Sex and muscle: the female bodybuilder meets Lacan', *Body and Society*, 2, 4, 45–57.

Armstrong, S. (1996) 'Cast against type', *The Guardian*, 3 June, 15.

Averett, S. and Korenman, S. (1996) 'The economic reality of the beauty myth', *Journal of Human Resources*, 31, 2, 304–30.

Baker, P. (1994) 'Under pressure: what the media is doing to men', *Cosmopolitan*, November, 129–32.

Bartky, S. (1990) *Femininity and domination: studies in the phenomenology of oppression*, New York: Routledge.

Beck, A.T. (1976) *Cognitive therapy and the emotional disorders*, New York: International Universities Press.

Bee, P. (1997) 'Starved of a chance', *Runner's World*, September, 48–51.

Bennett, W. and Gurin, J. (1982) *The dieter's dilemma*, New York: Basic Books.

Ben-Tovim, D. and Walker, K. (1991) 'Women's body attitudes: a review of measurement techniques', *International Journal of Eating Disorders*, 10, 2, 155–67.

Beren, S., Hayden, H., Wilfley, D. and Grilo, C. (1996) 'The influence of sexual orientation on body dissatisfaction in adult men and women', *International Journal of Eating Disorders*, 2, 135–41.

Berscheid, E., Walster, E. and Bornstedt, G. (1973) The happy American body: a survey report, *Psychology Today*, 7, 119–31.

Blair, A., Lewis, V. and Booth, D. (1992) 'Response to leaflets about eating and shape by women concerned about their weight', *Behavioural Psychotherapy*, 20, 279–86.

—— (1986) 'The forms of capital', in J. Richardson (ed.) *Handbook of theory and research for the sociology of education*, New York: Greenwood Press.

Bordo, S. (1990) 'Reading the slender body', in M. Jacobus, E. Fox Keller and S. Shuttleworth (eds) *Body politics*, New York: Routledge.

—— (1993) *Unbearable weight: feminism, Western culture, and the body*, Berkeley: University of California Press.

Boseley, S. (1996) ' "Anorexic" models cost *Vogue* ads', *The Guardian*, 31 May, 1.

Bourdieu, P. (1984) *Distinction: a social critique of the judgement of taste*, London: Routledge.

Bovey, S. (1989) *Being fat is not a sin*, London: Pandora Press.

Bradley, P. (1982) 'Is obesity an advantageous adaptation?', *International Journal of Obesity*, 6, 43–52.

Brand, P., Rothblum, E. and Soloman, L. (1992) 'A comparison of lesbians, gay men, and heterosexuals on weight and restricted eating', *International Journal of Eating Disorders*, 11, 253–9.

Bray, G.A. (1986) 'Effects of obesity on health and happiness', in K.D. Brownell and J.P. Foreyt (eds) *Handbook of eating disorders: physiology, psychology and treatment of obesity, anorexia, and bulimia* (3–44), New York: Basic Books.

British Heart Foundation (1994) *Coronary heart disease statistics*, London: British Heart Foundation.

Brown, J. and Lawton, M. (1986) 'Stress and well-being in adolescence: the moderating role of physical exercise', *Journal of Human Stress*, 12, 125–31.

Brown, L. (1987) 'Lesbians, weight and eating: new analyses and perspectives', in Boston Lesbian Psychologies Collective (eds) *Lesbian psychologies* (294–309), Urbana: University of Illinois Press.

Brownell, K.D., Greenwood, M., Stellar, E. and Shrager, E. (1986) 'The effects of repeated cycles of weight loss and regain in rats', *Physiology and Behaviour*, 38, 459–64.

Brownell, K.D. and Rodin, J.R. (1994) 'The dieting maelstrom: is it possible and advisable to lose weight?', *American Psychologist*, 49, 781–91.

Brownell, K.D., Rodin, J.R. and Wilmore, J. (1992) *Eating, body weight, and performance in athletes: disorders of modern society*, Philadelphia: Lea and Febiger.

Brownell, K.D. and Wadden, T. (1992) 'Etiology and treatment of obesity: understanding a serious, prevalent, and refractory disorder', *Journal of Counselling and Clinical Psychology*, 60, 505–17.

Brownmiller, S. (1984) *Femininity*, New York: Linden Press.

Bruch, H. (1962) 'Perceptual and conceptual disturbances in *anorexia nervosa*', *Psychological Medicine*, 24, 187–94.

—— (1973) *Eating disorders: obesity, anorexia nervosa, and the person within*, New York: Basic Books.

Buss, D. (1987) 'Sex differences in human mate selection criteria: an evolutionary perspective', in C. Crawford, M. Smith and D. Krebs (eds) *Sociobiology and psychology: ideas, issues, and application* (335–51), Hillsdale, NJ: Erlbaum.

—— (1989) 'Sex differences in human mate preference: evolutionary hypothesis tested in 37 cultures', *Behavioural and Brain Sciences*, 12, 1–49.

Butler, J. (1991) 'Imitation and gender insubordination', in D. Fuss (ed.) *Inside out: lesbian theories, gay theories* (13–32), New York: Routledge.

Button, E. (1993) *Eating disorders: personal construct therapy and change*, Chichester: Wiley.

Button, E., Sonuga-Barke, E., Davies, J. and Thompson, M. (1996) 'A prospective study of self-esteem in the prediction of eating problems in adolescent schoolgirls: questionnaire findings', *British Journal of Clinical Psychology*, 35, 193–203.

Caitlin, D. and Hatton, C. (1991) 'Use and abuse of anabolic and other drugs for athletic enhancement', *Advances in Internal Medicine*, 36, 399–424.

Caldwell, D. (1981) *And all was revealed: ladies' underwear 1907–1980*, New York: St. Martin's Press.

Carruth, B. and Goldberg, D. (1990) 'Nutritional issues of adolescents: athletics and the body image mania', *Journal of Early Adolescence*, 10, 122–40.

Cash, T. (1990) 'The psychology of physical appearance: aesthetics, attributes, and images', in T. Cash and T. Pruzinsky (eds) *Body images: development, deviance and change* (51–79), New York: Guilford Press.

Cash, T., Ancis, J. and Strachan, M. (1997) 'Gender attitudes, feminist identity, and body images among college women', *Sex Roles*, 36, 433–47.

Cash, T. and Pruzinsky, T. (eds) (1990) *Body images: development, deviance and change*, New York: Guilford Press.

Cash, T., Winstead, B. and Janda, L. (1986) 'The great American shape-up: body image survey report', *Psychology Today*, 20, 4, 30–7.

Chapkis, W. (1986) *Beauty secrets*, London: The Women's Press.

Chapman, R. (1988) 'The great pretender: variations on the new man theme', in R. Chapman, R. and J. Rutherford (eds) *Male order: unwrapping masculinity* (225–48), London: Lawrence and Wishart.

Charles, N. and Kerr, M. (1986) 'Food for feminist thought', *The Sociological Review*, 34, 537–72.

Chaudhary, V. (1996) 'The state we're in', *The Guardian*, 11 June, 14.

Chernin, K. (1983) *Womansize: the tyranny of slenderness*, London: The Women's Press.

Chesters, L. (1994) 'Women's talk: food, weight and body image', *Feminism and Psychology*, 4, 3, 449–57.

Christensen, L. (1997) *Experimental methodology* (7th edn), London: Allyn and Bacon.

Connell, R. (1987) *Gender and power*, Cambridge: Polity Press.

Conner, M., Martin, E., Silverdale, N. and Grogan, S. (1996) 'Dieting in adolescence: an application of the theory of planned behaviour', *British Journal of Health Psychology*, 1, 315–25.

Cooper, P., Taylor, M., Cooper, Z. and Fairburn, C. (1987) 'The development and validation of the Body Shape Questionnaire', *International Journal of Eating Disorders*, 6, 485–94.

Cowley, G. (1996) 'The biology of beauty', *Newsweek*, 3 June, 61–6.

Cox, B.D., Huppert, F.A. and Whichelow, M.J. (eds) (1993) *The Health and Lifestyle Survey: seven years on*, Aldershot: Dartmouth.

Crago, M., Yates, A. and Beulter, L.E. (1985) 'Height–weight ratios among female athletes: are collegiate athletics the precursors to an anorexic syndrome?', *International Journal of Eating Disorders*, 4, 79.

Crandall, C. (1995) 'Do parents discriminate against their heavyweight daughters?', *Personality and Social Psychology Bulletin*, 21, 724–35.

Crandall, C. and Martinez, R. (1996) 'Culture, ideology, and anti-fat attitudes', *Personality and Social Psychology Bulletin*, 22, 1165–76.

Cremer, S. (1997) 'The feel good food manual', *Men's Health*, May, 48–56.

Davis, C. (1990) 'Body image and weight preoccupation: a comparison between exercising and non-exercising women', *Appetite*, 15, 13–21.

Davis, C. and Dionne, M. (1990) 'Weight preoccupation and exercise: a structural equation analysis', paper presented at the *Fourth International Conference on Eating Disorders*, New York, April 1990.

Davis, C., Elliot, S., Dionne, M. and Mitchell, I. (1991) 'The relationship of personality factors and physical activity to body satisfaction in men', *Personality and Individual Differences*, 12, 689–94.

Davis, K. (1995) *Reshaping the female body: the dilemma of cosmetic surgery*, London: Routledge.

DeAngelis, T. (1997) 'Acceptance is the goal of the body image game', *APA Monitor*, March, 42.

Department of Health (1993) *The health of the nation*, London: HMSO.

Dewberry, C. and Ussher, J. (1995) 'Restraint and perception of body weight among British adults', *The Journal of Social Psychology*, 134, 609–19.

Dion, K., Berscheid, E. and Walster, E. (1972) 'What is beautiful is good', *Journal of Personality and Social Psychology*, 24, 285–90.

Dobson, R. (1997) 'Anorexia: now it's nineties man who suffers', *The Independent on Sunday*, 21 June, 3.

Donaldson, C. (1996) *A study of male body image and the effects of the media*, unpublished BSc dissertation, Manchester Metropolitan University.

Doy, G. (1996) 'Out of Africa: orientalism, "race", and the female body', *Body and Society*, 2, 17–44.

Dworkin, A. (1988) 'Not in man's image: lesbians and the cultural oppression of body image', *Women and Therapy*, 8, 27–39.

Eagley, A., Ashmore, R., Makhijani, M. and Longo, L. (1991) 'What is beautiful is good but . . . : a meta-analytic review of research on the physical attractiveness stereotype', *Psychological Bulletin*, 110, 109–28.

Elliot, S. (1994) 'Hunks in trunks hit a gap in the sports market', *The Guardian*, 17 February, 14.

Ellis, S. and Heritage, P. (1989) 'AIDS and the cultural response: the normal heart and we all fall down', in S. Shephard and M. Wallis (eds) *Coming on strong: gay politics and culture* (39–53), London: Unwin Hyman.

Emery, J., Benson, P., Cohen-Tovee, E. and Tovee, M. (1995) 'A computerised measure of body image and body shape', personal communication.

Epperley, T. (1993) 'Drugs and sports', in W. Lillegard and K.S. Rucker (eds) *Handbook of sports medicine* (249–58), Stoneham, Mass.: Andover.

Epstein, B. (1989) 'Women's anger and compulsive eating', in M. Lawrence (ed.) *Fed up and hungry: women, oppression, and food* (27–45), London: The Women's Press.

Epstein, L. and Wing, R. (1980) 'Aerobic exercise and weight', *Addictive Behaviours*, 5, 371–88.

Evans, C. and Dolan, B. (1992) 'Body Shape Questionnaire: derivation of shortened "alternate forms"', *International Journal of Eating Disorders*, 13, 315–32.

Ewing, W.A. (1994) *The body: photoworks of the human form*, London: Thames and Hudson.

Fallon, A. (1990) 'Culture in the mirror: sociocultural determinants of body image', in T. Cash and T. Pruzinsky (eds) *Body images: development, deviance and change* (80–109), New York: Guilford Press.

Fallon, A. and Rozin, P. (1985) 'Sex differences in perceptions of desirable body shape', *Journal of Abnormal Psychology*, 94, 1, 102–5.

Featherstone, M. (1991) 'The body in consumer culture', in M. Featherstone, M. Hepworth and B.S. Turner (eds) *The body: social processes and cultural theory* (170–96), London: Sage.

Ferguson, M. (1983) *Forever feminine: women's magazines and the cult of femininity*, Aldershot, Hants: Gower.

Festinger, L. (1954) 'A theory of social comparison processes', *Human Relations*, 7, 117–40.

Fisher, A.C., Genovese, P.P., Morris, K.J. and Morris, H.H. (1978) 'Perceptions of women in sports: psychology of motor behavior and sport', in D.M. Landers and R.W. Christina (eds) *The psychology of motor behavior and sport*, Champaign, Illinois: Human Kinetics.

Fisher, S. (1990) 'The evolution of psychological concepts about the body', in T. Cash and T. Pruzinsky (eds) *Body images: development, deviance and change* (3–20), New York: Guilford Press.

Forna, A. (1996) 'For women, or for men only?', *The Independent on Sunday*, 28 April.

Fox, P. and Yamaguchi, C. (1997) 'Body image change in pregnancy: a comparison of normal weight and overweight primagravidas', *Birth Issues in Perinatal Care*, 24, 35–40.

Francis, B. (1989) *Bev Francis' power bodybuilding*, New York: Stirling.

Frankel, S. (1998) 'The fashion of destruction', *The Guardian*, 7 February, 5.

Franzoi, S. and Shields, S. (1984) 'The body esteem scale: multidimensional structure and sex differences in a college population', *Journal of Personality Assessment*, 448, 173–8.

Freedman, R. (1986) *Beauty bound*, Lexington, Mass.: Lexington Books.

—— (1990) 'Cognitive-behavioral perspectives on body image change', in T. Cash and T. Pruzinsky (eds) *Body images: development, deviance and change* (272–95), New York: Guilford Press.

Furnham, A. and Alibhai, N. (1983) 'Cross cultural differences in the perception of male and female body shapes', *Psychological Medicine*, 13, 829–37.

Furnham, A. and Greaves, N. (1994) 'Gender and locus of control correlates of body image dissatisfaction', *European Journal of Personality*, 8, 183–200.

Furnham, A., Titman, P. and Sleeman, E. (1994) 'Perception of female body shapes as a function of exercise', *Journal of Social Behaviour and Personality*, 9, 335–52.

Fuss, D. (1989) *Essentially speaking: feminism, nature and difference*, New York and London: Routledge.

Gaines, C. and Butler, G. (1980) *Pumping iron: the art and sport of bodybuilding*, London: Sphere.

Gardner, R.M. and Moncrieff, C. (1988) 'Body image distortion in anorexics as a non-sensory phenomenon: a signal detection approach', *Journal of Clinical Psychology*, 44, 101–7.

Garfinkel, P. (1992) 'Evidence in support of attitudes to shape and weight as a diagnostic criterion of *bulimia nervosa*', *International Journal of Eating Disorders*, 11, 321–5.

Garner, D. and Garfinkel, P. (1981) 'Body image in *anorexia nervosa*: measurement, theory, and clinical implications', *International Journal of Psychiatry in Medicine*, 11, 263–84.

Garner, D., Garfinkel, P., Schwartz, D. and Thompson, M. (1980) 'Cultural expectations of thinness in women', *Psychological Reports*, 47, 483–91.

Garner, D., Olmsted, M. and Garfinkel, P. (1983) 'Does anorexia nervosa occur on a continuum?', *International Journal of Eating Disorders*, 2, 11–20.

Garner, D., Olmsted, M. and Polivy, J. (1983) 'Development and validation of a multidimensional Eating Disorder Inventory for *anorexia nervosa* and *bulimia*', *International Journal of Eating Disorders*, 2, 15–34.

Garner, D., Olmsted, M., Polivy, J. and Garfinkel, P. (1984) 'Comparison between weight-preoccupied women and *anorexia nervosa*', *Psychosomatic Medicine*, 46, 255–66.

Gillespie, R. (1996) 'Women, the body, and brand extension of medicine: cosmetic surgery and the paradox of choice', *Women and Health*, 24, 69–85.

Gittelson, J., Harris, S., Thorne-Lyman, A., Hanley, A., Barnie, A. and Zinman, B. (1996) 'Body image concepts differ by age and sex in an Ojibway-Cree community in Canada', *Journal of Nutrition*, 126, 2990–3000.

Gordon, R. (1990) *Anorexia and bulimia: anatomy of a social epidemic*, Oxford: Blackwell.

Gough, J. (1989) 'Theories of sexual identity and the masculinisation of the gay man', in S. Shepherd and M. Wallis (eds) *Coming on strong: gay politics and culture* (119–35), London: Unwin Hyman.

Greil, H. (1990) 'Sex differences in body build and their relationship to sex-specific processes of ageing', *Collegium Anthropologicum*, 14, 247–53.

Grogan, S., Donaldson, C., Richards, H. and Wainwright, N. (1997) 'Men's body image: body dissatisfaction in eight- to twenty-five-year-old males', paper presented to the European Health Psychology annual conference, Bordeaux, 3 September.

Grogan, S. and Wainwright, N. (1996) 'Growing up in the culture of slenderness: girls' experiences of body dissatisfaction', *Women's Studies International Forum*, 19, 665–73.

Grogan, S., Williams, Z. and Conner, M. (1996) 'The effects of viewing same gender photographic models on body satisfaction', *Women and Psychology Quarterly*, 20, 569–75.

Guillen, E. and Barr, S. (1994) 'Nutrition, dieting, and fitness messages in a magazine for adolescent women, 1970–1990', *Journal of Adolescent Health*, 15, 464–72.

Guinn, B., Semper, T., Jorgensen, L. and Skaggs, S. (1997) 'Body image perception in female Mexican American adolescents', *Journal of School Health*, 67, 112–15.

Hanna, C.F., Loro, A.D. and Power, D.D. (1981) 'Differences in the degree of overweight: a note on its importance'. *Addictive Behaviors*, 6, 61–2.

Harris, M.B., Walters, L.C. and Waschull, S. (1991) 'Gender and ethnic differences in obesity-related behaviors and attitudes in a college sample', *Journal of Applied Social Psychology*, 21, 1545–66.

Harris, S. (1994) 'Racial differences in predictors of college women's body image attitudes', *Women and Health*, 21, 89–104.

Hatfield, E. and Sprecher, S. (1986) *Mirror, mirror: the importance of looks in everyday life*, New York: SUNY Press.

Heinberg, L. and Thompson, J.K. (1992) 'Social comparison: gender, target importance ratings, and relation to body image disturbance', *Journal of Social Behavior and Personality*, 7, 335–44.

Heinberg, L. and Thompson, J.K. (1995) 'Body image and televised images of thinness and attractiveness: a controlled laboratory investigation', *Journal of Social and Clinical Psychology*, 14, 325–38.

Hill, A., Oliver, S. and Rogers, P. (1992) 'Eating in the adult world: the rise of dieting in childhood and adolescence', *British Journal of Clinical Psychology*, 31, 95–105.

Hodkinson, W. (1997) 'Body image stereotypes: the idealisation of slimness and perceptions of body image and occupational success', unpublished BSc dissertation, Manchester Metropolitan University.

Hofstede, G. (1980) *Culture's consequences: international differences in work-related values*, Beverley Hills, Cal.: Sage.

Horm, J. and Anderson, K. (1993) 'Who in America is trying to lose weight?', *Annals of Internal Medicine*, 119, 672–6.

Hough, D.O. (1990) 'Anabolic steroids and ergogenic aids', *American Family Physician*, 41, 1157–64.

Hsu, L. (1990) *Eating disorders*, London: Croom Helm.

Huon, G. (1988) 'Towards the prevention of eating disorders', in D. Hardoff and E. Chigier (eds) *Eating disorders in adolescents and young adults* (447–54), London: Freund.

—— (1994) 'Towards the prevention of dieting-induced disorders: modifying negative food- and body-related attitudes', *International Journal of Eating Disorders*, 16, 4, 395–9.

Huon, G., Morris, S. and Brown, L. (1990) 'Differences between male and female preferences for female body size', *Australian Psychologist*, 25, 314–17.

Illman, J. (1997) 'Plastic maketh the man', *The Guardian*, 8 February, 8.

Institute for the Study of Drug Dependence (1993) *Steroids*, London: The College Hill Press.

Irving, L. (1990) 'Mirror images: effects of the standard of beauty on the self- and body-esteem of women exhibiting varying levels of bulimic symptoms', *Journal of Social and Clinical Psychology*, 9, 230–42.

Itzin, C. (1986) 'Media images of women: the social construction of ageism and sexism', in S. Wilkinson (ed.) *Feminist social psychology* (119–34), Milton Keynes: Open University Press.

Iwawaki, S. and Lerner, R.M. (1974) 'Cross-cultural analyses of body–behavior relations: 1. A comparison of body build stereotypes of Japanese and American males and females', *Psychologia*, 17, 75–81.

Kannel, W.B. (1983) *Health and obesity*, New York: Allyn and Bacon.

Katz, J.L. (1986) 'Long distance running, *anorexia nervosa* and *bulimia*: a report of two cases', *Comparative Psychiatry*, 27, 74–8.

—— (1988) 'Eating disorders', in M. Shangold and G. Mirkin (eds) *Women and exercise: physiology and sports medicine* (248–63), Philadelphia: F.A. Davis.

Kenrick, D.T. (1989) 'Bridging social psychology and socio-biology: the case of sexual attraction', in R.W. Bell and N.J. Bell (eds) *Sociobiology and social sciences* (5–23), Lubbock, Texas: Texas Tech University Press.

Keys, A., Brozek, J., Henschel, A., Michelsen, O. and Taylor, H.L. (1950) *The biology of human starvation*, Minneapolis: University of Minnesota Press.

Kirkpatrick, S.W. and Sanders, D.M. (1978) 'Body image stereotypes: a developmental comparison', *Journal of Genetic Psychology*, 132, 87–95.

Kitzinger, C. (1987) *The social construction of lesbianism*, London: Sage.

Klapper, J. (1960) *The effects of mass communication*, New York: Free Press.

Koff, E. and Bauman, C. (1997) 'Effects of wellness, fitness, and sport skills programs on body image and lifestyle behaviors', *Perceptual and Motor Skills*, 84, 555–62.

Korkia, P. (1994) 'Anabolic steroid use in Britain', *The International Journal of Drug Policy*, 5, 6–9.

Krasnow, M. (1997) *My life as a male anorexic*, London: Harrington Park Press.

Lakoff, R.T. and Scherr, R.L. (1984) *Face value: the politics of beauty*, Boston: Routledge and Kegan Paul.

❧ Lamb, C.S., Jackson, L., Cassiday, P. and Priest, D. (1993) 'Body figure preferences of men and women: a comparison of two generations', *Sex Roles*, 28, 345–58.

Lazarsfeld, P., Berelson, B. and Gaudet, H. (1948) *The people's choice*, New York: Columbia University Press.

Lerner, R.M. and Korn, S.J. (1972) 'The development of body build stereotypes in males', *Child Development*, 43, 912–20.

Lewis, R. (1996) *Gendering orientalism: race, femininity and representation*, London: Routledge.

Lewis, V., Blair, A. and Booth, D. (1992) 'Outcome of group therapy for body-image emotionality and weight-control self-efficacy', *Behavioural Psychotherapy*, 20, 155–65.

McAlpine, J. (1993) 'Mr Muscle cleans up', *The Scotsman*, 13 August, 4.

Major, B., Testa, M. and Bylsma, W. (1991) 'Responses to upward and downward social comparisons: the impact of esteem relevance and perceived control', in J. Suls and T. Wills (eds) *Social comparison: contemporary theory and research* (237–60), Hillsdale, NJ: Erlbaum.

Maloney, M., McGuire, J., Daniels, S. and Specker, B. (1989) 'Dieting behaviour and eating attitudes in children', *Pediatrics*, 84, 482–9.

Mansfield, A. and McGinn, B. (1993) 'Pumping irony: the muscular and the feminine', in S. Scott and D. Morgan (eds) *Body matters* (49–68), London: Falmer.

✳ Markus, H. (1977) 'Self-schema and processing information about the self', *Journal of Personality and Social Psychology*, 35, 63–78.

Marshall, J. (1981) 'Pansies, perverts and macho men: changing conceptions of male homosexuality', in K. Plummer (ed.) *The making of the modern homosexual* (133–54), London: Hutchison.

Mazur, A. (1986) 'U.S. trends in feminine beauty and overadaption', *Journal of Sex Research*, 22, 281–303.

Meredith, B. (1988) *A change for the better*, London: Grafton.

Metropolitan Life Assurance Company (1983) *Statistical bulletin*, New York: Metropolitan Life Assurance Company.

Meyer, R. (1991) 'Rock Hudson's body', in D. Fuss (ed.) *Inside out: lesbian theories, gay theories* (259–90), New York: Routledge.

Miller, C.T. (1984) 'Self schemas, gender and social comparison: a clarification of the related attributes hypothesis', *Journal of Personality and Social Psychology*, 46, 1222–9.

Mintz, L. and Betz, N. (1986) 'Sex differences in the nature, realism, and correlates of body image', *Sex Roles*, 15, 185–95.

Mishkind, M., Rodin, J., Silberstein, L. and Striegel-Moore, R. (1986) 'The embodiment of masculinity: cultural, psychological, and behavioural dimensions', *American Behavioural Scientist*, 29, 545–62.

Mitchell, J. (1989) ' "Going for the burn" and "pumping iron": what's healthy about the current fitness boom?', in M. Lawrence (ed.) *Fed up and hungry: women, oppression, and food* (156–74), London: The Women's Press.

Morgan, D. (1993) 'You too can have a body like mine: reflections on the male body and masculinities', in S. Scott and D. Morgan (eds) *Body matters* (69–88), London: Falmer.

Morgan, K. (1991) 'Women and the knife: cosmetic surgery and the colonization of women's bodies', *Hypatia*, 6, 25–53.

Morris, D. (1985) *Bodywatching*, New York: Crown.

Mort, F. (1988) 'Boys own? Masculinity, style and popular culture', in R. Chapman and J. Rutherford (eds) *Male order: unwrapping masculinity*, London: Lawrence and Wishart.

Muller, M. (1998) *A part of my life – photographs*, London: Scalo.

Myers, B.S. and Copplestone, T. (1985) *Landmarks of Western art*, Middlesex: Newnes.

Myers, P. and Biocca, F. (1992) 'The elastic body image: the effects of television advertising and programming on body image distortions in young women', *Journal of Communication*, 42, 108–33.

Myers, R. and Roth, D. (1997) 'Perceived benefits and barriers to exercise and stage of exercise', *Health Psychology*, 16, 277–83.

Nayak, A. (1997) 'Disclosing whiteness in Haagen-Dazs advertising', *Body and Society*, 3, 33–51.

Neff, L., Sargent, R., McKeown, R., Jackson, K. and Valois, R. (1997) 'Black–white differences in body size perceptions and weight management practices among adolescent females', *Journal of Adolescent Health*, 20, 459–65.

Nisbett, R.E. (1972) 'Hunger, obesity, and the ventromedial hypothalamus', *Psychological Review*, 79, 433–53.

Nochlin, L. (1991) 'The imaginary Orient', in *The politics of vision*, London: Thames and Hudson.

Ogden, J. (1992) *Fat chance: the myth of dieting explained*, London: Routledge.

O'Kelly, L. (1994) 'Body talk', *The Guardian*, 23 October, 30–2.

Orbach, S. (1993) *Hunger strike: the anorectic's struggle as a metaphor for our age*, London: Penguin.

Pennycook, W. (1989) 'Anorexia and adolescence', in M. Lawrence (ed.) *Fed up and hungry: women, oppression, and food* (74–85), London: The Women's Press.

Pliner, P., Chaiken, S. and Flett, G. (1990) 'Gender differences in concern with body weight and physical appearance over the life span', *Personality and Social Psychology Bulletin*, 16, 263–73.

Polivy, J. and Herman, C. (1983) *Breaking the diet habit*, New York: Basic Books.

Pope, H., Katz, D. and Hudson, J. (1993) '*Anorexia nervosa* and "reverse anorexia" among 108 male bodybuilders', *Comprehensive Psychiatry*, 34, 406–9.

Prentice, A. (1995) 'Don't blame the metabolism', *MRC News*, Autumn, 27–31.

Prentice, A. and Jebb, S.A. (1995) 'Obesity in Britain: gluttony or sloth?', *British Medical Journal*, 311, 437–9.

Pruzinsky, T. and Cash, T. (1990) 'Integrative themes in body-image development, deviance and change', in T. Cash and T. Pruzinsky (eds) *Body images: development, deviance and change* (337–49), New York: Guilford Press

Pruzinsky, T. and Edgerton, M. (1990) 'Body image change in cosmetic plastic surgery', in T. Cash and T. Pruzinsky (eds) *Body images: development, deviance and change* (217–36), New York: Guilford Press.

Pultz, J. (1995) *Photography and the body*, London: Orion.

Raudenbush, B. and Zellner, D. (1997) 'Nobody's satisfied: effects of abnormal eating behaviours and actual and perceived weight status on body image satisfaction in males and females', *Journal of Social and Clinical Psychology*, 16, 95–110.

Richins, M. (1991) 'Social comparison and the idealised images of advertising', *Journal of Consumer Research*, 18, 71–83.

Rickert, V., Pawlak-Morello, C., Sheppard, V. and Jay, S. (1992) 'Human growth hormone: a new substance of abuse among adolescents?', *Clinical Pediatrics*, December, 723–5.

Robinson, T., Killen, J., Litt, I., Hammer, L., Wilson, D., Haydel, F., Hayward, C. and Taylor, B. (1996) 'Ethnicity and body dissatisfaction: are Hispanic and Asian girls at increased risk for eating disorders?', *Journal of Adolescent Health*, 19, 384–93.

Rodin, J., Silberstein, L.R. and Streigel-Moore, R.H. (1985) 'Women and weight: a normative discontent', in T.B. Sonderegger (ed.) *Nebraska Symposium on Motivation, vol. 32, Psychology and Gender* (267–307), Lincoln: University of Nebraska Press.

Rosen, J. (1990) 'Body image disturbances in eating disorders', in T. Cash and T. Pruzinsky (eds) *Body images: development, deviance and change* (190–214), New York: Guilford Press.

Rothblum, E. (1990) 'Women and weight: fad and fiction', *The Journal of Psychology*, 124, 5–24.

Rozin, P. and Fallon, A. (1988) 'Body image, attitudes to weight, and misperceptions of figure preferences of the opposite gender: a comparison of men and women in two generations', *Journal of Abnormal Psychology*, 97, 342–5.

St Martin, L. and Gavey, N. (1996) 'Women's bodybuilding: feminist resistance and/or femininity's recuperation', *Body and Society*, 2, 45–57.

Sanders, T. and Bazelgette, P. (1994) *You don't have to diet*, London: Bantam.

Schilder, P. (1950) *The image and appearance of the human body*, New York: International Universities Press.

Schoemer, K. (1996) 'Rockers, models, and the new allure of heroin', *Newsweek*, 26 August, 50–6.

Schulman, R.G., Kinder, B.N., Powers, P.S., Prange, M. and Glenhorn, A. (1986) 'The development of a scale to measure cognitive distortions in bulimia', *Journal of Personality Assessment*, 50, 630–9.

Secord, P.F. and Jourard, S.M. (1953) 'The appraisal of body cathexis: body cathexis and the self', *Journal of Consulting Psychology*, 17, 343–7.

Shapiro, H. (1992) 'Adjusting to steroid users', *Druglink*, 7, 16.

Shilling, C. (1993) *The body and social theory*, London: Sage.

Siever, M. (1994) 'Sexual orientation and gender as factors in socioculturally acquired vulnerability to body dissatisfaction and eating disorders', *Journal of Consulting and Clinical Psychology*, 62, 252–60.

Silverstein, B., Peterson, B. and Purdue, L. (1986) 'Some correlates of the thin standard of physical attractiveness of women', *International Journal of Eating Disorders*, 5, 898–905.

Singh, D. (1993) 'Adaptive significance of female physical attractiveness: role of the waist-to-hip ratio', *Journal of Personality and Social Psychology*, 65, 293–307.

—— (1995) 'Female judgement of male attractiveness and desirability for relationships: role of the waist-to-hip ratio and financial status', *Journal of Personality and Social Psychology*, 69, 1089–1101.

Slade, P. (1982) 'Toward a functional analysis of *anorexia nervosa* and *bulimia nervosa*', *British Journal of Clinical Psychology*, 21, 167–79.

Slade, P. and Russell, G. (1973) 'Awareness of body dimensions in *anorexia nervosa*: cross-sectional and longitudinal studies', *Psychological Medicine*, 3, 188–99.

Smeets, M.A.M., Smit, F., Panhuysen, G.E.M. and Ingleby, J.D. (1997) 'The influence of methodological differences on the outcome of body size estimation studies in *anorexia nervosa*', *British Journal of Clinical Psychology*, 36, 263–77.

Smith, D. (1990) *Texts, facts and femininity: exploring the relations of ruling*, New York: Routledge.

Smith, M.C. and Thelen, M.T. (1984) 'Development and validation of a test for bulimia', *Journal of Consulting and Clinical Psychology*, 52, 863–72.

Snyder, E.E. and Kivlin, J.E. (1975) 'Women athletes and aspects of psychological well-being and body image', *Research Quarterly*, 46, 191–5.

Snyder, E.E. and Spreitzer, E. (1974) 'Involvement in sports and psychological well being', *Research Quarterly*, 44, 249–55.

Sobal, J. and Stunckard, A. (1989) 'Socio-economic status and obesity: a review of the literature', *Psychological Bulletin*, 105, 260–75.

Sorell, G.T. and Nowak, C.G. (1981) 'The role of physical attractiveness as a contributor to individual development', in R.M. Lerner and N.A. Bush-Rossnagel (eds) *Individuals as producers of their development: a life-span perspective* (389–446), New York: Academic Press.

Staffieri, J.R. (1967) 'A study of social stereotypes of body image in children', *Journal of Personality and Social Psychology*, 7, 101–4.

Strauss, R.H. and Yesalis, C.E. (1991) 'Anabolic steroids in the athlete', *Annual Review of Medicine*, 42, 449–57.

Striegel-Moore, R.H., Silberstein, L.R. and Rodin, J. (1986) 'Toward an understanding of risk factors for bulimia', *American Psychologist*, 41, 246–63.

Striegel-Moore, R.H., Tucker, N. and Hsu, J. (1990) 'Body image dissatisfaction and disordered eating in lesbian college students', *International Journal of Eating Disorders*, 9, 493–500.

Stunckard, A.J., Harris, J.R., Pedersen, N.L. and McClearn, G.E. (1990) 'A separated twin study of the body mass index', *New England Journal of Medicine*, 322, 1483–7.

Stunckard, A.J., Sorensen, T. and Schulsinger, F. (1983) 'Use of the Danish adoption register for the study of obesity and thinness', in S. Kety (ed.) *The genetics of neurological and psychiatric disorders*, New York: Raven Press.

Taylor, C. (1997) 'Does my bum look big in this?', *The Independent on Sunday*, 11 May.

Taylor, S. (1995) *Health psychology* (3rd edn), London: McGraw-Hill.

Thomas, T. (1993) 'Slimming eats into new man's soul', *The European*, 12 November.

Thompson, J.K., Penner, L. and Altabe, M. (1990) 'Procedures, problems, and progress in the assessment of body images', in T. Cash and T. Pruzinsky (eds) *Body images: development, deviance and change* (21–46), New York: Guilford Press.

Thompson, J.K. and Spana, R.E. (1988) 'The adjustable light beam method for the assessment of size estimation accuracy: description, psychometrics and normative data', *International Journal of Eating Disorders*, 7, 521–6.

Thompson, J.K. and Tantleff, S. (1992) 'Female and male ratings of upper torso: actual, ideal, and stereotypical conceptions', *Journal of Social Behavior and Personality*, 7, 345–54.

Thompson, S., Corwin, S. and Sargeant, R. (1997) 'Ideal body size beliefs and weight concerns in fourth grade children', *International Journal of Eating Disorders*, 21, 279–84.

Thornhill, R. and Gangestad, S.W. (1994) 'Human fluctuating asymmetry and sexual behavior', *Psychological Science*, 5, 297–302.

Tiggemann, M. (1992) 'Body-size dissatisfaction: individual differences in age and gender, and relationship with self-esteem', *Personality and Individual Differences*, 13, 39–43.

—— (1996) ' "Thinking" versus "feeling" fat: correlates of two indices of body image dissatisfaction', *Australian Journal of Psychology*, 48, 21–5.

Tiggemann, M. and Pennington, B. (1990) 'The development of gender differences in body-size dissatisfaction', *Australian Psychologist*, 25, 306–13.

Tiggemann, M. and Rothblum, E. (1988) 'Gender differences and social consequences of perceived overweight in the United States and Australia', *Sex Roles*, 18, 75–86.

Toro, J., Castro, J., Garcia, M., Perez, P. and Cuesta, L. (1989) 'Eating attitudes, sociodemographic factors, and body shape evaluation in adolescence', *British Journal of Medical Psychology*, 62, 61–70.

Touyz, S.W., Beaumont, P.J.V. and Collins, J.K. (1984) 'Body shape perception and its disturbance in *anorexia nervosa*', *British Journal of Psychiatry*, 144, 167–71.

Tricker, R., O'Neill, M.R. and Cook, D. (1989) 'The incidence of anabolic steroid use among competitive body-builders', *Journal of Drug Education*, 19, 313–25.

Turner, B. (1992) *Regulating bodies: essays in medical sociology*, London: Routledge.

Turtle, J., Jones, A. and Hickman, M. (1997) *Young people and health: the health behaviour of school-aged children*, London: Health Education Authority.

Tyler, C.A. (1991) 'Boys will be girls: the politics of gay drag', in D. Fuss (ed) *Inside out: lesbian theories, gay theories* (32–70), New York: Routledge.

Ussher, J. (1993) *The psychology of the female body*, London: Routledge.

Viner, K. (1997) 'The new plastic feminism', *The Guardian*, 4 July, 5.

Wadden, T., Brown, G., Foster, G. and Linowitz, J. (1991) 'Salience of weight-related worries in adolescent males and females', *International Journal of Eating Disorders*, 10, 407–14.

Wannamethee, G. and Shaper, A.G. (1990) 'Weight change in middle-aged British men: implications for health', *European Journal of Clinical Nutrition*, 44, 133–42.

Ward, T. (1983) *Against ageism*, Newcastle: Search Project.

Wardle, J., Bindra, R., Fairclough, B. and Westcombe, A. (1993) 'Culture and body image: body perception and weight concern in young Asian and Caucasian British women', *Journal of Community and Applied Social Psychology*, 3, 173–81.

Wardle, J. and Marsland, L. (1990) 'Adolescent concerns about weight and eating: a social-developmental perspective', *Journal of Psychosomatic Research*, 34, 377–91.

Warren, C. and Cooper, P.J. (1988) 'Psychological effects of dieting', *British Journal of Clinical Psychology*, 27, 269–70.

Watney, S. (1995) 'AIDS and the politics of gay diaspora', in M. Dorenkamp and R. Henke (eds) *Negotiating lesbian and gay subjects*, New York and London: Routledge.

Weiderman, M. and Prior, T. (1997) 'Body dissatisfaction and sexuality among women with *bulimia nervosa*', *International Journal of Eating Disorders*, 21, 361–5.

Wells, W. and Siegel, B. (1961) 'Stereotyped somatotypes', *Psychological Reports*, 8, 77–8.

Werlinger, K., King, T., Clark, M., Pera, V. and Wincze, J. (1997) 'Perceived changes in sexual functioning and body image following weight loss in an obese female population: a pilot study', *Journal of Sex and Marital Therapy*, 23, 74–8.

Whitehead, M. (1988) 'The health divide', in P. Townsend, N. Davidson and M. Whitehead (eds) *Inequalities in health* (217–357), Harmondsworth, Middlesex: Penguin.

Wiggins, J., Wiggins, N. and Conger, J. (1968) 'Correlates of heterosexual somatic preference', *Journal of Personality and Social Psychology*, 10, 82–90.

Wilcosky, T., Hyde, J., Anderson, J.J.B., Bangdiwula, S. and Duncan, B. (1990) 'Obesity and mortality in the Lipid Research Clinics Program Follow-up Study', *Journal of Clinical Epidemiology*, 43, 743–52.

Wilson, E. (1997) 'Why are more men having cosmetic surgery?', *The Express*, 18 February, 48–9.

Wilson, G.T. and Smith, D. (1989) 'Assessment of *bulimia nervosa*: an evaluation of the eating disorders examination', *International Journal of Eating Disorders*, 8, 173–9.

Wolf, N. (1991) *The beauty myth: how images of beauty are used against women*, New York: William Morrow.

Wooley, O., Wooley, S. and Dyrenforth, S. (1979) 'Obesity and women', *Women's Studies International Quarterly*, 2, 81–92.

Yeselis, C. and Bahrke, M. (1995) 'Anabolic-androgenic steroids', *Sports Medicine*, 19, 326–40.

Yingling, T. (1991) 'AIDS in America: postmodern governance, identity and experience', in D. Fuss (ed.) *Inside out: lesbian theories, gay theories* (291–310), New York: Routledge.

Zellner, D., Harner, D. and Adler, R. (1989) 'Effects of eating abnormalities and gender on perceptions of desirable body shape', *Journal of Abnormal Psychology*, 98, 93–6.

Zigmond, A. and Snaith, R. (1983) 'The hospital anxiety and depression scale', *Acta Psychiatrica Scandinavica*, 67, 361–70.

Name Index

Subject index